JUGGERNAUT

John Wardroper

JUGGERNAUT

Temple Smith · London

First published in Great Britain in 1981
by Maurice Temple Smith Ltd
37 Great Russell St, London WC1

© John Wardroper 1981

ISBN 0 85117 207 5   Cased ✓
      0 85117 208 3   Paper

Photoset by Margaret Spooner
in 10½ on 12pt Melior

Printed in Great Britain by
The Blackwell Press Ltd
London, Guildford, Worcester, Oxford

Contents

1

The view from Marsham Street

A civil servant in need of an answer will look first in a file, or if the question is too large for that he will refer to a deeper source of wisdom, less definable but still more precious, known as the departmental view. This is understandable: it is a sound way to get through the day's business. The danger is that the departmental view becomes enshrined, a perfected body of unquestionable truths. That transient person, the minister, is instructed in these truths from the day he arrives, and he must be forceful and adroit to alter them in any lasting way. He will be wise to note that ambitious civil servants are guided by the need to keep the good opinion of their departmental head, the permanent secretary, the 'view' personified, who is also the man to whom they will owe their advancement.

At the Department of Transport the view has prevailed for twenty years and more that an ever-growing use of heavy-weight lorries is good for Britain and must be encouraged. Controls must be minimal and taxes modest, and awkward questions must be silenced. The result, it is claimed, is 'cheap transport': a surprisingly superficial claim for trained minds to make, as I propose to show. Ever since the maximum lorry weight was raised to 32 tons in 1964, the department and British lorry makers and operators have been at one in contending that still bigger lorries would be even better. Ministers of transport have generally been persuaded to believe that this view is (to use one of the civil servants' favoured mild words) sensible. But a difficulty has tried the department's patience. Each time a proposal to permit heavier lorries has become known, the outcry of ungrateful citizens has made ministers pause. This first happened in 1970, when the lorry industry, after private talks with civil servants, demanded an increase to 44 tons. Amenity groups all over the country let the minister know that the rise to 32 tons had had an impact that was dismaying enough. The age of the juggernaut had arrived. Every year thousands more 32-tonners were running millions more miles through Britain, with scarcely any curb on where they could go. The protesters wanted these lorries to be tamed, and they condemned the idea of anything bigger. In December 1970 the minister, John Peyton, refused to go above 32 tons; furthermore, he said the time had come to deal with 'a growing and undoubted nuisance'.

How little was done about the nuisance will be made clear in this book. Although the 44-ton dream was postponed, the departmental allies of the lorry men did a good deal to shield them from troublesome regulations. Soon, too, the lorry men were cheered by the revival of their dream, thanks to Britain's joining the Common Market. The Brussels secretariat, guided by an international lorry lobby, was determined to have uniformly large lorries throughout the Community. The word was harmonisation. There was no thought of harmonising downwards to Britain's 32 tons, or even of adopting West Germany's and France's 38 tonnes (one tonne = 0.984 of a ton). Forty-four tonnes was the aim—chiefly because that would allow lorries to carry containers packed to a weight of 31 tonnes which would otherwise have to go by rail. Knowing that the question might not be settled quickly, the department privately encouraged British lorry operators to count on being consoled with a lesser interim increase. During the years 1973–80, records of the motor industry show, nearly 73,000 lorries designed to operate at more than 32 tons were registered. This investment mounting to nearly £2,000 million (in 1980 prices) in machinery that could not be fully exploited—not legally, at any rate—was a constant incentive for British action.

Even an interim increase, however, would clearly encounter great opposition. By 1978, when the nine-nation argument at Brussels had advanced only as far as a draft directive, the number of lorries operating in Britain at over 28 tons, the kind that people see as juggernauts, had risen to 94,000—three times as many as in 1970. And though these lorries made up less than a fifth of all lorries on the road, they had become by far the chief goods-movers. They were performing 60,500 million tonne-kilometres a year (these metric statistics are unavoidable), or more than three-fifths of all road freight. The lorry lobby and the department produced soothing assertions, such as 'Big lorries mean fewer lorries'. It was true that middle-weight lorries, pushed out of business, were declining sharply in numbers. Soon the department was able to declare, misleadingly, that 'lorry traffic' was decreasing in towns. 'Traffic' here means 'mileage run by all lorries'. A more apposite fact for people living, shopping or working in busy roads was that in the period 1973–8 there was one category of lorry, and one alone, whose mileage in built-up areas went up (and by a fifth): four-axle articulated lorries. A prudent civil servant could see that it might be hard to persuade people that lorries of 38 or 40 tons, let alone 44, would make their lives pleasanter.

Besides, an election was not far off. The transport minister, William Rodgers, dared not announce anything so unpopular. Instead he did what ministers often do in a difficulty: he proposed a committee of inquiry. What happened next reveals a good deal about the transport department, and about the civil service mind.

One of the strongest weapons of a civil servant is his power to move slowly, but when his heart is in something he can be a quick worker. On 9 October 1978 the department's permanent secretary, Sir Peter Baldwin, had in front of him a cutting from *The Times* about the arguments for a weight increase, with a scribbled question in the margin from Rodgers: 'Should we have an inquiry?' Baldwin sent a minute to his freight directorate, the departmental division that deals with lorry policy, asking for suggestions. The under-secretary in charge of the directorate, Joseph Peeler, and an assistant secretary, David Lyness, put their thoughts into shape and had a talk with Baldwin on Friday the 13th—a talk that evidently gave Peeler clear enough guidelines to enable him, the following Monday (presumably after some weekend overtime), to send up a 1,200-word note by way of his immediate superior, Peter Lazarus, deputy secretary. It was intended for the eyes of only a few, but thanks to an unknown traitorous dissident and a copying machine it was leaked, to the enlightenment of students of public administration.

At this point it is important to record that the freight directorate is officially not a protector and advocate of hauliers' and lorry-makers' interests. It is meant to oversee

road freight in the interests of the community as a whole, and
the fields of action formally set down for it include 'lorries and
the environment'. Nowhere in Peeler's note, however, is there
a hint that he felt the least need to seem to his superiors to be
proposing an impartial inquiry that would help the minister
and the public to make up their minds whether heavier lorries
would or would not be on balance a good thing for Britain.
The only question was how to manage the inquiry so as to
produce the result that Baldwin wanted as much as Peeler.
This knowledge made Peeler remarkably forthright. He wrote:
'For the purpose of this note it is assumed that we wish . . .
to move, as soon as parliamentary and public opinion will let
us, to a maximum gross weight of thirty-eight or forty tons.
Ideally we should do this in harmony with our EEC partners
. . . but there is a strong case for doing it anyway.' An inquiry
would be 'a means of getting round the political obstacles'
since 'the more straightforward approach' (simply announcing
a decision) was politically unacceptable.

   The main advantage of an inquiry, Peeler said, would be
'presentational'—the civil servant's gentle word for 'good for
getting our case over'. He went on: 'At the end of the day,
recommendations would be made by impartial people of
repute who have carefully weighed and sifted the evidence
and have come to, one hopes, a sensible conclusion in line
with the department's view.' But could things possibly go
wrong? 'The worst risk, if not the most likely, is that the
inquiry would produce the wrong answer, or come to no clear
conclusion within a reasonable time.'

   The wrong answer! How could one avoid that and still
make the inquiry look fair? Peeler wrote: 'Gross lorry weights
and their direct and indirect effect on the environment,
including road surfaces, would be the main theme. It would be
open to the inquiry to consider, and for those interested to
press for, the reduction of maximum lorry weights. The
possible diversion of traffic from rail would also be relevant . . .
It might be difficult not to consider axle weights [which
govern a lorry's road-damaging power] . . . but it would be
undesirable to allow the inquiry to get into the complex
technicalities of axle weights . . . There will be pressure to
extend the inquiry to cover such matters as lorry routing,
lorry noise and lorry safety generally.' Here was the chief
worry: 'In general, the more the scope of the inquiry is

extended, the longer it will take and the greater the danger that the main issue will be lost sight of. On the other hand, any artificial restriction could well give colour to the accusations of "rigging" which are likely to be made anyway.' Peeler's final point was again presentational: 'Although the establishment in the public mind of a clear and overwhelming case on balance for heavier lorry weights is seen as the main end of the inquiry, it could well have wider effects. It should provide a focus for the various road haulage interests to get together, marshal their forces, and act cohesively to produce a really good case which should not merely establish the main point at issue but should do good to their now sadly tarnished public image. This would make it easier for the government to propose legislation (on lorry weights and other matters) in their favour.'

When John Horam, Rodgers's junior minister, read his copy of the Peeler note his first thought was, 'My God, if someone leaks this—' Within a fortnight someone did. It arrived in the post at the office of Transport 2000, a rail-backed organisation that delights in opportunities to tarnish the road lobbies' image, and it was passed to *The Guardian*. On the day it published the Peeler story, the newspaper said: 'If the government chose to do, it could prosecute us . . . Absurd though it may seem, Section 2 of the Official Secrets Act is so sweeping that the story . . . based as it is on documents leaked from the Department of Transport, would easily fall within its ambit.' Although the leak sent tremors through the department and angered Rodgers, he did not venture to prosecute. To do so would only have drawn even more attention to the reasonings of Peeler. In a letter to *The Guardian,* Dr Peter Levin of the London School of Economics referred to the controversies over another sort of transport inquiry, into motorway schemes, and said: 'This latest evidence of official attitudes can only undermine those who have trusted that decisions will be made on the basis of rational argument . . . During the past two years I have been urging objectors at the Archway Road [London] inquiry to put their case to the inquiry rather than boycott or disrupt it. How shall I answer would-be disrupters now?' A letter to *The Times* said the Peeler note raised an important general point about civil servants: 'When they are given a particular responsibility—as for road haulage, or for Concorde or the nuclear industry, to take two other examples—they almost inevitably perceive the public interest as requiring them to promote the vigorous development of their charge.' Or as another letter put it: 'With civil servants like Sir Peter Baldwin, Peter Lazarus, Joseph Peeler and David Lyness, who needs a British Road Federation?'

The reference to the nuclear industry is apposite. Officials at the Department of Energy made up their minds years ago, in close accord with the industry, that the future was nuclear. When Tony Benn became energy secretary in 1974, he was handed a 172-page brief 'dressed up to look like a range of options', he told the Royal Institute of Public Administration when he was once more out of power; but 'beneath the presentational language' he found the departmental view. He quoted this one sentence: 'In principle it is desirable that all new orders for base-load power stations should be nuclear.' Benn also quoted a letter to The Times from an eminent civil servant, Sir William Hayter: 'If expert opinion in this field is unanimous in favour of a particular course, is it likely that a minister, and one without any scientific qualifications, would be right and all the experts wrong?' Benn's comment was: 'This argument amounts to a declaration that democratic control cannot extend to technical matters and is only tolerable in the shrinking areas of policy that laymen can comprehend. It is a recipe for technocracy' (Benn, 1980).

Some people may discount this as the over-critical talk of a leftish Labour man. But Rodgers himself, well to the right of Benn, also offered some cautionary thoughts when in his post-ministerial freedom he spoke to the same institute: 'I refer to the equivalent of "going native" for an expatriate serving in a foreign post. In my experience, there are occasions when an official gets too close to the interest group with which he deals and becomes instinctively resistant to ministerial proposals hostile to it. It is important that personnel policies should recognise this and strike the right balance' (Rodgers, 1980). In this last sentence Rodgers meant that no man should spend too many successive years dealing, for example, with lorry men. It is a question, however, whether shifting men would make a great difference: Peeler had come to transport from housing (where he was known for his dislike of rent subsidies) and had become a spirited advocate of the departmental view on lorries during little more than five months as head of freight directorate.

At the time of the leak, of course, Rodgers had to stand up in the Commons and defend Peeler. 'I have complete confidence in that official,' he said, 'and in the loyalty and integrity of civil servants as a whole.' Peeler himself was puzzled to find that his note was thought arrogant. In his mind, people simply needed educating to see the light. A couple of months later he even made the point publicly at a London hauliers' meeting: 'I don't wish to enter too much into this highly controversial issue, but there is a major task of educating the public's opinion over this issue.' Perhaps a less self-confident official would have kept his head down, for Rodgers was still in favour of an inquiry. Moreover, he was not fully convinced of the economic advantages of heavier lorries and was not happy about the freight directorate's view of environmental concern as a mere presentational problem to be overcome. Indeed, he had earlier ordained that people from leading amenity associations should occasionally be admitted to the department in Marsham Street, Westminster, to put their views to civil servants whose chief callers until then had been lorry lobbyists.

In March 1979 two things happened: Peeler was shifted sideways and Rodgers announced an inquiry with terms of reference that displeased his officials, for they were much wider than they would have been if the leak had never occurred: 'To consider the causes and consequences of the growth in the movement of freight by road and, in particular, of the impact of the lorry on people and their environment; and to report on how best to ensure that future developments serve the public interest.' Not a word there about 38, 40 or 44 tonnes; but when Rodgers's Conservative successor, Norman Fowler, set the inquiry in motion two months later, he said: 'It must face squarely the issue of whether there should be any change in the present limits.' Fowler said he did not want the inquiry to be 'unduly protracted', but that was not much consolation for the big-lorry advocates. Until the inquiry panel had taken evidence, pondered and written a report, and until Parliament had given a verdict in the light of public opinion, no British transport minister could go to a meeting in Brussels of his Common Market colleagues and vote to unleash heavier lorries on Britain's roads. And what if the inquiry produced 'a sensible conclusion' but also brought so many negative ideas into the open that in the end Parliament still said no?

The turn of events was unwelcome, too, at the Common Market headquarters in the Rue de la Loi, Brussels, where officials of Directorate-General VII (Transport) had been trying since the late sixties to produce a package of 'harmonised' maximum gross weights and axle weights that all member countries would accept. They had worked closely with two committees of lorry manufacturers, but had not consulted railway managements or trade unions and had had only grudging contact with environmentalists. Harmonisation meant that no EEC country would be allowed to bar lorries up to the agreed maximums. Thus it was an especially controversial matter for Britain (and Ireland too): it would abolish the 32-ton limit.

The terms of the EEC draft directive of 1978 are best understood if one first grasps the nature of the big lorries with which it is chiefly concerned. They are known as articulated lorries (artics for short) because they consist of two linked elements, a compact tractive unit and a long trailer. The 32 tons of a top-weight British lorry are distributed over only four axles: two on the tractive unit to take its own weight plus the front end of the trailer, and two at the trailer's rear end. As later chapters will show, this 32-tonner has many questionable qualities. They would in most cases be more questionable still in the range of vehicles proposed in the directive: with four axles, up to 35 tonnes; with five axles, up to 42 tonnes; with six axles, up to 44 tonnes. There was also a questionable axle-load proposal. It is individual axle-loads that decide how much a lorry damages the road. The addition of just one ton enormously increases the damage (as explained in Chapter 7). The legal limit in Britain, Ireland, Germany, Denmark and the Netherlands was 10 tons, which is far from gentle; but the EEC proposal was for a drive axle of a much more damaging 11½ tonnes. Directorate-General VII called this 'moderate', a word justified only by the fact that Italy had 12-tonne axles and France, Belgium and Luxembourg inadvisedly even had some lorries running with 13-tonne axles.

DG VII argued that harmonisation was 'necessary' if the EEC were to have a common transport policy—which itself remained undefined. It did not point out that within one single nation, the US, and another single nation, Canada, a great range of state and provincial weight limits prevailed (and all of them kinder to the roads than what DG VII proposed). DG VII said its plan would create 'a more homogeneous market' for lorries. The need for that odd word 'more' became clear when it was seen that the proposal contained 'heads I win' clauses. The countries with axle-loads above 11½ tonnes would be allowed to go on using them within their borders, and they and other countries would also be able to retain vehicles that conflicted with the 'harmonisation' in other ways. The package was open to criticism on other grounds, too, so the officials of DG VII worked hard to create favourable opinions.

Under their close guidance, a vote in favour, with minor reservations, was obtained in 1979 from the EEC Economic and Social Committee, which vets all proposals of the Brussels bureaucracy. For officials who know exactly what they want, this vetoless body of scores of nominated men and women representing business, trade unions and, in theory, the general public in all member countries is a convenient instrument. For guidance on technical matters such as axle-loads and road damage, committee members depend on experts. For the British, the expert was Tony Gaffney, West Yorkshire's county surveyor, a believer in heavier lorries. At least one British member, Roderick Doble, a retired town clerk, began 'dead against a weight increase' and ended voting yes. He said afterwards that a large multi-nation committee was a difficult place to analyse a complex question: 'This is the harmonisation you get sitting round the table.'

For hauliers, the chief attraction of higher weights is that one driver can shift 22 tonnes of payload with a 32-ton lorry, 28 tonnes with a 40-tonner and over 31 tonnes with a 44-tonner. Harmonisation would simplify cross-border transport (but the EEC is not Europe: Switzerland, for example, has a 28-tonne lorry limit). DG VII, in its efforts to persuade all concerned that its package was on balance a good thing, argued that it would save energy and bring a net benefit to the economy, though DG VII did not hint that thousands of millions of extra spending might be needed on roads and bridges. As for environmental impact, DG VII spoke of tighter controls over noise, fumes and braking (which, however, could be achieved, and more easily, with more moderate vehicles). It also spoke of bans in 'environmentally sensitive areas, such as centres of old towns', but this was not a new notion.

DG VII's case failed to convince the European Environmental Bureau, a body representing nearly fifty amenity
groups throughout the EEC. Its submission to DG VII brought
together most of the opposition arguments. It called for a
wide-ranging 'impact assessment' in which the following
questions would be considered:

'Will the proposal encourage yet more freight to travel
longer distances by road? Allowing greater payloads . . . is
likely to generate more road freight and attract freight from
the railways. What parallel measures are being proposed to
encourage more freight to travel by rail or water?

'What is the effect on energy consumption? . . . The heavier
a lorry, the more likely it is to be used partially laden. Heavier
lorries partially laden use more fuel than lighter lorries . . .'
(These two topics are dealt with in Chapter 8.)

'What is the direct environmental effect of allowing increases
in gross weight? . . . A heavier lorry will do more damage if it
goes out of control or is involved in an accident . . . It may be
significant that it is the flattest member-state (the Netherlands)
that allows the greatest gross weight. There is also evidence
that heavier lorries are more likely to overturn since the centre
of gravity is higher . . .' (For accidents, see Chapter 4.)

'Is the increase in use and weights of lorries being matched
by progress in reducing noise and vibration?' (See Chapter 5.)

On environmental bans: 'How effectively are such restrictions already applied in different member-states?' (See Chapters
6 and 8.)

'How effectively are the existing licensing systems in
member-states operating to minimise the use of lorries?' (See
Chapter 3.)

The bureau also presented a ten-page analysis challenging
DG VII's claim that its proposals would 'minimise damage to
the infrastructure'. The bureau questioned the basis of DG
VII's assumptions about road damage. If DG VII insisted on
harmonisation, it said, it should harmonise on the existing
British limits (which are far from ideal, as Chapter 7 shows).

A DG VII official, John Edsberg (English despite his name),
had given the bureau an undertaking that as his office had
published a paper in which the lorry manufacturers and
hauliers had set out their case for heavier vehicles, it would
also publish the bureau's views. But when he saw the bureau's
submission, his response was: 'I am not sure the [EEC]

Commission can be expected to publish a paper which says that its proposals are unacceptable.'

Among the challengers of DG VII's package, the British environmentalists were the most active, and with good reason. It was not only that Britain faced a gross weight increase of 35 per cent. Britain was already the most lorry-battered country. The fact that Denmark and Italy already permitted lorries up to 44 tonnes, and the Netherlands a few to 50 tonnes, was misleading. Continental countries severely controlled long-distance lorries; Britain's transport department encouraged them to proliferate. West Germany provides the best example of the send-it-by-rail philosophy. On trips of more than fifty kilometres, its lorries recorded 55,900 million tonne-kilometres in 1978, against 80,000 million in Britain; its railways recorded 57,500 million against 19,980 million. So in West Germany the long-distance lorries carried less than half the total; in Britain more than 80 per cent. Furthermore, the transport department's forecasts said that by 1990 the British lorries' tonne-kilometres would increase by between 17 and 35 per cent. Medium and small lorries would actually be doing less, and the most-hated big ones much more: by 1990 the mileage run by lorries over 25 tonnes would increase by at least a half and perhaps by two-thirds.

It was no wonder that Britain was the country where politicians found it wise to have an inquiry and let people speak their minds about the 'causes and consequences' of this growth. After the Peeler fiasco, the civil servants were still able to influence the inquiry in several quiet ways. William Rodgers had had in mind a full eight-man committee, a body sometimes known to produce awkward minority reports, or even to come round to a way of thinking that displeases its makers. When Norman Fowler took over he appointed one man, Sir Arthur Armitage, professor of law and vice-chancellor of Manchester University, with four assessors to advise him. The assessors were Sir Henry Chilver, civil engineer and vice-chancellor of Cranfield Institute of Technology; Professor Patrick Lawther, head of a Medical Research Council toxicology unit; Audrey Lees, Merseyside's chief planning officer; and Professor Ray Rees, an economist of University College, Cardiff. Because Chilver was a member of the Royal Commission on Environmental Pollution and Lawther was active in

the Clean Air Society, the lorry-men's associations asserted
that the assessors had an environmental bias. However, the
environmentalists had some reason to say the opposite.
Cranfield does a good deal of manufacturer-sponsored
research on heavy vehicles, and Chilver was a director of
several companies heavily involved in road freight—especially
English China Clays, whose forty-odd subsidiaries range
from Associated Asphalt through Heavy Transport and Sludge
Tankers to Western Express Haulage. As for Lawther, the
Clean Air Society was dominated by manufacturers and others
with pollution problems; and he was noted as an opponent of
stringent action against exhaust emissions. Still more important to the department was that it supplied the secretary to the
inquiry and also his assistant—both of them officials on first-
name terms with the freight directorate.

An inquiry chairman has never before, perhaps, set to work
with clearer knowledge than Armitage had of what his
appointing ministry wanted of him. However, he had no lack
of opportunity to learn both sides of the argument. More than
1,800 submissions came in from round the country, and
Armitage asked a number of organisations, ranging from the
Road Haulage Association to the Campaign Against the Lorry
Menace, to give oral evidence. The chief issues will be fully
discussed in later chapters, but it will be useful here to present
some basic thoughts from a 27,000-word submission that was
part of Armitage's reading on the environmentalist side: that
of the Civic Trust, an uncombative and some would say too
gentlemanly body, which serves as a focus for 1,200 amenity
societies.

The key question for Armitage, the trust said, was: 'Is the
nuisance in general getting worse or are such measures as are
being taken reducing the nuisance—or at least keeping it
within bounds?' With the benefit of talks with freight directorate men, the trust said: 'A view held within the department
... is that "we are steadily improving the situation", and a
picture of the year 2005 is of "a great reduction in the
nuisance ... perhaps a few more lorries and a greater pre-
ponderance of long vehicles, but the vehicles will be as quiet
as today's cars, and through traffic should be largely removed
from towns and villages".' This view, the trust said, was
'more than implausible'. What of the department's own
freight forecasts? What invisible hand would stop the rising

graph? 'Will it be the benign hand of government or will it be the hand of Opec? Will the appetites of consumers be surfeited or will manufacturers not move goods so far? . . . Will public resistance to lorries force the government's hand?' And the trust asked Armitage to imagine what the forecasts would mean by 2005:

> Stand at the roadside in a typical urban shopping street or small town carrying through traffic and watch the lorries as they pass. The first step is to imagine the majority of the smaller and medium lorries replaced by the largest . . . The next step is to imagine half as many lorries again. The picture is not a pleasant one.

If the transport department was against changing the present 'general freight regime', to use its phrase, it should 'state categorically that it is prepared to accept a steady environmental deterioration'.

Here was the point: the most sacred part of the department's freight regime was its refusal to limit the number of big lorries in continental style, but it averted its eyes from the consequences. Over the years the department had if anything come to sound more complacent. In 1972, when Geoffrey Rippon, hardly a campaigning minister, was overlord of the environment/transport complex, he told the Commons: 'The government fully accept that we cannot just go on as we are and that the price in terms of noise, fumes and congestion is quite unacceptable.' We did just go on; yet in 1979, when the transport department presented its own thoughts to Armitage, it avoided any such outright statement. The most it could bring itself to do was to ask a series of questions, such as: 'Would existing programmes be adequate to contain the effects of the increased traffic? . . . Could the increasing amount of freight movement by road be moderated: by what means, with what benefits, and at what cost?'

Still, a question that even implied the possibility of such action was probably thought daring enough. The department offered Armitage a modest view of its powers: 'Most changes and developments in the freight transport industry have been unconnected with any steps taken by government.' More seriously, nearly every paper the department produced for Armitage was worded to put big lorries in a good light.

In most matters to do with the commercial and industrial
world, civil servants have to look for information and
guidance to the very people who have axes to grind. Long
before the public knows that a proposal is under discussion—
whether a positive one, such as to invest £1,000 million in an
airliner, or a negative one, such as to control or ban a noxious
chemical—men from the industry concerned are visiting the
ministry and giving their lessons. A past history of such visits
will have helped to create the departmental view or philosophy
against which wise officials do not contend. As Michael
Meacher, MP, said in a letter to *The Guardian* commenting on
Tony Benn's lecture on mandarin power: 'I remember once
being told by a civil servant that after his successful interview
before a civil service board he was advised, "Serve your
minister well, but don't forget *we* are responsible for your
promotion".' A man who knows the transport department
well put it to me like this: 'Officials who resist the departmental line harm their prospects. They get shifted aside. There
is no public shame, but people in the canteen may know. Most
of them favour a quiet life.'

Of course, civil servants do engage in arguments. Opposing
views are put. But in the end no permanent secretary or
minister will thank a man for an inconclusive statement of
pros and cons. Here is where the philosophy and the lobbies
can combine to have great power. In the case of transport,
men with files of calculations about payloads or lorry export
prospects can easily outweigh objectors (if any are heard) with
unquantifiable worries about environmental impact. A minister
may say, as ministers have, We must civilise the lorry. But
officials with clear ideas, who enjoy the sensation of dealing
in a hardheaded way with hardheaded hauliers and lorry
makers, can outwit such orders. In the words of Jack Straw,
MP—who as political adviser to Barbara Castle in two
ministries was able to study civil servants in action—things
can happen that are 'deeply worrying'. Straw said in a lecture
at the University of Leeds in 1978: 'It is not surprising that
sometimes an official or group of officials may seek to
influence the outcome of deliberations in an unacceptable or
improper way: by delays, by the foreclosing of options, or by
being downright misleading . . . Ministers lead high-pressure
lives, and can easily become isolated . . . from alternative
sources of advice. In these circumstances they can be "got at",

or be subject to a slow drip one way by officials bent on securing their own pet schemes.' In Straw's view, which echoes Rodgers's remarks on civil servants 'going native', they are always in danger of enjoying too cosy a relationship with lobbyists who, unlike politicians, have access to departments and are seen by officials as their 'clients'. It too often happens, he says, that policy-making is influenced 'more by the desire for a quiet life with the department's "clients" than any other consideration' (Straw, 1978).

At the Department of Transport, whose chief direct function has always been roadbuilding, there has long been evidence of cosiness with those who build roads and with the makers and operators of the vehicles that justify the roads. For years it has been customary for monthly visits to be made to the department by, in particular, officials of the Freight Transport Association, which represents 15,750 firms from manufacturers to retailers which transport their own goods; and of the Road Haulage Association, which enrols two-fifths of the 46,000 hauliers who operate lorries for hire. Such officials have lunches with civil servants, and there was formerly even a civil servant who played golf with Freight Transport Association men. George Mitchell, an official of the other association, who began dealing with the department in the thirties, told me in 1979: 'I've been dealing with them so long I'm almost part of the furniture.' Every year the RHA goes to the department with a list of road schemes that it wants to be given priority. 'The department asks, Which scheme do you want moved?' Mitchell said. 'The department treats us very well on this. We have been able to get certain roads built.' He did not have a high opinion of the chief road lobby, the British Road Federation, which relies more on direct public relations and subsidised local pressure groups: 'It's more effective to work quietly.'

When the Armitage inquiry was announced, with its terms of reference going so worryingly beyond what presentational purposes required, astute minds in the department could see that the long history of kindnesses to the lorry men created a difficulty. So little had been done for the public (the department's true clients) that heavier lorries might be hard to sell. The department began showing signs of bureaucratic paranoia. My own small experience sheds further light on the civil service mind.

Although lobbyists can easily see officials in the triple-
towered complex in Marsham Street which Transport shares
with Environment, it is another matter for someone intending
to write a book that might well question the departmental
view. Control of information is the officials' best means of
influencing both ministers and the outside world. Ministers
themselves are of course constantly giving private briefings to
journalists; but as Tony Benn said in the lecture I have already
quoted: 'The power of the civil service to arrange for its view
of policy to be transmitted discreetly to the media is every bit
as great.' He could have added: 'Still greater is its power to
withhold.'

In 1979, when I began the research for this book, I was
known in Marsham Street as a result of articles I had written
in *The Sunday Times* since 1976 on transport matters: articles
that often publicised facts the department would have liked to
see ignored. As a newcomer to the subject in 1976 I had had
my first lessons in the information system when the department's press office, through which everything has to be
arranged, laid on 'non-attributable briefings' for me with
several officials: an assistant secretary who enthusiastically
told me about the motorways he still had to build, an under-
secretary for railways who spent most of his time knocking
railways, and an assistant secretary in the freight directorate
who said, in defiance of the reigning government's policy,
'We don't *want* to shift long-distance freight on to rail', and
who added, 'We do not believe that heavy lorries on good
roads designed for them are not a good thing.' (This man,
Gerry Flanagan, after having spent years dealing with lorry
operators, moved to the National Freight Corporation, Britain's
biggest haulage business, as director of corporate planning.)
When I asked the press office to find me someone whose job
was to deal with the environmental impact of lorries, I was
told that no particular person was responsible: each environmental question was considered as it arose. It was only much
later that I discovered that the department had avoided telling
me that 'lorries and the environment' came under Flanagan
and his directorate colleagues.

My approach in 1979 produced (after exchanges of letters
and a talk with the chief information officer) some foundation-
laying interviews with the head of the promising-sounding
Transport Policy Review Unit and with two economists, and a

short session with the successor to Joseph Peeler as head of
freight directorate, who even at this sensitive time had no
thought of adopting a 'lorries and environment' mantle, for he
began with these memorable words: 'We are the sponsor
directorate for the road-haulage industry.'

Three months after my first approach I was still waiting to
talk to officials on such matters as vehicle safety, highway
policy and research. I had also written in vain to the Transport
and Road Research Laboratory in Berkshire, on which the
department spends more than £10 million a year, for interviews there about a number of current research topics: road
damage, safety, vehicle design, fuel economy, environmental
impact, freight forecasts. I was beginning to have cold-
shoulder sensations. In the fourth month I discovered that all
my correspondence had gone up to Sir Peter Baldwin himself.
I was honoured with a letter from him:

> I am in a bit of a difficulty. On the one hand, it is nice to be
> helpful, and sensible also since you could take it out of us if
> you thought we had been unhelpful. On the other hand, if
> we tried to slake the thirst for information among authors
> of books on our affairs, we could find ourselves giving up
> too much time from other duties . . . The question for me is
> where to draw the line. One guide for me is that the only
> policy which we can expound is that of the minister. There
> is no point in our spending time telling you what the
> minister has said when we can draw your attention to his
> own statements or to papers which he has authorised to be
> issued. If there are subjects . . . about which you cannot tell
> whether you know the minister's mind, we will consider
> whether there is any more material to which we can refer
> you . . .

That argument would almost rule out the practice of non-
attributable briefings, which departments generally find so
useful. However, some of the turns of phrase were enjoyable:
it was good to see that I must not think the department
unhelpful. I replied as urbanely and humbly as possible,
understanding his difficulty but still desiring interviews. This
head of a £3,000-million-a-year department responded with
further talk of his difficulties: 'They do not only bear on the
assistance which we seek to give, as a matter of some priority,

to journalists and authors, but on all aspects of the many tasks of this department. I hope that you will agree that we have already given you considerable help . . . and that you will understand that you have not been singled out for special treatment . . .' That phrase recurred when I spoke on the phone to the chief information officer: 'I assure you, you haven't been singled out for any special treatment.' It was a piquant use of positive-sounding words for something negative; and it suggested a bad conscience, for at no time had I said anything to suggest that the department was being 'unhelpful' or was singling me out.

Baldwin made one offer: I could see his director-general of research as 'the way of dealing' with my request to see people at the Road Research Laboratory. This man talked for much of the time—impressively, but not, for me, with much relevance— about future technology. I said I still wished to see people at the laboratory, a place that normally welcomes inquiring writers, for few make the effort to go there. At his suggestion I sent him a list of the research items I still wished to discuss. He took nearly six weeks to find a way to say no: '. . . I do not feel that it would be right for us to give you privileged access to research workers at a stage when their studies are far from complete . . . It is an established principle at the laboratory to treat all authors equally, and to make an exception in your case might be to establish a precedent . . .'

In all, six months had passed. Somehow the department was not eager to load me with information about the virtues of its policies. I would have to manage as best I could. If I now err from time to time in my facts or my interpretation, I hope the department will not blame me. I had to press on without having been able to ask people in the highway planning directorate about the effect that ever-increasing juggernauts were having on road surfaces, or in the vehicle safety directorate about stability problems with 40-ton lorries, or in freight directorate about how big lorries on their door-to-door business were to be kept out of 'sensitive' roads, or at the Road Research Laboratory about its work on bursting gas mains or the damaging power of high axle-loads or juggernaut accidents or noise and vibration or people's attitudes to lorries or freight transfers to rail or the long-term future of the freight industry. I had to guess why it was that the laboratory's environmental section had been dismantled; and decide for myself whether to accept the department's assurance that decisions on lines of research to be pursued or abandoned were in no way political. I had to try to draw no dangerous conclusions when I heard that people at the laboratory had been known to say, 'If we let these results out to the public it will cause trouble'; and that a senior man there had been ordered to do a hurried study on freight policy for the next twenty years which he called 'very important—a very political thing'; or when I was told by a professor of transport studies, 'In the civil service, research is highly political.'

I knew I could not free myself of the conviction that information itself is highly political. I was not alone in thinking so. Here again is the Civic Trust in its evidence to Armitage: 'Ministers, recognising that the lorry problem is thorny—that what electors want may conflict with what industry wants—have preferred to leave it alone. Instead of the last ten years . . . having been a period of fruitful discussion . . . and thus having paved the way for sound policies, we have seen government allowing constructive points of criticism to go unanswered, failing to explain the reasons for some of its policies, and often being reluctant to supply even quite simple information.' And this is the trust's comment on the department's failure to produce any useful research into the effect of lorry vibration on buildings: 'The trust is left with the feeling that many find ignorance convenient.'

The department has from time to time gone on record with words of goodwill. In a public consultation document of 1976, *Transport Policy*, it said that transport 'cannot be left solely to market forces'. The government must 'ensure that all members of the community had reasonable opportunities for mobility'; it must protect the environment, 'for the movement of goods and people imposes real costs on the community'; and it must encourage economic efficiency, as 'the market does not prevent the extravagant use of scarce resources, notably energy'. A White Paper of the following year returned to the theme: 'A wholly free market in transport could be brutal . . . Each mode of transport must be judged on the same criteria and encouraged to do what it can do best in terms of both economic and social costs.' The White Paper was drafted under the eye of William Rodgers, after a struggle with some officials over, among other things, lorry impact. It was a

compromise, and did not go on to say, for example, that one of
the things the railways 'do best' is reduce the brutal effect of
road traffic. In any case the benign phrases did not come to
much in practice; and soon, under Norman Fowler, the
department had a minister eager for a free market, and fully in
tune with freight directorate's short way with social costs.
'The customer must decide,' said the directorate, and so said
Fowler in public. It sounded like a good rule; but in fact it
made sense only if the providers of freight services were
covering all their costs. In fact the lorry operator's customer
has not been paying his share of the 'real costs' of environmental damage and accidents, or even the full cost of the
lorries' use of the roads.

And the community cost goes wider. When the customer
makes his freight-moving decisions on this false basis, he is
not only thrusting social costs upon people who have no say in
the matter; he is also distorting their future. He is causing
what economists call 'a misallocation of resources'. Falsely
cheap road transport, whether of people in cars or of goods in
lorries, stimulates investment in roads and vehicles, and
creates a way of life too dependent on transport. That is far
from preventing 'the extravagant use of scarce resources,
notably energy'. In the eyes of too many people in the
department, however, the vast growth of road traffic is a
robust argument for yet more growth. When officials look at
the national accounts, in which lorries are insufficiently
charged with road costs and in which the cost of noise, fumes,
vibration, blight, fear and accidents is scarcely visible, but in
which railways are listed as a debit, they see an unending
increase in road traffic as healthy, almost a proof of departmental virility. Thus it is that although the 1977 White Paper
spoke up for the improvement of public transport, for greater
use of the railways, for conservation of energy and even for a
decrease in 'our absolute dependence on transport', vehicle-
miles still rule.

Lorry operators, reasonably enough taking advantage of
the kindly framework provided for them and ignoring the
occasional community-conscious words of transport ministers,
have made Britain far more dependent on road freight than
any other European industrial country. They are eager,
naturally, to emphasise this dependence. In the words of John
Silbermann, the Road Haulage Association's chairman in

1979–80, 'We must remind ourselves that Britain is nationally entirely dependent upon the lorry to maintain our way of civilised life. There is little these days that is not transported by commercial vehicle at some time during its manufacturing or distributive processes . . . I have repeatedly claimed that Britain enjoys a lorry-based economy . . . It is difficult to say something like this without appearing to blow our trumpet, but it is a fact that the haulage industry gives such a high standard of performance to its customers that it is simply taken for granted.' The Freight Transport Association put similar thoughts to Armitage, and said: 'The overwhelming dependence on the lorry is increasing.' It is true that lorries perform a great deal of essential work, and that ways will have to be found to continue some forms of road transport when the oil runs out. However, there are many questions. Must not the dependence on long-distance lorries be reduced now, so that the country is less committed to a production and distribution infrastructure that will make the coming transition more difficult? Should not the department's be-kind-to-lorries philosophy be abandoned? And more immediately embarrassing to the lorry lobby: Even in these present years of plentiful diesel, have big lorries brought increased efficiency? Ask the head of freight directorate and he will say yes. Ask him why and he will say: There are thousands of sharply competing hauliers, so they must be efficient.

However, the facts challenge him. Two weeks after Silbermann spoke the words quoted above, Peter Thompson, chief executive of the National Freight Corporation (now National Freight Company), analysed the payloads carried during the period 1973–8, when the number of lorries under 16 tons declined and the number over 16 went up by 79 per cent, and he said: 'The effective use of the heavier vehicles has quite significantly declined . . . Whilst the industry has improved its productivity when measured by output per vehicle . . . the industry has been less efficient at ensuring that the larger vehicles are being filled to capacity.' This efficiency question will be discussed in Chapter 8. For the moment it is enough to record the implications pointed out by Thompson, who commands nearly 20,000 lorries. A 40-tonne lorry would be a cheaper freight-carrier, he said, only when loaded to 90 per cent of its maximum; but experience showed that as vehicles had grown larger 'they tended to be used less efficiently'.

When the campaign for heavier lorries gave rise to a searching inquiry, and then brought forth statements such as this, the campaigners began to feel some anxiety. However well-inclined Sir Arthur Armitage himself might prove toward the 'right answer', he would be the target of serious counter-views. The display of contending arguments might not reform the thinking of the civil servants (though public inquiries had been known to shift departmental views), but it might well open the eyes of the public and politicians. Where might it end?

2

Roads for all reasons

There are men nearing retirement in Marsham Street who
gave the prime of their lives to the fulfilment of a dream: the
creation by 1985 or 1990 of a road network on which thirty
million vehicles would be able to move almost free of
congestion in town as well as country. The dream looks
childish now, but its effects are very much with us, not only in
the ruined hearts of such places as Birmingham, but also in a
flawed and uncoordinated transport system, and in the
departmental mind. The department's roadbuilders are like a
nation that has not come to terms with the dwindling of an
empire. The new roads on which they are still spending many
hundreds of millions of pounds annually are designed to last,
and to justify their cost, into the next century. Some years
before that century comes, according to almost every forecast,
oil production will have passed its peak. No longer is it the
presentational strategy to maintain public approval for the
costly programme by offering a vision of liberated citizens
in fast cars flowing untroubled throughout the land. Life is
more serious; lorries rule. 'Our roadbuilding strategy is to
put first emphasis on the regeneration of the economy,' said
Norman Fowler in 1980. 'I am giving top priority to the completion of industrial routes, and in particular the routes to
the ports.'

In 1960 the selling line was different. The transport minister,
Ernest Marples (of Marples Ridgway, civil engineers and
roadbuilders), told his party conference: 'We have to rebuild
our cities. We have to come to terms with the car. The
pedestrian must be segregated from the motorist.' The future
was bright for roadbuilders. Marples had an 'advisory group'
deciding how to cut back the railways, a group made up
largely of big industrialists of whom the best-remembered is a
man from Imperial Chemical Industries, Richard Beeching.
Britain's first motorway, the M1, was a year old, and more

were soon to follow. Marples, and his department, were determined that motorways through the country would be complemented by motorways in towns. He had a planning group at work who were creating, he said, 'a design for living'. This notion was straight from the mind of another engineer, the guiding spirit of that planning group, Colin Buchanan.

Although ministers and the men who advise them tend to have a happy confidence in their own wisdom, the mere announcement of a plan to do the world good is not enough. Parliament and the public have often to be cajoled and worried into seeing the truth. It is true that in 1960 millions of people were motorists and millions more wished to be; but they were not ready to welcome the painful consequences of their own desire. Means of persuasion were needed, such as a well-chosen inquiry committee. But before a committee sits, climate-creating measures are helpful, such as the convening of a seminar or symposium, preferably at a university and attended by a mixture of public officials, academics and foreigners. So it was in April 1961: a symposium on Urban Survival and Traffic was held at Newcastle upon Tyne, organised by Durham University's department of civil engineering and planning 'in collaboration with the Roads Campaign Council'.

Little is heard of this council now, but in 1961 it was the most active road lobby, and especially with MPs. In the late fifties it had organised MPs of both sides into an All-Party Roads Study Group which helped to achieve the approval, almost without debate, of a programme of motorway and trunk road building totalling 4,200 miles. Its Tory joint-chairman of those days, Geoffrey Wilson, said afterwards that the group 'worked extremely well and has done much to ease the bitterness of the controversy'.

Colin Buchanan was a star of the Newcastle symposium. It is a piquant fact, however, that he had recently undergone an agony of spirit that could have ended with his abandoning his 'design for living', and then some city-bashing would never have happened. He told the symposium that his approach to problems was 'constructional': 'When I observe a snarl-up of traffic I instinctively ask what can be done by way of physical re-arrangement.' One day at the ministry, though, he had had a shock: 'I was poring over some plans and an economist came along and looked over my shoulder and said, "But, my dear boy, I could solve that for you in such a simple way."' The economist said he would 'tax three-quarters of that traffic off the road altogether'.

The constructional mind was unnerved. 'It took me months to recover . . . and pick up my confidence again,' said Buchanan. The reasoning that saved him was this: 'Sooner or later, people will demand towns that cater properly for what has probably been the most fantastically successful invention in history, and . . . will be prepared to pay for it.' Having overcome the subversive thought of that economist, Buchanan also managed not to draw subversive conclusions from the evidence of his eyes and ears. Although in 1961 the world was a quieter place than now, the noise round his ministry office in Southwark, he said, was 'tremendous' and nearly everybody in the building suffered. Then at the end of the day he had to walk through 'a turmoil of traffic' to Waterloo. 'I regard the crossing of every street as a potential death-trap . . . The total picture of sordid confusion is quite terrifying . . . This new means of getting round involving the use of a fast-moving, noisy, smelly and (unless properly provided for) extremely dangerous vehicle has—'

What has it done?

'—has made the traditional arrangement of streets and of buildings completely out of date.' People might fight, he said, to preserve this or that 'much-loved and admired locality' but if such people got their way that would stop us from 'getting the most out of the motor'. First frighten, then cajole: the most important thing about his engineered townscape, with pedestrians pushed out of the vehicles' way, would be 'its power to delight'.

In those days people in authority (people who tended to be motorists) seldom asked troubled questions. One at the symposium who did was Wilfred Burns, then Newcastle's chief planning officer. He asked: 'Are we to destroy all that a city means, forgetting its pleasantnesses, its attractions and its stimulations, and instead concentrate on only one aspect of life—the movement and parking of four-wheeled vehicles?' Marples's department was deaf to such doubts. It told Buchanan and his planning group to produce a report, and it dignified them with a 'steering group' of architects and other eminent outsiders. One of these was Councillor T. Dan Smith of Newcastle, who within a few years, and before his

questionable ways of expediting redevelopment contracts
sent him to jail, was to destroy some of the pleasantnesses of
that city, in spite of Burns.

When Buchanan's design for living, Traffic in Towns,
emerged in 1963, with its vision of urban motorway grids, and
of shops and people pushed up above, and of Oxford Street a
six-lane throughway, it was given an official fanfare. 'We
have no reserve in commending it,' said the steering group. 'If
the coming flood of vehicles means freer and easier transport
of goods and persons, it cannot help but be beneficial.' The
report constantly displayed its goodheartedness. Here, for
example, is Buchanan on road accidents: 'It may be that
future generations will regard our carelessness in allowing
human beings and moving vehicles to use the same streets . . .
with the same horror and incomprehension with which we
recall the indifference of earlier generations to elementary
sanitation.' His equating of traffic and sewage was bold; but
neither he nor his masters asked, What is a city street from
which human beings are banned except for those sitting in
fast-moving, noisy, smelly and dangerous vehicles?

It was not a time when trained minds were making anti-
constructional connections. A member of the steering group,
the architect Sir William Holford, was impressed by the result
of a rush-hour race, organised in 1963 by BBC Panorama,
from Putney to Charing Cross: 1st, motor scooter; 2nd,
bicycle; 3rd, car; 4th, horse; 5th, walker. In an article in Traffic
Engineering he said: 'But no one drew the moral—'

That scooters and cycles should be encouraged?

'—that a thousand more cars are available for use every day
and there is not a single urban channel designed to use them
properly.'

Similar thinking prevailed in other countries, of course,
during the third quarter of this century, which will come to be
seen as the golden age of the motor vehicle. Cheap petroleum
meant that road improvements and new roads were indeed
needed, and that there was everywhere a shift of passengers
and freight from rail to road. The question was (as civil
servants put it): Where should the balance be struck? The idea
of giving motor vehicles the freedom of towns by means of
vast rebuilding was hardly balanced. It was damaging nonsense, and impossibly expensive. (One sceptic, the economist
Christopher Foster, calculated in 1964 that to give the

Buchanan treatment to all towns of more than 20,000 inhabitants would cost at least £18,000 million, or over £85,000
million in 1980 prices.) The point is that it was nonsense
warmly advocated by highly-placed men. When the dream
faded, the most searching analyses of what had gone wrong
came, as is often the case, from America. For example, here is
an American academic, Gordon Fellman, writing in the
journal *Transportation* (December 1975): 'In highway planning as in urban renewal . . . the very rich and powerful
pursue their financial and power interests partly on their own
and partly through the offices of upper middle-class professionals, who often *think* they are acting objectively when
actually they provide the technical planning and ideological
rationalisation for the interests of the rich and the powerful.'

The anger of less powerful people in their 'much-loved and
admired localities' or merely in humbler streets helped to end
the dream; but it did not die in Buchanan's own mind. In
retirement on a Gloucestershire hillside, down a road marked
Private, he wrote down some thoughts in 1979. He said the
argument of *Traffic in Towns* was 'absolutely sound': if
people did not wish to give up their cars, you had to rebuild the
towns for the sake of the environment. 'Furious opposition' to
motorways in general had meant the loss of 'long-term
environmental benefits'. 'The greatest tragedy was the un-
scrupulous jettisoning for electoral advantage of the road
proposals [inner-ring motorways] for Greater London.'

Even in the sixties, the highway-minded professionals in the
transport department had had to do some fighting for their
views. Barbara Castle, who became the minister at the end of
1965, was a different person from Ernest Marples. Some
years later, she recalled in an address to senior civil servants
that she found 'an atmosphere of ill-concealed hostility' in the
department. 'It took me several months to get my civil
servants even to be able to mouth the words "integrated
transport policy". There they had all been, you see, in the
Marples and Beeching tradition for the past four or five years,
and they did not believe in an integrated transport policy.'
Their disbelief even decided the wording of the draft answers
they gave her in readiness for Commons questions: 'We do not
believe in an integrated transport policy,' they wrote.

'I took this for a bit,' she said, 'but finally wrote across the

official memorandum, "Pardon me, we do" in large letters. I
crossed out the "not". After that, my view faithfully appeared
in every supplementary [Commons answer]: "We do believe
in an integrated transport policy." But does anybody believe
that an attitude of mind had changed?' (Castle, 1973).

It had not changed. Barbara Castle had come to the
department determined on a shake-up. In particular she
wanted the department to cease to be a ministry of roads. Her
first call for integrated thinking was: 'Produce evidence on
which all investment in roads, rail and ports should be based.'
However, the civil servants' natural resistance to new thinking
was sharpened by two things: she brought in an outsider,
Christopher Foster, as director of economics; and there was a
leak (not of her doing) that she wanted to get rid of her
permanent secretary, Sir Thomas Padmore, the chief non-
believer in integration. As a result of the leak he stayed on for
two years, seldom going to departmental meetings. For a
time, nevertheless, there were signs of change. Mrs Castle,
not being anti-rail like Marples, slowed down the Beeching
axe. Her first White Paper, *Transport Policy*, 1966, contained
assertions of goodheartedness. The development of the motor
vehicle, it said, was bringing benefits but also congestion,
misery, noise, fumes, danger, death 'and a threat to our
environment in both town and countryside which, if it
continues unchecked, will ensure that the pleasure and
benefit for which we use the car will increasingly elude us.
The aim of a rational transport policy must be to solve this
paradox.' The White Paper also promised a lorry licensing
system that would be 'an effective instrument of a modern,
national freight policy' (more on this in the next chapter) and
'urgent action' to make lorries safer and less unpleasant.

But what of the paradox? Here Buchanan, and no doubt the
thought of votes, still ruled. *Traffic in Towns* was gospel: 'As
Professor Buchanan has pointed out . . . to protect the environment and to relieve congestion, our large cities and towns
will need over the next generation a modern network of high
capacity traffic routes . . . We now have an expanded urban
road programme, growing and gathering momentum.' This
was 'no more than a beginning', and there would also be a
thousand-mile inter-urban network by 1970. At the same time
rail investment, small though it was, was falling. Following
Barbara Castle's call for evidence on which all investment

should be based, Christopher Foster, the early sceptic about the cost of Buchananism, had a team at work to discover the likely comparative returns on investment in road and in rail on trunk routes. This research-for-integration included an Inter-Urban Transport Costs Model. It was particularly concerned with freight, and detailed studies were done on the London–Newcastle and Preston–Glasgow routes to try to decide the investment split that would move freight to the greatest benefit of the economy as a whole. These studies ended in a departmental pigeonhole when Foster parted from the ministry in 1970. Ten years later the opinion of the department's chief economist was: 'The studies should have ended after a few weeks.'

Barbara Castle returned to the paradox in a 1967 White Paper, *Public Transport and Traffic,* in which she spoke of the need for 'a new dynamic role for public transport' and said: 'Unless we recognise this we shall pull down the centres of our towns in an attempt to get rid of congestion; and at the end of the day we shall find congestion is still with us.' She did establish local passenger transport executives, but she kept to her road programme; and when she was succeeded by a weaker minister, Richard Marsh, the department produced a White Paper, *Roads for the Future,* 1970, that promised more roads than ever—'a comprehensive national system of trunk roads on which commercial traffic and private cars can move freely and safely and on which congestion and the frustration and economic costs it creates have been virtually eliminated'. New motorway routes were drawn across the map . . . Bristol–Southampton, Swindon–Milton Keynes . . . By 1985 or so, the promise was, motorways and other prime trunk roads would total 4,200 miles, at a cost of about £13,500 million in 1980 prices, plus the equivalent of a further £10,250 million for lesser rural roads and for the urban motorway dream. With Edward Heath's coming to power in that year, the roadbuilders' future looked brighter still. Highways were henceforth to be justified more and more as freight-movers to enrich the economy. 'Strategic network' was the catchphrase.

Difficulties were arising, however. Even though a large part of the dream was no more than lines on maps, people directly exposed to the paradox were rebelling. Anger was erupting at public motorway inquiries. Agitation had begun against the rapid spread of big lorries. One response was to

dignify (or emasculate) the word 'environment', a conveniently
imprecise term, by the creation of the Department of the
Environment. In that time of Whitehall gigantism, the department was made to include transport—with the result that the
public could easily have the illusion that all the proposals of
highway planners and of lorry promoters were subject to the
kindly restraint of environmental experts.

MPs began asking whether a little less should be spent on
roads and a little more on buses and railways. At a hearing of a
Commons environment sub-committee in 1972, one motive
force behind roadbuilding was admitted by the head of the
transport planning body for south-east Lancashire and north-
east Cheshire. He agreed with an MP who suggested that it
would take 'quite an act of self-denial' by motorists sitting on
local committees to decide against new roads and say they
would 'cater for the so-called masses who cannot afford cars'.

The sub-committee also raised a question that has still not
been satisfactorily settled: when assessing the relative benefit
of investing in a road or buses or a railway, how do you
evaluate social costs (noise, congestion, misery, death) and
social benefits? A man from the environment department's
urban policy appraisal directorate told the MPs: 'At the
moment one is not able, I think, to quantify the full social
cost . . . We go as far as we can.'

Q: How far do you go?

A: One quantifies those things which in a sense we can
measure and put a value on, such as time, operating costs and
convenience—and obviously the capital costs.

In short, 'as far as we can' meant that they were not
quantifying any social costs, only benefits. Time-saving in
particular was, and is, by far the greatest single plus item in
the cost/benefit equation used to justify spending the money.
Officials put exact prices on an hour of leisure time or
working time, add up all the millions of such hours which
(according to other officials' forecasts) will be saved over the
years by building a road, and this remarkable quantification
provides 80 per cent of the justification for investing the
needed millions.

The sub-committee called for an urgent reassessment of all
urban highway schemes, and for a number of measures to
reduce the demand for roads: rapid-transit schemes, bus
lanes, parking limits, pedestrian precincts, lorry routing. In

its response, the department conceded that it would be impossible to provide for 'maximum car use' in Britain's cities, and it made a statement that tellingly reveals the state of the departmental mind: 'Even by the 1980s many people will still be dependent on public transport for some or all of their journeys.'

The department's 'tails you lose' procedure of quantifying and not quantifying was questioned again in 1973 at a symposium—once more at a department of engineering, this time at Southampton University—on the newly fashionable theme, Transportation and Environment. Geoffrey Searle, a transport department economist, said: 'You quantify what can be quantified.' And then, perhaps more frankly: 'What we try to quantify are the direct benefits to travellers.' The department's deputy director of highways soothed further questioners by saying that a lot of research was being done on 'evaluating noise, visual intrusion and severance' (no such evaluations ever took effect); and his message for people who wanted to 'stop all major roadbuilding', for there were such dissenters even then, was: 'More harm will be done to the environment by not making proper provision for the motorcar.' A blunter statement came from a British Road Federation man, Sir George Middleton: 'Plans must be the work of experts . . . Selling those plans and making them acceptable is a public-relations exercise where much skill is needed.'

Part of the skill was in having road-minded men in influential positions. One such was Alfred Goldstein of the engineering and highway consultants Travers Morgan, who for many years was chairman of the department's Planning and Transport Research Advisory Council, a quango heavy with roadbuilders. In 1975, when motorway protesters were an increasing annoyance, Goldstein used a lecture to the Royal Town Planning Institute to offer some 'thoughts to help the highway promoters'. Steps should be taken to rally 'the silent majority', he said. 'We must also seek to set some limit to the extent of public discussion. Government policy cannot be productively debated anew at each of fifty public inquiries a year . . . I am second to none in supporting individuals and their rights. But roads are being and should continue to be built.' The advisory council, unsurprisingly, rarely proposed lines of research that might question the road strategy.

The limits set to discussion were already narrow enough.

No proposed motorway was ever exposed to public inquiry in its entirety, so objectors could not raise what the Americans call the 'no build' alternative. They were told that they could merely argue over the precise line to be followed, and as each inquiry dealt only with a short section, there was little leeway even in that. Inquiries were in charge of inspectors appointed and paid by the transport department (until 1977), and privately instructed to keep a tight rein on objectors who tried to cross-examine departmental witnesses. When the road-planners presented masses of computerised figures to show that the cars and lorries forecast to use the proposed road over the next twenty years would save more than enough quantified, evaluated hours to justify the investment, objectors could hardly challenge the figures without access to the planners' 'input' and 'methodology'—and a computer. And even if an inspector advised against a scheme, a rare occurrence indeed, the department overruled him in its own favour. It is no wonder that feelings of injustice erupted in angry scenes.

This embarrassed the department a little. It was trying to seem environmentally goodhearted. In 1973 an apparent concession was made: at an inquiry into a proposed section of the M42 through green belt land south of Birmingham, the inspector said objectors could question the need for the road. This had hitherto been ruled out on the ground that 'need' was a matter of national policy and could be debated only in Parliament. By this date objectors were spending thousands of pounds to hire lawyers and advisers to face the department's publicly-paid experts, and they had learned about the methodology. They sought to cross-examine a departmental official on a manual called the Red Book, whose 'input' included forecasts of vehicle traffic. The inspector's concession immediately proved minimal. He upheld a claim by the department that the content of the Red Book was 'policy', and that cross-examination on policy was barred. This claim meant that only Parliament (which in fifteen years had scarcely discussed motorways) was permitted to debate, and reach intelligent conclusions on, such subtle things as logistic growth curves with formulas like this:

$$x = \frac{aX}{X + (a-X)e^{-art/(a-X)}}$$

The forecasts were and are fundamental. To spend hundreds of millions a year of the taxpayers' money can be justified, on the department's own terms, only if enough high-speed car and lorry trips are made in the years to come. While the M42 inquiry was still being held, a Middle East war produced the first oil crisis. The forecasts were adjusted—and have since been sharply adjusted further. The department, however, has fought to preserve its dictum that what it calls 'the wisdom of the methodology' is policy and its officials must not be cross-examined about it.

In the name of a farmer, Jack Bushell, one of many people whose land the M42 threatened, the objectors went to the High Court, where the judge upheld the department, chiefly on the ground that when a minister is promoting his own scheme he is not bound by rules of natural justice. The case had become a test of ministerial power. In 1979 in the Appeal Court, Lord Denning pronounced: 'There has been a deplorable loss of confidence in these inquiries. We must use our authority to see that they are conducted fairly in accordance with the requirements of natural justice . . . The objectors should not be brushed off with the remark, "It is government policy." I do not regard the traffic forecasts as government policy at all. They are predictions about the future.' He found against the department. It appealed to the Lords, for official power was in peril. There the department argued that the objectors had not suffered any encroachment of natural justice or any 'substantial prejudice' from the bar on cross-examination, but *even if they had,* the department was still in the right. By four law lords to one, administrative majesty was upheld. The sole consolation of believers in justice was that the one dissenter, Lord Edmund-Davies, said: 'Matters of fact and expertise do not become "policy" merely because a department of government relies on them . . . The refusal . . . to permit cross-examination on what, by common agreement, was evidence of cardinal importance, was indefensible and unfair and, as such, a denial of natural justice.' The department, absolved of the need to be fair, named 1982–3 as its date to build the M42.

The years since 1973 had, however, brought changes. Restraints on oil and cash saw to it that by the mid-seventies the questions asked by the M42 objectors and by many others at least came to be discussed within the department. Hitherto

the director-general of highways had reigned almost un-
controlled in his realm within a realm, producing roads to
meet forecasts which could become true only if the roads were
built. Now he had to respond to the painful suggestion that
changes of policy, such as a shift of investment to bus and rail,
could reduce the unquestionable need. The director-general,
John Jukes, fought hard. When William Rodgers's 1977 White
Paper was being written, Jukes was still so far from accepting
that the lists of future roads which he had nursed for so long
could be questioned that he said he could not see why the
White Paper needed a highway chapter. Despite him, it said
this: 'The strategic network concept will be modified . . . The
government intends to adopt a more flexible approach . . .
This is a matter not of building to lines superimposed on maps
and to rigid standards but of deciding on the right standard for
each section of route.' Rodgers told his roadbuilders: 'You are
transport men, not highways men only.' Jukes retired and his
realm was put under an overlord with a less narrowly
constructional role, 'local transport and highways'. By the
eighties, however, there was still no sign that the department
might accept the idea that all transport investment should be
judged by parallel criteria, including social costs and benefits
now and in the future, and a full long-term valuation of those
finite resources, oil and land. (The department thinks so little
of land that it is unable to say how many thousands of acres
have been taken for roadbuilding. It 'keeps no comprehensive
records', it told an MP in 1980.)

Little is now heard about time-savings for millions of
motorists. It is just as well, for the man whom Norman Fowler
appointed in 1979 as his outside adviser, the transport
economist Ian Heggie, had said in an article that the department's methods of evaluating time-savings were far-fetched,
unduly simplistic and 'grossly over-estimate the tangible
benefits of road improvements' (Heggie, 1979). I have already
quoted Fowler on 'regeneration of the economy'. In his 1980
White Paper on roads he used road freight as his chief
argument for an increase in construction to the highest level
since 1976, even though more and more millions would also
be needed to rebuild motorways and trunk roads breaking up
under the heavy lorries. Fowler's second objective was 'to fit
in as many bypasses as possible' to help 'hard-pressed towns
and villages'. The White Paper showed, however, that at least

eighty proposed trunk road bypasses had been put in a dateless limbo. Twenty-four of these figured on a list the department had just given Sir Arthur Armitage's lorry-and-environment inquiry as evidence of bypass progress. In its evidence to Armitage on ways of easing the impact of lorries, the department had neatly combined the regeneration and environment arguments to justify more trunk roads: 'Major road schemes designed to meet the needs of industry are likely to carry the heaviest traffic and so bring both the largest traffic benefits and substantial relief to existing roads and the communities through which they pass.'

Furthermore, it will no longer be much use for objectors to a road to demonstrate (if they can get at the necessary figures) that in the department's own cost-benefit analysis the cost of a scheme is greater than the promised benefits in time-saving and reduced accidents. The department told Armitage: 'Where a scheme does not produce a positive economic benefit . . . a broader judgment must be made about whether it provides good value for money. The disturbance caused by lorry traffic would be an important factor here. In special cases, for example historic towns like Berwick-on-Tweed, the environmental advantages of a bypass may outweigh a negative economic return.'

It is a striking point. The highways programming directorate, it seems, need never lose an argument, so long as freight directorate keeps more and heavier lorries coming. The highway economists could even begin to think wistfully that if only they had after all got round to quantifying environmental damage, all unbypassed towns would yield such vast figures that an embarrassing 'negative economic return' would never be seen. However, they have to dash such thoughts, for if an environmental cost can be quantified where the department wishes, it can be quantified everywhere else, and the national total would be sure to debit juggernauts with a huge allocation of social costs.

The department gave Armitage a list of 74 towns of more than 10,000 population, in England alone, which it planned to relieve with bypasses or with bigger schemes; and a further 166 English towns and villages on non-trunk roads which county councils proposed to bypass. For many of these, however, nothing could happen until the 1990s. As for coping with lorry traffic within towns, 'the scope for major construction in central areas is limited' and not much more could be done in the suburbs; and yet 'significant numbers of schemes exist . . . which would provide communications for industry and commerce, reduce traffic delays and divert heavy traffic around residential developments, if sufficient funds were available'.

Contradictions in the department's thinking on roads and lorries, or rather in its presentational wording, were shown in other statements to Armitage: 'The motorway and trunk road programme, particularly over the last fifteen years, has done much to reduce the impact of lorry traffic on urban areas . . . The programme has reduced travel times and . . . has also encouraged different patterns of location and distribution which are related increasingly to the road network. It has thus facilitated the growth of road freight.' 'The proportion of goods vehicle traffic in built-up areas should continue to decrease . . . The continuing trunk road construction programme will have a significant effect.' The devious reasoning of the first sentence quoted has been exposed in the previous chapter: a fall in the number of small and medium lorries reduced total vehicle-miles ('traffic') on built-up roads, but the mileage there of the biggest lorries, those with greatest 'impact', had increased; thanks to the road programme, as the passage goes on to make clear. The word 'proportion' in the second passage is equally devious: the mileage of the big lorries will merely increase at a lower rate in towns than on the ever-extending trunk roads.

The department naturally prefers to emphasise the non-urban traffic: 'Sixty-five per cent of the mileage of four-axled lorries . . . is now on motorways and trunk roads in non-built-up areas' (which is a little like saying that most of the mileage of Concorde is over the Atlantic). Haulage spokesmen press the same point. This can be observed when the Road Haulage Association prepares material for members to give in evidence at motorway inquiries. ('We write it for them and they learn it by heart,' said George Mitchell, the veteran official quoted earlier.) Here are sentences from the briefs of two hauliers at an M25 inquiry: 'We believe the public in general prefers the lorries to use the motorways'; 'The general public finds the large commercial vehicle more acceptable on the motorways.' They may be wise to say so less often, for fear of stirring up the town-dwellers' obvious comment.

The question was begged with even greater enthusiasm by Robert Phillipson, director of the British Road Federation (an umbrella group for all builders and users of roads), in his evidence to Armitage: 'So-called environmentalists who have successfully delayed the road programme have directly contributed to the deterioration of the environment . . . An acceleration of the road programme will bring relief from heavy lorries.'

Neither the department nor the RHA nor the BRF ventured publicly to talk with delight about the actual juggernauts. For that one must turn again to Sir Colin Buchanan on his Gloucestershire hillside. When he set down his thoughts in 1979—it was for a draft of a speech—he said: 'I adore juggernauts in themselves—a fine sight, don't you think, to see one steaming along a wet motorway in its cocoon of spray?' He wished he could have his time again: 'I would be the owner-driver of the biggest juggernaut permissible . . . It would be a marvellously designed truck with compact living accommodation for myself and wife, with a compartment for a co-driver . . . Half the world would be our hunting ground . . . What exquisite delight to roll to a halt atop the Kulujamshid Pass in the moonlight . . . and doze off whilst gazing out at that stupendous panorama . . . My trouble is that I like juggernauts . . . How anyone could be bored with motorway driving is beyond my comprehension when there is so much to look at.'

It is time to look at the adorable juggernauts and their operators.

3

Unharried hauliers

The bright vision of Colin Buchanan, juggernaut-driver manqué, must not be dismissed as mere eccentric romanticism. It is a reminder of an important truth about the road-haulage business. For a working-man of spirit, a job as a long-distance lorry driver offers an escape from menial tasks or from the deadening labour of the assembly-line. He need not aspire to a sunset vista on a mountain pass: his destination may be Glasgow or Middlesbrough, but when he sets off with a day's driving ahead of him he can feel a cheering sense of independence. For hours to come, there will be no boss to tell him what to do. Here are the thoughts of some long-distance men: 'You are your own guv'nor. No one breathes down your neck . . . Where else can you get the freedom? . . . You're on your own—your own gaffer.' This is all the more true of men who drive to the continent and beyond. 'I do it for the money, the adventure and, let's be honest, the ego-trip,' says one. 'It is a hell of a feeling driving one of these things.'

One of the ways for an enterprising wage-earner to advance to self-employment, furthermore, is to become the owner-driver of a lorry. In Britain, men owning just one or two lorries make up more than 70 per cent of the 124,000 licensed lorry operators. In no industrialised country is it easier than in Britain to set oneself up in the haulage business. Once this was not so: Britain, like other countries, had a licensing system that limited the numbers of long-distance hauliers. That was abolished in 1968. Road haulage became a free-enterprise scene, and for many hauliers that meant a cut-throat life. For the public it meant that before long Britain had far more long-distance lorries for its size then any other country; and yet the operators of this vast fleet have been under fewer restraints than elsewhere to civilise its effects. When competition is fierce and margins are narrow, only a heroically benign haulier will voluntarily spend money on kindlier vehicles or order his drivers to be bywords for moderation.

The liberated lorries also put the state railways under much sharper competition than elsewhere. And the irony was that all this was achieved by a Transport Act devised under a Labour minister, Barbara Castle, who presented it as the means of giving Britain 'an integrated transport system'. How this came about is another revealing example of how lobbyists and civil servants can get their way.

The basis for the 1968 Act was a report from a committee under Lord Geddes, at a time when the road programme was accelerating and the Beeching axe was swinging. Geddes recommended that the long-standing system of restricting the number of long-distance lorries, known as 'quantity licensing', should no longer be used—whether for diverting freight to the railways, easing congestion, increasing safety or reducing the environmental impact of lorries. Quantity licensing, he concluded, caused inefficiency and should be swept away. The only purpose of a licensing system should be to ensure that lorries operated safely: the new phrase became 'quality licensing'. Geddes did not suggest that other matters, such as lorry impact, were beyond the concern of government. 'The lorry is not the perfect servant going almost unseen and unheard about its business,' he said. But he thought that should be a matter for direct controls (on noise and smoke, for example, and on lorry routing), and if the government was concerned about the cost of road damage or congestion, or wanted to shift freight to rail, it could impose extra taxes rather than limit numbers by licensing (Geddes, 1965).

Barbara Castle began by rejecting part of Geddes's liberationist reasoning. In a White Paper of 1967, *The Transport of Freight*, she said her objective was 'to make the maximum economic use of our railways as well as our roads by promoting the transfer of all suitable traffic from congested roads to the railways'. This was 'still a valid objective of licensing'. It was 'plain common sense to keep some form of quantity licensing as one of the means of encouraging industry to use rail transport where it can get a service which in overall terms of speed, reliability and cost is at least as good'. She proposed two complementary measures. A system christened 'freightliner' would be developed to carry container-packed goods for most of their journey by rail, with lorries taking them to and from terminals; and everyone who wanted to operate lorries over 16 tons gross weight on trips further than 100 miles would have to apply for a special licence, to which the railways could object (a retention, in fact, of quantity licensing). Her hope was that within a few years a freightliner network with fifty terminals using container-lifting cranes would win 4,500 million ton-miles of traffic then going by road (that would have increased the railways' ton-mileage by a third); and that by 1980 the figure would be 6,000 million ton-miles. In fact by 1979 it was only about 1,500 million.

In the freight world, these proposals were to be the heart of the promised integration. Barbara Castle was already committed to set up a national authority. When a resolution of the National Union of Railwaymen at Labour's 1966 conference had called for legislation to implement an election promise of integrated transport, she had given a pledge: 'You will get the legislation for which you ask, and I hope in the next session of Parliament.' She had also set economists to work calculating 'road track costs'—that is, the lorries' share of the cost of the roads they used. She had asked other economists to find the answers to interesting questions that nobody in the transport department had asked before: What are the true relative costs, both economic and social, of carrying goods by road and by rail? What are the likely returns from investing in rail or in road on trunk routes? These are the questions that the department resisted then and has pushed aside since.

It has already been seen in Chapter 2 that Barbara Castle could scarcely get her civil servants to speak the words 'integrated transport policy'. She also recalled, in the same address to a seminar of civil servants, that she did not think she could have got her Transport Act through—'through the department, that is, not the House of Commons'—if she had not had her own team of political advisers, people with an 'interventionist approach' like her own, 'ready to do battle with the very laissez-faire philosophy that I inherited'. She went on: 'It was uphill, uphill all the way. Quantity licensing: I might have been proposing publicly-financed sin or something. The whole instinctive reaction of the department was against three-quarters of that Act. I'm not saying anybody sabotaged it . . . You've got negative power; you can work without enthusiasm' (Castle, 1973).

In the 1968 debates she called the freightliner system 'technical integration in practice'. It emerged, however, that it was not to be run by British Rail but by a National Freight Corporation in command of all state-owned lorries. The Act required the two bodies 'to provide a properly integrated goods service' (though the corporation had only a fraction of the country's lorries). Liaison between British Rail and the corporation would be entrusted to a Freight Integration Council, which would 'see to it', Barbara Castle said, 'that integration really got off the ground'. In due course it became clear that the civil servants had devised a system that would do no such thing. In the hands of lorry operators, freightliners developed very slowly. And when at the end of 1968 Barbara Castle's successor, Richard Marsh, was asked in the Commons when he proposed to bring in the hundred-mile licensing, which was central to the integration idea, he said, 'Not before 1970 . . . The date will depend on the satisfactory development of the freightliner service.' The phrase 'not before' is a favourite of civil servants: if something never happens they have told no lie. The Freight Integration Council, having been given no powers to 'see to' anything, met a few times, talked about parcels, and issued two brief reports. The second (three pages) in 1973 said it was 'not the appropriate time' for it to investigate freightliners and it had nothing else to study. No more was heard from this quango until 1979, when Norman Fowler announced that it was to die, aged ten. The following year he removed from the Act the dormant hundred-mile licensing clause, which had not been killed sooner only because the department did not want to draw attention to its existence.

In abolishing the Castle relic, Fowler said quantity licensing would 'add to bureaucracy'; his aim was 'to put the interests of the customer first'. He did not, of course, state that continental countries are happy with their system, by which the number of lorries licensed to carry long-distance freight is carefully limited and freight rates are controlled as well to prevent undercutting. The original aim was to protect the railways (and now there is an energy incentive as well); but there is almost equal emphasis on the environmental advantages and on the prosperity of the hauliers themselves—which in turn, as this chapter will show, is good for the community. West Germany has one of the strictest systems, with only 45,000 lorries licensed to ply for hire beyond a 50-kilometre (31-mile) radius, a detailed scale of charges per ton for various consignments, and incentives for using rail. Without cut-throat chasing of business, the Germans say, their lorries are more efficiently used. The hauliers prosper. 'They are astonished that we think they should have our system,' a frank Road Haulage Association official told me. The contrast is not confined to Europe. In many Canadian provinces and American states, a man who wants to become a long-distance trucker must satisfy conditions of 'public convenience and necessity' and existing truckers can oppose him. In parts of Canada and all of the US there are also fixed tariff rates.

Britain's wide-open entry and fierce competition have led some hauliers to dare to speak in favour of similar restraints. The National Freight Corporation's chief, Peter Thompson, said in 1977 after a visit to the US: 'We were convinced that road haulage in the United States was more efficient than here and was certainly in a healthier overall condition.' As for the customer, 'competition on service is fierce' and standards were 'higher than anything we experience in the UK'. And he suggested a form of quantity licensing: 'Each year a jury of experts drawn from the industry and also from the customers should sit and advise the Secretary of State on whether it is sensible for a quota of new operators' licenses to be established for the year ahead.' The British haulage industry was in bad shape and getting worse, he said. 'I believe that part of this deterioration has come from the liberalisation that occurred in the 1968 Transport Act. We now have the most liberal road haulage system in Europe and possibly any of the large industrial nations of the world. I believe it is not working' (Thompson, 1977).

An industry as public as road transport, moving 32-ton machines at speed on the roads, can be an especial peril if its entrepreneurs are in bad shape. This was recognised by the 1968 Act. The Geddes report had found a worrying state of affairs. Although lorry-drivers could then legally work a fourteen-hour day, with eleven hours at the wheel, those generous limits were 'widely disregarded' and the enforcement system was 'quite inadequate'. In one year, an under-manned force of inspectors had found more than 8,000 vehicles in such bad condition that they were ordered off the road, and had brought 26,000 prosecutions for overloading or for breaking the hours rules. The punishment that hauliers feared, said Geddes, was the loss of use of a vehicle—yet not one licence was revoked and the use of only eleven lorries was suspended. Fines levied were 'usually well worth paying for the financial gain from the offence'—which is just as true now. Geddes recommended that hauliers' licences should be revoked or suspended often enough 'for every operator to realise that his livelihood is in very real jeopardy if he does not conform to safety regulations'.

Barbara Castle agreed. She said in introducing her Bill: 'We should get the killer lorries off the roads . . . Is it not time that we stopped operators scratching a living by buying a lorry or two on the never-never and putting them on the roads without the resources to maintain them properly?' She laid down that every haulier must show that he had a proper depot and maintenance facilities, and adequate finances. She also announced that the eleven-hour driving day, in force since 1934, was long overdue for a cut: she would make it nine hours. To help enforce the hours rules, she would have lorries fitted with tachographs—super-speedometers that continuously record a vehicle's speed, its halts and the distances run in the course of each day. The tachograph clause in the Bill, however, never became reality, for that valued supporter of the Labour Party, the Transport and General Workers Union, was denouncing tachographs as 'spies in the cab' (and was to go on doing so for a dozen years). There were other small retreats. A proposed 'wear and tear' tax on heavy lorries to pay for the extra damage they did to the roads was dropped. The nine-hour day became a ten-hour day—and remained so until December 1978. And the chief questions were yet to be answered: Would the enforcement staff cease to be inadequate? Would lorry operators really be required to be capable and trustworthy and to have proper depots? Would offenders be put 'in very real jeopardy'?

Control had been so lax before that there was indeed improvement, chiefly as a result of stricter vehicle maintenance, with annual tests supplemented by spot-checks at the roadside. The involvement rate of lorries in fatal accidents fell by 1977 to 55 per cent of the 1969 rate (though it must be noted that vehicles were improving technically, and during the same period the rate for cars fell to 68 per cent). The important point is that the accident record of lorries was still bad, as the next chapter will show; and the great liberalisation brought many ills, both for the public and for the trade itself. The 1968 Act proved to be a good example of the 'heads I win, tails you lose' procedures of the transport department. Free entry quickly created sharp competition: that was 'efficiency' in action. The promise of integration served only to help Labour MPs and railway unions swallow the pill. And the promise to the public of careful vetting of hauliers and strict punishment of wrongdoers: that required time, money, staff and stern directives from on high. Here what Barbara Castle called the civil servants' 'negative power', their skill at 'working without enthusiasm', could take command. They did not believe in putting serious offenders in real jeopardy. The prevailing view has always been that to take away a haulier's licence, which Geddes rightly said was the most effective sanction, was too cruel a blow. Lorry men must not be 'harried'. One of the results of the non-harrying policy is that lorry-drivers themselves often lead harried lives. There has been plenty of evidence in recent years, both in court cases and in letters to trade journals such as *Motor Transport* and *Commercial Motor*:

A Dunfermline haulier: 'Generally hauliers love to moan and groan day in and day out, and are in fact in their glory stretching the law, their drivers and their vehicles to the utmost to make ends meet.'

A Bristol lorry-driver's wife, commenting on a researcher's remark that the dangers of driver fatigue were 'pure hypothesis': 'Of course I am biased after seeing my lorry-driver husband fall asleep over his evening meal . . . Are you not aware that employers expect the impossible, starting at 4 a.m., home perhaps 7 p.m. if you're lucky? . . . Obviously, if you were to ask drivers or employers the truth, they would not admit this because of the threat of prosecution and loss of livelihood . . . Because of the meagre subsistence allowance, many drivers catnap in their cabs. They cannot sleep, their makeshift beds are hard and cold and the hunger pains creep on about 2 a.m. . . . Get on the road, look at the wrinkled, wizened, heavy-eyed man of fifty-five who has been on the road for thirty-five years!'

A young lorry-driver: '. . . I cannot get work because I want to keep my licence clean. I have been interviewed around Surrey and London for jobs, but the first thing they ask is, "Are you willing to break the law for us?", and hint about the extra money that can be made . . . All I am asking for is a decent employer, a good truck and a decent wage . . . A job I went to in London, he asked me to break the law, so I said I wanted the price of my licence, £300. He told me to find the door.'

Veteran driver with large firm: 'Having seen some of the "chancers" at work, it never ceases to amaze me how they manage to stay in the industry and very often become their firms' star drivers. They get all the benefits of new vehicles and excessive overtime. More experienced persons, who want to work only legal hours and observe the various codes . . . can usually expect to get older vehicles and, very often, the more mundane work with no bonuses . . . These are but a few of the many ways in which a company such as ours can play one driver against another . . . It thinks only of keeping the motors moving as many hours as it can persuade drivers to work.'

Money is the crux. These bad practices are widespread because the fierce competition which the department blesses compels hauliers to take on work at rates that often hardly pay their current costs, let alone the cost of replacing their lorries. There will always be 'cowboy' operators. It is when the risks of being caught are low that the evil spreads: the 'chancers' undercut good firms, so they in turn become chancers. Low basic pay is part of the system. In 1980 the basic rate for a Class 1 driver, a skilled man in top-weight lorries, was between £75 and £78 for forty hours. By working a 55-hour week, *Motor Transport* calculated, he earned £5,571 in the year. The trade runs on overtime, bonuses and 'dodgy nights out'—a phrase meaning that a man on a long journey gets an untaxed overnight subsistence allowance (under £9, however, in 1980) but either sleeps in his cab or flogs his lorry home illegally and sleeps in his bed. Some drivers like this system—while their health lasts, or until they have a crash, or have the rare bad luck to be caught by a ministry official. Others clearly do not, and are willing to say that the public, too, suffers. In the midst of the lorry strike of January 1979, a man then getting a basic London wage of £53 for a forty-hour week driving 32-ton tankers of hazardous chemicals had this to say: 'All we want is a decent basic wage so that we can live without being dependent on bonuses . . . If we get back to the depot at say 4.30 we are given another run and paid for this on a bonus system . . . Now, in order to get back in time to be given another run you can see lorries flying about the road . . . Bonus schemes like this create cowboys.'

Every motorist who has experienced an urgent lorry hot on his tail will now see that the department's non-harrying of lorry operators can cause the harrying of others, including himself.

The department's responsibility goes deep. The licensing and supervision of more than half a million lorries is in the hands of eleven regional licensing authorities—men ranging from former town clerks to retired generals. They are called independent, but are chosen by the department and are guided by the freight directorate, 'the sponsor directorate for the road-haulage industry'. Barbara Castle had wanted an end of the practice by which a man without capital or depot could become a haulier by 'buying a lorry or two on the never-never', but official negative power made it easy to do just that. With little more than the money for a down-payment, a man has been able to acquire a secondhand 32-ton juggernaut and get a licence to operate it from his private house. The wording of the application form actually encouraged this: 'If the operating centre is your house address, give that address.' Many of the eleven authorities have not even insisted that an applicant had to have somewhere to park his lorries off the street; or else have condoned the basing of lorries on municipal car-parks.

Applicants were required to demonstrate that they would be able to keep their lorries in good condition, but if they had no facilities of their own they merely produced a maintenance contract with a garage, and licensing officials did not investigate the garage. Many authorities failed to satisfy themselves that an applicant had enough money in hand to reduce the temptation to operate illegally. The trade was opened, in effect, to anyone who promised to be good (not to overload, or break the hours law, or run unsafe vehicles); but then the department did not ensure that there would at least be effective policing. The enforcement staff (traffic examiners to check on loading and hours, vehicle examiners to check lorries) have been kept undermanned year after year. When serious offenders were brought before the licensing authorities —the moment when they were supposed to have been put 'in very real jeopardy'—what happened? To the chagrin of well-intentioned examiners, and indeed of those law-abiding hauliers who were suffering from the cowboys' corner-cutting, the man dispensing justice too often wagged a finger and said in effect, 'You have been a bad boy. Go away and be good.' When the same offender came up a second or third time, he still generally suffered little more than a further exhortation. The difference between what jeopardy meant in one region and in another is a further oddity of the system. In the five years 1975–9 in all Britain, 690 operators' licences were revoked; but half of these were in just one region, the West Midlands. In Yorkshire in the same period only 11 were revoked. Nobody has suggested that hauliers in Yorkshire (or in the other regions, where this punishment was not much more frequent) were far less wicked than those of the West Midlands.

Life has nevertheless not been too difficult even in the West Midlands for men operating on a shoestring. Take the case of a haulier who owned two articulated lorries, and who applied in 1979 for permission to operate three more. It emerged that he ran his business from a council house and paid the council £30 a year to let him base the lorries in a council car-park, where a freelance mechanic did what maintenance he could. The licensing authority, Arthur Crabtree, said this was absurd, and refused to allow extra lorries. However, the man's existing licence stood: he was given a year to find a better depot.

A similar twelve-month extension was granted by the north-western authority to a Lancashire haulier who had been in trouble more than once over the bad condition of his six lorries, for which the maintenance was done in a railway arch measuring 20 ft by 9 ft. In London, a Hackney haulier was better provided, having a yard and five railway arches, but he had 26 lorries and 50 trailers and sought permission to have 10 more big artics. An examiner said the firm had a record of convictions for overloading and other offences, and had failed to produce records or answer letters. But the extra lorries were allowed.

Time and again hauliers surprisingly escape punishment by pleading that they misunderstood or were ignorant of a regulation; or that their lorries were in bad shape because they were working on tough terrain; or that if they had to give up some of their lorries they would be put out of business. When a Norfolk firm was accused of 'outrageous' offences of failing to keep hours-of-work records for a six-month period, the excuse offered was that a girl clerk had not asked the drivers to produce them. The firm was fined £60, three drivers a total of £65: very little in relation to the money that can be made working excess hours.

The freight directorate's devotion to an untramelled road freight system is further demonstrated by the way it has used its negative power to delay the introduction of two refinements designed to curb hard-driving hauliers: the reduction of permitted working hours and the use of the tachograph.

Since 1970 drivers of heavy lorries (and long-distance buses) in the Common Market have been limited to four hours at the wheel before taking a break, and eight hours in any day. The fitting of all such vehicles with the tachograph to help police and other officials to catch lawbreakers was completed by 1977. When Britain entered the Market in 1973 she was given three years to adopt the hours limits and to get the fitting of tachographs under way. A long heel-dragging act followed. The lorry-drivers' unions (chiefly the Transport and General) and the lorry-owners' associations were allied in opposition, with the transport department as their collaborator. On the continent, and especially in West Germany, the tachograph was commonly seen not as the driver's enemy, a spy in the cab, but as an instrument to defend him from bad employers and to justify pay increases from more efficient working (the information it records can help a firm optimise its routing, and show drivers how not to misuse their lorries). In Britain the unions took the line that whatever the continentals might do, here the unions were strong and could look after their members without the help of foreign devices.

At times the men made points that demanded sympathy. For example, the Transport and General's largest lorry-driver branch, No. 5/35, put out a leaflet in 1979 saying: 'The eight-hour day we welcome . . . Enforcement of the eight-hour day has a simple solution: a basic forty-hour weekly wage that drivers and their families can live on . . . The prime objective of the tachograph is to give management complete control over rhythms of work . . . The tachograph turns driving into assembly-line-type work, and as such can make it not worth doing at all . . . A major tragedy of modern industrial life is that many jobs have been *deskilled* and stripped of any interest. Driving heavy goods vehicles is one of the few industrial jobs that have been upgraded in recent years.'

However, the union hostility was chiefly based on much narrower reasoning: the knowledge that it would rob men of excessive overtime, bonuses and dodgy perks. Hard men in the branches overrode anyone who might have favoured using the introduction of tachographs as a bargaining point to bring basic earnings a little nearer to those of their continental brothers. As for the employers, most of them were happy to have the policing of hours depend on logbooks inventively filled in by the drivers. The employers' public contention was that reduced hours and the use of the tachograph would add hundreds of millions of pounds a year to transport costs.

Unions and employers saw themselves as defending their interests. But the transport department aided and abetted them: that is harder to justify. Under a succession of ministers, it stonewalled at Brussels against obedience to the law. Its more sensible officials were put in a shamefaced position, especially when they were required to argue that the tachograph was not really an aid to safety—for plenty of evidence kept appearing in the transport press about what was really at issue.

Driver of twenty years' service: 'Bending rules always was the norm and always will be. Most of the opposition to the tachograph stems from the fact that it is virtually fiddle-proof.'

Columnist in *Motor Transport*: 'The malpractices that are rife in the haulage industry are well known to all . . . For the government to be saying to Brussels that it can see no justification for tachographs in the UK must mean that it is either totally ignorant of the extent to which the hours laws are being broken—which is hardly credible—or that at the behest of the unions it is deliberately abandoning any pretence of seeing that its own laws are properly enforced.'

Evidence at inquest: The driver of a Staffordshire gravel lorry began work at 6.56 a.m., drove three successive loads to the Manchester area, then two loads to Huddersfield, setting off on the last trip after midnight. In the twenty-second hour of that driving day, he plunged off a viaduct on the M62 and fell to his death. A director of his firm said it had no knowledge of the hours he was putting in. Verdict: accident.

Driver for more than thirty years: 'Lorry drivers today are the scum of the road. They have the biggest vehicles on the road and they let every other road-user know it . . . Tachographs would give this industry some standing. All the time you use logbooks, drivers will fiddle them. Lorry owners will encourage them to do so . . . I have friends who tell me the big petroleum companies are encouraging them to work to a system of job and finish—encouraging them to drive 6,300 gallons of petrol at dangerous speeds. Has everybody gone mad? . . . The only people who don't want tachographs are greedy and dishonest drivers and owners.'

When this man, Harry Coburn of Erith, Kent, said all this and more in a letter to *Commercial Motor,* I wrote to him and he replied with enthusiasm—and with more thoughts straight from the cab:

'Strange as it seems, it's not the one-lorry owner-drivers who are at fault. They take pride in their one vehicle, maintain it perfectly and don't break the law because they have invested their life savings in it. No, it's the big companies. Transport is big business.

'I say vehicles carrying petroleum spirit, gases and chemicals should be governed by law to a maximum speed of 45 m.p.h. on motorways, not 60. Speed kills, it always has and always will.

'What's behind this dodgy running is money. The employers say, You do a bit more and we'll see you all right. The other day I was talking to a man in the café who had driven a load of meat from Lowestoft to Ipswich—then he had come to London—and he was going to drive to Somerset the same day. The tachograph will be the best thing that ever happened to transport.

'A road I use a lot is the A12. You go down there and watch these container lorries. You won't get by them—they're doing 60 and 70. On that road their legal limit is 40. With the modern lorries you've got to be doing about 45 to get into top gear—it's as simple as that. In one fortnight on the A12 I saw three lorries overturned.

'Dodgy running: they start at 6 a.m., should be off the road at 5, shouldn't be back in the lorry till 6 next morning—but they're back in the lorry at midnight. There's nobody to check up on them. You tell me where you're going to find the ministry men [traffic examiners]. There aren't enough ministry men, there aren't enough police. The Department of Transport is to blame for quite a lot of what goes on. I've tried to get through to them. I wrote suggesting it was about time they had men on the roads at night. Most of this dodgy driving is carried on at night. I got no answer. Oh, I did get a phone-call from their local office. They're very crafty—they phone you, they'll never say anything in writing. The ministry are not interested. They don't want to know.'

Another advocate of the tachograph was Leonard Fagg of Otley, West Yorkshire, a driver of forty years' standing. By 1979 some British firms had come round to using the device without being compelled. Fagg wrote to *Motor Transport*: 'My firm bought a new vehicle and with it came the dreaded "spy in the cab". But it isn't really! I consider my tachograph my friend.' I wrote to him as well, and on his Sunday off he typed an 1,800-word letter making many points like Coburn's and some additional ones: 'Yes, the tach must contribute to road safety. A driver who now works perhaps fourteen to fifteen hours (even more too!) a day may only drive the lawful number with a tachograph fitted—and what's even more important in my view, he must also take his proper breaks. I know that most drivers (this is no guesswork, I've talked to hundreds) take only a few minutes for their supposedly half-hour breaks. Some even take no break at all. Like the fellow the other week in Nantwich . . . who said to me that he'd got about forty "drops" to do that day, and although a lot were close together, it still meant he could not take a meal-break, and must really slog on like a slave in order to get them done.

'It's only a matter of time before the TGWU see that the tachograph is really quite a godsend for all concerned, and they will be better employed in seeing to it that their members lose no actual financial benefits from its use—for instance, those paid by tonnage or by mileage, both systems to be banned as soon as possible. Bonuses too—if for rushing about and "getting more done"—are bad. Driver education is the best answer. After all, a lorry is big and heavy and can cause terrible havoc when crashing.'

The end of the department's long fight against the tachograph was that in 1979 Britain was declared in breach of the EEC law and undertook to conform. Nobody could say that the requirement came as a surprise, yet the department ordained, after visits from the haulage associations, that the fitting of lorries with tachographs should proceed at an easy pace and that their use should not be compulsory until the end of 1981, four years late (and six years after the original date for newly-registered lorries and for those carrying dangerous goods). As for permitted hours, a similar drawn-out fight meant that it was 1979 before British lorry drivers were limited to the nine-hour driving day that Barbara Castle had wanted in 1968; and they were not to match the continental eight hours until January 1981. The threat of a national lorry strike if the tachograph law were accepted—a fear much emphasised by William Rodgers as a reason for defying the EEC—came to nothing. The Transport and General's leaders prudently polled their members. Out of more than 100,000 drivers, 19,175 voted for a strike and 33,937 said no.

It must not be thought that there was any anti-Market philosophy behind the department's long resistance. The department is eclectic. It can just as easily smile upon a Market regulation even before it actually exists. The guiding principle is, Don't harass the haulier.

For years, part of the Market's 'harmonisation' proposals, strongly backed by British lorry men, has been an increase in the permitted length of juggernauts from 15 metres to 15½ (almost a 20 in. increase, to 50 ft 10 in.). Without the extra, it is almost impossible to carry a 40-foot container or other maximum payloads and also have a cab with room for a bunk—and a bunk is a great profit-maximiser on long hauls. During the late seventies thousands of illegal over-length artics came on to Britain's roads. The department's role has emerged in a few cases in which they have been prosecuted; for example, at Middlesbrough in 1979. A firm with fifty-two lorries, Flowers Transport of York, was charged with operating 15½-metre lorries. Its solicitor said it had had assurances from the department that the EEC harmonisation would come into force in 1977. On the strength of this it had bought nine Mercedes lorries with sleeper cabs. Now the firm was 'faced with this problem of excessive length'. The solicitor spoke of the thousands of other offenders and said it would be 'morally iniquitous for the company to be fined for buying up-to-date machines giving a greater degree of driver comfort'. The magistrates decided that the firm was a victim of 'an unfortunate set of circumstances'. Verdict: absolute discharge.

Prosecutions have been rare. The department's policy has been to turn a blind eye. 'We are not supposed to make a fuss,' one official told me. When an MP raised the question, the answer drafted by someone in freight directorate was: 'There may be cases in which some lorries slightly exceed the legal limits but I have no evidence of any substantial and wide-spread infringement . . . or that the law is not being reason-ably enforced.' The Road Haulage Association's view of reasonableness is that 'the slightly excessive lengths of sleeper-cab-unit artics should be tolerated'. When in 1979 it heard that in a few places unreasonable people were checking artic lengths, it decided that 'a further effort should be made at departmental level' to have the permitted length increased.

A more serious offence over which the department did not show excessive zeal was overloading. Its prevention is important for three reasons: it is dangerous, it increases road damage and it exposes law-abiding hauliers to unfair com-petition. The great growth in the numbers of large lorries made strict enforcement all the more important; yet once more the department gave a masterly display of negative power. When in the sixties it legalised lorries nearly fifty feet long, it did nothing about the fact that very few of Britain's 2,300 weighbridges were able to cope with them; and even on those few, the important job of weighing separate axle-loads was, in the department's own words, 'a complex and some-times impossible process'. Furthermore, nobody in the depart-ment troubled to see that the network of motorways and near-motorway dual carriageways, on which the lorries were establishing their much-approved ton-mileage records, were supplied with weighbridge sites, so they became for the offender a vast region of immunity. Checks on other roads were rare enough. They were not even under unified direction: the department's understaffed traffic examiners did what they could, and in some counties separate checks were done by trading standards officers or by police. The counties greatly outshone the ministry men. In 1978, traffic examiners through-out Britain weighed 29,295 lorries of all sizes, but the officers of only nine counties weighed 61,316 (17,000 of them in Kent alone), a contrast revealed to the Armitage inquiry, but only at the insistence of a senior Kent official.

The lack of weighbridges was well known in the department.

Responsible men were concerned. 'A well-maintained goods vehicle can be turned into a lethal weapon if it is overloaded,' a former licensing authority chairman, John Else, told the Road Haulage Association in 1977. Annual reports of the licensing authorities had shown for many years, Else said, 'that they have a feeling of frustration . . . about the absence of adequate weighing facilities in the places where they are required.'

The means to put things right existed: a modern, portable machine that could weigh a juggernaut in twenty seconds, producing an electronic print-out axle by axle. This Weighwrite machine had been in use at Dover harbour and elsewhere (though not for prosecution purposes) since the early seventies. In 1976, in an effort to overcome representations against it by the Freight Transport Association and the Road Haulage Association, it was put through exhaustive tests to show that it could record axle-loads within a tolerance of 50kg. The department said it hoped to bring in regulations within months to enable the Weighwrite to be used for prosecutions. But then it allowed the FTA and RHA to engage in a long delaying action. The department offered to allow a 100kg tolerance in prosecutions. Not good enough, said the associations. Time passed. Oh, well, let's make it 150kg, said the department. All right, said the FTA, happy with this generosity. Not good enough, said the RHA. Time passed. The Weighwrite firm was busy selling the machines in Hungary, Australia and elsewhere. British motorways, especially in the Midlands, were cracking up before their time, thanks partly to overloaded axles (a mere ton over the ten-ton axle limit increases the damage by about 50 per cent). Weighwrite's chief, Len Gorman, wondered what was happening at the department. 'We want to gain the confidence of the industry,' an official told him. Gorman thought outsiders might take the view that the department was being supine. The RHA was now arguing that the machine should be used only as a screening device: it would spot apparent offenders which would then be sent along to an old-style weighbridge. Such a procedure would of course have nullified the speed and flexibility of the Weighwrite. Even departmental officials began to wonder whether the RHA was eager to have lorries weighed effectively. At last, in the latter half of 1978, the department did its duty by the public, overruled the hauliers and brought in the necessary regulations. The original intention had been to have a hundred machines in action by 1977. In 1980 the department told Sir Arthur Armitage that it 'has encouraged' the machine's development and 'has already installed nineteen'.

The department's kindly patience made a gift to the hauliers of many millions of illegal ton-miles, whose cost to the public is shown by a statement to Armitage by the County Surveyors' Society that 'overloading accounts for a 50 per cent increase in total damaging power' and on some roads it might exceed 100 per cent. In recent years between a quarter and a third of laden vehicles checked have been overloaded—one in sixteen of them so dangerously that it was prohibited from travelling further. 'Chancers' know the odds against their being stopped are good. Even at ports in the south-east, officials seldom manage more than one check a week; yet Norman Fowler asserted in 1980: 'The law is strictly enforced.'

When an offender is caught, his fine is often under £50: less than one overload earns for him. The fines exacted in some other places would terrify British hauliers. In Hungary, if the Weighwrite shows a one-ton excess the penalty is £1 for each kilometre the lorry travels. Not long ago, *Commercial Motor* reported a crackdown in Pennsylvania and commented: 'Imagine the outcry from the Road Haulage Association and the Freight Transport Association if penalties on this scale were exacted in Britain . . . Spot fines of over £800 for three-ton overloads on thirty-two-ton artics would soon dispose of the cowboys—' Here came a surprising 'but': '—but would put many unimpeachable small hauliers out of business too.'

By 1977 the questionable results of lorry liberation plus inadequate enforcement were gaining the attention of William Rodgers. When he saw leading RHA men, including John Silbermann, and pressed them to improve their image by having cleaner, better-maintained and more carefully driven lorries, Silbermann told him, We can't afford it. He said that easy entry to the trade by men with little money and few qualifications or principles was squeezing honest operators so much that they could scarcely finance new vehicles. Silbermann told me that haulage was 'a cut-throat game' and 'a commercial jungle'. He calculated that the annual costs of a responsible haulier were so much higher than those of 'Mr

Nasty' that the cowboy could offer to carry a load on his juggernaut for less than half the fair price. When a leading haulier began to talk like this, the few men in the department who wanted a tighter grip on the system had their hands strengthened. Rodgers set up a committee under the economist Christopher Foster to inquire into the operation of the 1968 Act. Foster knew well that the department would spurn any proposal for quantity licensing in the continental or American style; and in his report he rejected it as 'impracticable and misguided'. The freight directorate and the lorry operators echoed each other in saying that this was the most important thing in the report. They were less enthusiastic about the committee's ninety other recommendations. They particularly disliked a proposal that licensing authorities should have power to declare a lorry depot unsuitable for environmental reasons, and that they should accept evidence on the question from neighbouring householders and even from 'any person offended by the activities of vehicles from that operating centre'.

Some of the recommendations, by the mere fact that they were needed, displayed what odd gaps there were in the enforcement system. Foster proposed, for example: that in deciding whether to approve a man as 'of good repute', a licensing authority should take account of criminal convictions, evasion of lorry excise duty, or bankruptcy; that every lorry should bear a special plate, clearly visible, showing that it had not had its licence revoked (a thing officially recommended as long ago as 1932); that roadside checks should be done at nights and weekends; that there should be facilities for checks on motorways and fast trunk roads; that a driver caught breaking the hours law should be barred from driving on; that offences known to the police should be passed on to the licensing authorities; that records of every operator, his lorries and any past offences should be on a national computer system. There were recommendations, too, that more departmental examiners should be appointed; that police should give more time to lorries; that magistrates should be advised of the seriousness of hours and other offences; that the authorities should have power to impound illegally operated vehicles; that lorry-drivers should be liable to lose their licences if caught driving illegal vehicles or breaking the hours law.

On wider issues, Foster recommended that a permanent committee should be set up to decide annually how much tax lorries should pay to meet their full public costs; and he proposed some wide-ranging action on the social impact of lorries, which I shall quote in Chapter 6.

The 162-page report reached the department in November 1978. The following summer Norman Fowler said he hoped to publish a 'detailed response' in a few months. He did not. In February 1980 he promised the Civic Trust that, as his views on the social/environmental issues were relevant to Sir Arthur Armitage's inquiry, he would convey his detailed response to Armitage, and 'quite soon'. In May 1980 Foster told me: 'We thought we wrote a good report. I am very disappointed that there's been no action, and I know several members of the committee are. What on earth has been happening?' He soon got a disappointing answer. In August 1980, after twenty-one months of Marsham Street gestation, Fowler produced a very limited response indeed. He would introduce roadside checks at night and at weekends. He would not order checks on motorways and fast trunk roads, but planned more checks 'on the main routes to and from motorways'. However, both these changes would mean less enforcement elsewhere (he was actually cutting staff). 'As a matter of urgency' he would introduce a more conspicuous lorry licence disc. He agreed that computerised records would be valuable; they were 'under consideration'. Official receivers were being asked to inform licensing authorities when lorry operators were bankrupted or put in liquidation. However, there was to be no general instruction to police to pass on information about criminal offences.

And that was about it. Fowler ruled out measures that would be 'expensive' or impose 'unreasonable burdens on the industry'. As for environmental control, far from giving Armitage a verdict on Foster's proposals, Fowler now said he would decide nothing until Armitage had reported. It looked as if 'negative power' had reduced Foster's 162 pages to very little.

4

A load of danger

A driver of 32-ton artics talks about night-shift trunking up and down the motorways: 'I was managing on about three hours' sleep a day . . . The lines start crossing and then, bang, you are on the hard shoulder . . . If you could pull off for a nap, that's the best thing to do, but on the motorway you can't, you have to get to the next pull-off. That's probably five miles down the road. By the time you get there you have woken up again so you say, well, I'll make the next one . . . and of course in between you might go again. This has a lot to do with accidents.'

Bang, you are on the hard shoulder: which helps to account for a striking statistic from Northamptonshire police. In the period January 1976 to March 1979, of forty-four people killed on the M1 within the county, thirteen were on the hard shoulder. Many of the deaths were on downhill stretches, where big lorries quickly reach an excessive speed if a driver is dozy, and on curves, which are tricky when 'the lines start crossing'. The heavy toll brought an official warning to motorists that if they had to stop beside the motorway they should quickly get as far as possible from their cars. A traffic superintendent at his headquarters near the M1 told me: 'I'm absolutely appalled by the things that go on out there. I would like to have a special group with emphasis on effective enforcement. If you gave me ten extra men I bet I'd make a profit in fines in the first year. Our emphasis is on the excessive hours—in my opinion the biggest single cause of multiple accidents and other serious accidents.'

The words of long-distance drivers, especially those on shift-work, support what he says. In a job that is at once sedentary and wearing, punctuated by quick breaks for ill-cooked greasy food, they commonly suffer from neck ache, backache, leg ache, indigestion and piles. But worst of all is the lack of a good night's sleep. Here are some further remarks from drivers interviewed by an academic researcher, Nick McDonald, for a thesis on fatigue: 'If I can get at least three hours sleep I can work, but will have to have a bit of a sleep later in the day—twenty minutes stretched out in the cab.' 'At night when you are coming back, then you start going. Sometimes you have to pull up. Only ten minutes, that's all you need.' 'In my dinner-break I might shut my eyes. I don't feel I'd get back without doing so. The return journey from three in the morning is heavy going.' Men often have the experience of 'missing the miles'—suddenly realising where they are and not remembering how they got there. 'When you drop off you dream you are awake and that you are driving.' Sometimes drivers hallucinate: 'One time I saw a furniture pantechnicon across the motorway and slammed on my brakes . . . It wasn't there.' 'I saw a kangaroo crossing the road. I still maintain that I saw it. But I was tired.'

This must not be thought a minority problem. The big artics, 28 tons and up, do 30 per cent of their ton-mileage on trips of more than 300 kilometres (187 miles). If men in charge of freight trains were known to be frequently in this condition, or even if it were a common, lawful practice for them to sleep in their cabs, there would be an outcry. Yet the lorries, unlike the trains, are a danger to the public both on the motorways and when completing their exhausting journeys on other roads and in urban streets. It is only the trains, however, that are subject to statutory accident inquiries followed by reports: a process that reveals what went wrong and suggests preventive action. A fatal lorry accident is scarcely worth a paragraph. Lorry operators and manufacturers have thus been able to avoid having attention drawn to the reforms, both human and mechanical, that would make their trade safer.

What the operators repeatedly emphasise is that the involvement rate of lorries in injury accidents, when judged on the basis of annual mileage run, is lower than that of cars. This is true, and is the least one could expect of professional drivers going about their commercial business. However, it is not the whole truth. Of the accidents in which lorries are involved, a high proportion are nasty ones. Their involvement in serious-injury accidents equals that of cars. More important, mile for mile a lorry is twice as likely as a car to be involved in a fatal accident. The reason is simple. 'In nearly all accidents involving heavy goods vehicles,' says a recent report from the

Road Research Laboratory, 'the involvement of the HGV can be blamed for the fatality or serious injury because of its mass, size and rigidity' (Riley and Bates, 1980). This report shows that lorries were involved in 6 per cent of pedestrian deaths, 12 per cent among two-wheeler riders and 16 per cent among car occupants.

Lorry-drivers themselves are less vulnerable. This is an unchanging fact. Back in the sixties, an analysis of 181 fatal car/lorry accidents in the West Midlands showed that 224 car occupants were killed and only 5 lorry-drivers. In 1976, according to the Riley/Bates report, lorries of more than three tons unladen were involved in 678 accidents in which other road-users died. This was the toll: car occupants, 391; pedestrians, 159; motorcyclists, 112; pedal cyclists, 47; small goods vehicle occupants, 46; bus or coach occupants, 22. In those accidents how many lorry-drivers died? Just eight, or one per cent of the total. The only real risk to a lorry-driver was when he hit another heavy lorry (28 killed) or crashed on his own, chiefly in roll-over accidents (31).

The reason for the disproportion is simple: 'mass, size and rigidity'—and especially mass. The authors of the West Midlands study wrote: 'In view of the proposal that lorries of even greater size and with heavier loads might be permitted on our roads, it is important to appreciate the implications . . . of this mixing of cars and heavy vehicles' (Gissane and Bull, 1973). The bigger the lorry, the worse the peril. If a car and a juggernaut crash head-on, the lorry slows slightly and the car is slammed backwards—a violent reversal sufficient to kill, even without the lorry's high front smashing into the car's tender top. A University of London analysis of 18,668 head-on collisions is revealing about the killing power of extra weight (Grime and Hutchinson, 1979). When there was little or no difference of mass, the percentage of drivers killed or badly hurt on either side was about the same. The percentages changed dramatically with the disproportion in mass. In accidents involving lorries between ten and twenty times as heavy as cars, the percentages killed or injured worked out like this:

	Fatal	Serious	Slight	Uninjured
In lorry	0	1.7	9.1	89.2
In car	11.9	38.7	46.8	2.6

When the lorries were more than twenty times as heavy (which includes the juggernaut class) the percentages were:

	Fatal	Serious	Slight	Uninjured
In lorry	0	0	5.4	94.6
In car	14.3	48.3	33.9	3.6

The moral for the juggernaut driver is: If I move out to pass on a three-lane road and see a car coming toward me, I have a 95 per cent chance of escaping without a scratch if I brazen it out. The moral for the motorist is: Yield or risk death or disablement.

The transport department has failed to publish statistics to show exactly how much the fatal-accident involvement of lorries increases in the higher weight categories, even though the police have been recording accidents by weight-bands since 1974. A few years ago, however, I managed to obtain from the Transport and Road Research Laboratory an analysis of 799 fatalities involving lorries in 1974, showing that 44 per cent of them involved those over 8 tons unladen (roughly 24 tons gross). In 1976, British Rail researchers were able to obtain enough figures to show that the fatality rate, mile for mile, among the biggest lorries was twice that of medium ones and nearly three times that of the smallest. They calculated the probable effect of sending a given tonnage of freight in 32-ton lorries instead of in trains carrying 450 tons each, and said: 'It appears likely to result in twelve to seventeen times as many deaths and thirty-five to fifty times as many serious injuries'. Even when the trunk haul was only 100 miles and the goods had to be delivered for a final 10 miles by lorry, the accident advantage for rail was reckoned to be more than fourfold (British Rail, 1976).

It was noted in the previous chapter that the accident rate of lorries fell more sharply than that of cars after the 'quality licensing' controls were introduced. However, drivers who proudly speak of themselves as 'professional' ought to be able to point to an accident record far superior to that of others. It is not only that they are professionals, with special driving tests (for vehicles over 7½ tons gross). Consider: their vehicles are subject to far sharper scrutiny than the average car; sitting high in their cabs, they are in a much better position to anticipate hazards, especially at intersections; they do their

mileage as workers, whereas a large proportion of car
accidents occur after convivial evenings; and a far larger
proportion of lorry mileage than car mileage is on motorways
and dual carriageways, with less risk of conflict, especially
with vulnerable pedestrians and two-wheelers. (Incidentally,
because of the department's statistical method, its figures for
lorry involvement rates 'may be significantly understated',
according to the Foster report, Appendix C.)

In view of all this, the road-haulage record remains bad.
Even for the lorry-driver himself, relatively safe though he
is, it is a hazardous occupation as the industrial world goes.
The researcher cited above, Nick McDonald, has estimated
that in 1976 the annual casualty rate among British lorry-
drivers was at least 8.8 fatal and 375 injured per 100,000. In
two especially hazardous industries, engineering and construction, the fatality rates were 13.3 and 15.3; but for
manufacturing as a whole it was only 3.4. The lorry men's
figure, moreover, did not include occupational accidents they
had when not driving. Yet lorry-drivers are not included,
oddly enough, in the annual 'accidents at work' statistics and
the Health and Safety Executive does not concern itself with
them.

The economic pressures in the industry are to be seen in the
state of the vehicles as well as the men. Even though
mechanical failure on the road costs a haulier dear, maintenance is erratic. When officials check lorries at the roadside,
they find that about 6 per cent have defects so serious that
they are given 'immediate prohibition' notices. In the north-
western area in 1979 the percentage was 7.66, and even when
lorries were inspected at testing stations, or at depots with
prior warning, 4 per cent were in a dangerous state. This and
other areas reported a decline in standards.

Lorries are dangerous, furthermore, even when in good
condition. This is especially true of the big articulated ones.
They are designed not to be as safe as technology permits, but
to be as low in price and as high in payload capacity as the
regulations will allow.

Compare these two statements: 'The safety standards of
lorries are second to none' (Freight Transport Association
submission to Armitage). 'Heavy goods vehicles make a
disproportionate contribution to most categories of road-user
casualties' (*Accidents Involving Heavy Goods Vehicles,* Trans-

port and Road Research Laboratory, 1979). The TRRL study, by a team led by Ian Neilson, was presented at a Paris conference on lorries in 1977, but for some reason two years passed before the laboratory published it. Perhaps someone thought it was too thorough in setting out the ways in which lorries are not quite second to none. Here are Neilson's chief points, supplemented by material from other sources.

Tyres

Those made for lorries have a much poorer grip than car tyres. Roads with surfaces smooth from use 'may be hazardous for large vehicles at an earlier state of wear than for cars'. The reason for the difference is that lorry tyres are not made of the high-grip, non-skid rubber that is a selling point for cars, because it does not give nearly as much mileage. As an earlier TRRL report put it, 'Heavy commercial vehicle tyres are normally treaded with polymers from the lower end of the scale, influenced by operator requirements for the greatest possible mileage.' That is, economy before safety.

Brakes

On a good dry surface, and with brakes in good condition, fully-laden lorries tested at TRRL needed about twice the stopping distance of cars. In Neilson's words, 'Most cars can achieve an overall average deceleration throughout a braking stop of 0.8g, but heavily laden goods vehicles often do not reach much above 0.4g.' (Many cars in fact attain 1g or 2½ times the stopping power of many lorries.) Lorry brakes, 'being only just powerful enough for the demands on them,' says Neilson, need frequent maintenance, 'which is not always carried out'. Being air-operated, lorry brakes need up to one second to take full effect after the driver steps on the pedal. But most important is the fact that a 32-ton lorry, with a mass perhaps thirty times a family car, does not have thirty times the tyre contact with the road. If the EEC proposal for four-axle artics of 35 tonnes took effect, the disparity would be even greater. In the words of Alan Bunting, a writer on lorry technology, 'If a man from Mars saw cars and lorries on the same road, he would wonder why the law permits different braking.'

Stability when braking

A special problem for lorries is that the load on various axles varies greatly when they are laden or unladen. If the braking power needed by a 32-tonner is applied when it is part-laden, or running empty at about 11 tons, its wheels will lock. This is a particular danger with an artic's second axle (its drive axle): on a wet road it can easily send the artic into a jack-knife crash. The danger can largely be overcome by means of load-sensing valves which automatically modify the braking according to the load on an axle. The tractive units of most new artics are now fitted with this device—not all, because the transport department has merely laid down a 'code of practice' for lorry-makers. Jack-knifing is less common than it was; but the valves need strict maintenance. There is a more advanced system to prevent wheel-lock no matter how hard brakes are applied or how slippery the surface. By 1979 only about 6,000 lorries were fitted. The reason why there were so few is chiefly that this system costs up to £400 per axle and it increases brake wear. Again, the department does not demand its use. The demand comes instead from responsible operators, such as the National Freight Corporation or Bass-Charrington. 'The department tends to sit back a bit and watch what Europe does,' said a spokesman for the Motor Industry Research Association in 1980. 'So many developments tend to hang about until you get legislation.'

Roll-over

Articulated lorries with high loads can easily overturn on bends even at low speeds. This weakness is inherent in the machine. An artic's trailer, which in the case of a laden 32-tonner is about four-fifths of its total weight, has only its rear bogie wheels on the ground, nearly forty feet behind the driver in his cab. Its centre of gravity is much higher than that of the tractive unit to which it is coupled. When a driver takes a bend too fast, he feels no warning that his trailer is going over until too late. Non-cowboy-like driving is the basic cure. But the pursuit of bigger payloads increases the risk by raising the trailer's centre of gravity. 'Increased vehicle weights may well result in higher loads,' Neilson says. May well indeed: if a 44-tonne lorry is only fractionally longer than Britain's 32-tonners but is carrying about 10 tons more payload, its centre of gravity must be higher.

Power jack-knife

An artic can jack-knife not only through wheel-lock but also from a too-sudden surge of power. Investigations by the laboratory suggested that this happened on wet roads at 40 m.p.h. or more when the driver of a high-powered unladen artic accelerated sharply. Neilson says the tendency highlights 'the importance of wet road grip' in lorry tyres and the need for 'a minimum load on the drive axle at all times'.

The outcome of all studies is that the proposed EEC lorries would add to safety problems for many more reasons than the increase in mass. In its evidence to Armitage the department played this down. On the question of braking stability it conceded that 'the problem . . . may be greater' but it said that the fact that the proposed lorries above 35 tonnes would have a fifth axle would help. 'If the extra axle is fitted on the trailer this should reduce the tendency for "trailer swing" to develop, and if it is fitted on the tractive unit it will reduce the tendency to jack-knifing.' But of course it cannot do both. Besides, each option presents further problems on which the department was silent. If the trailer rides on a group of three axles instead of two there is 'wheel scrub' when cornering (bad for tyres, bad for road surface) and not enough of the lorry's total weight is on its drive axle (jack-knife danger). As for having a three-axle tractive unit instead, the EEC, in kindness to the hauliers, is against requiring that except when a lorry exceeds 40 tonnes, because it adds weight and cost (economy before safety again). By contrast, the much safer practice generally followed in the US is to use a three-axle tractive unit for trucks of more than 28 tons; and the second and third axle of the unit are both drive axles—the preferable option, though heaviest and dearest.

The department is well informed on the problems because in 1979 it published a report, *Comparative Trials of Articulated Goods Vehicles Between 32.5 and 44 Tonnes*, following tests on seventeen lorries, British and foreign, supplied to the Road Research Laboratory by manufacturers and vehicle hire firms.

When braking, many of the larger vehicles took longer to stop than the 32-tonners. Sixteen of the seventeen showed a tendency to jack-knife 'even though many were fitted with load-sensing valves'. Artics with three-axle tractive units showed 'less violent instability' than those with three-axle

trailers. 'Two of the seventeen combinations were completely
unstable, jack-knifing even when fully laden on the dry
surface.' In a parking-brake test on a hill, one 44-tonner slid
backwards.

As the vehicles' weights rose, they were 'progressively less
resistant to overturning' because of their higher centres of
gravity: 'Higher gross weights will therefore increase the risk
of roll-over accidents.' In technical terms, a five-axle lorry of
40/42 tonnes 'might overturn under a minimum lateral acceleration of up to 20% less than that needed to overturn' a 32-
tonner. The report recommends 'some form of in-cab device to
warn the driver when the trailer is reaching a critical angle'.

The lorry industry criticised the report, asserting that the
vehicles were not fairly chosen and that some of the tractor-
trailer combinations were not well matched. The Society of
Motor Manufacturers and Traders organised some tests of its
own, but in 1980 it said the results 'are not available', which
suggests that they were not much help to it.

The transport department assured Sir Arthur Armitage that
it wants to improve safety 'by matching standards of performance to advances in technology'. It has failed to demonstrate
its concern, however, even over something so basic as
mudguards. Any motorist who has enjoyed the challenge of
passing articulated lorries on a fast road in a rainstorm has
quite likely been too preoccupied to notice an odd fact: in
most cases the trailer wheels, with their eight huge tyres, have
no mudguards. In Britain, though not in Denmark, Sweden
and some other continental countries, if a trailer has a flat-
based body above its wheels it is permitted to wear no more
than rear mudflaps. Spray from the wheels hits the trailer's
underside and plumes outwards. The regulations say that
lorry trailers 'shall be equipped with wings or similar fittings'
to contain the spray, 'unless adequate protection is afforded
by the body of the trailer'. The department, after consultation
with lorry lobbyists, long ago ordained that the mere flat
underside of the trailer was 'adequate', thus flouting the
intention of the law by quiet bureaucratic edict. It is not
surprising that, as shown by a social survey reported to
Armitage by the department, 'many car drivers consider
that . . . the worst problem caused by lorries is the spray from
their tyres'.

The department has never tried to say that spray does not

matter. As long ago as 1966 the Road Research Laboratory concluded that spray contributed to at least one in seventy-seven motorway accidents—and at a time when the big artics were rare. Tests by the laboratory showed, as one would expect, that adding mudguards greatly reduced spray. However, the lorry lobby resisted a change in the rules: mudguards add weight and cost. Ten years passed. More and more people complained. We are doing research, the department said. In 1977, aerodynamics men at Southampton University handed the department a 100-page report with 22 diagrams and some spools of ciné film—the fruit of four years' work during which model lorries built to one-eighth scale were tested in wind tunnels and real lorries were filmed on the M3. In 1979 the department made known its conclusion from the report that there was still 'no satisfactory solution'. It also published a report on tests at the Road Research Laboratory in which laser-beam equipment recorded the spray produced by lorries with no trailer mudguards and others with sophisticated ones with deep valances (Transport, Department of, April 1979). For some reason the report did not print comparative laser traces for these vehicles, though it did do so for vehicles travelling at various speeds (showing, usefully, that spray varies according to the cube of speed, so that if a lorry on a rainswept motorway slows from sixty to forty it makes only three-tenths as much spray). The addition of the mudguards, the report said, reduced spray by 30 to 40 per cent—puzzlingly less than similar tests elsewhere had shown.

By then, in any case, mudguard technology had moved on. Two companies had developed ways of achieving more spray-reduction than ever before. The trick was to have the water thrown up by the tyres hit a material that threw it down again in heavy droplets instead of outwards in swirling spray. The American-based Monsanto chemical company produced a polyethylene-surfaced sheet resembling a sturdy doormat; and the Featherwing mudguard company of Burnley, Lancashire, devised a fine steel mesh. After several years of tests, both went on the market in Britain in 1980, the first as Clear Pass, the second as Spray Breaker. Large firms that cared about safety and about their image were fitting them. Amazed motorists were asking what the secret was—and the lorries' drivers were enjoying much-improved rear vision, a great extra safety point. The makers of Clear Pass said tests with lorries of Roadline showed that visibility through the wind-screen of a car passing an unfitted lorry was about 30 per cent, but Clear Pass made it about 70 per cent. Spray Breaker claimed equal success, and its price was lower. By the end of the year, the Road Research Laboratory began testing the well-tested new mudguards. In the meantime, the EEC had adopted a directive specifying mudguards of a minimum standard for all wheels. However, there was a catch: it was up to each country to make the directive mandatory. British hauliers could follow the old definition of 'adequate' so long as the transport department refrained from making an order. If it wished, the department could do better and require mudguards of a Clear Pass or Spray Breaker standard; but first its officials would have to forsake the habit of devising artful non-reasons for non-action. In 1980 their advice, MPs were told, was that 'the perfect solution has not yet been found'.

Government departments have a further line of defence against demands for life-saving measures: cost/benefit analysis. How much ought one to require a factory or a chemical-maker or a lorry operator to spend to save a certain number of lives? The department produced an example of the method for Sir Arthur Armitage when he asked what could be done to reduce the number of motorists and others killed or injured through under-running the high, unyielding structures of big lorries. If lorries were made to fit rear under-run guards, it said, the balance would work out like this, in 1979 prices: Cost of guard, £60; 'present value' per lorry of extra fuel used during lorry's life as result of extra weight, £44; total £104. Benefit from annual saving of 30 lives at £68,500 each, 180 serious injuries at £4,100 and 600 slight injuries at £100, a 'present value' of £50. However, the department got the benefit side all wrong. The Riley/Bates report suggests that rear under-run guards might save the lives of up to 50 car occupants, plus others in vans and on motorcycles—say 60 in all. Moreover, in 1979 the official cost of a fatality was £101,100 and of a serious injury £4,270. Result: benefit actually exceeds cost. Happily, desiccated miscalculations will eventually not prevail: rear under-run guards are to become compulsory on new lorries, perhaps by 1982. Not out of departmental benevolence, however, but in conformity to an EEC directive. One must wonder, though, what other measures have been blocked by similar arithmetic.

Economic arguments also come into official policy on speed limits. In view of lorry braking and roll-over problems, one might expect cautious limits and strict enforcement. Once again, though, the department is kind to the lorry. On motorways the limit is 60 m.p.h., higher than in virtually every European country (or the US, with its universal limit of 55). When Armitage asked about speeds, the department failed to point out that in West Germany, the Netherlands, France (above 19 tonnes), Sweden, Switzerland and several others it is 50, and that several countries have a special limit of 37½ for artics, as they are unstable.

Off the motorway, Britain's lorry limit is 40, but people are generally astonished to learn this. Where is it seen to be enforced? It is almost universally given the blind-eye treatment. On the A1 and no doubt on other dual carriageways, traffic examiners have told lorry-drivers, 'We don't mind around 50.' A national survey in 1977 showed that well over 70 per cent of lorries were exceeding 40 on dual carriageways; and a survey on de-restricted roads in the London area in 1979 showed that 89 per cent were offenders. For some time the operators' associations have been pressing to have 50 m.p.h. made legal for lorries on dual carriageways. The department told Armitage that one of the operators' arguments is that the present limit is widely infringed, 'so there is no risk to road safety in raising it'. The chief argument, of course, is that higher speeds enable lorries to run more profitably. In its evidence the department largely favoured the operators' reasoning, though it did point out the braking/stability hazards and also said that lorries 'reach optimum speed from an energy-conservation standpoint at speeds nearer to forty than fifty'.

Continental lorry-drivers are delighted with the speeds they can get away with in Britain. Lorry-watchers will note that the backs of most continental lorries carry two large discs giving their maximum kilometre-speeds on motorways and other roads, usually 80 and 60 (50 and 37½ m.p.h.). People whose memories go back before 1957 will recall that British lorries had a similar disc saying 20. In that year, when the limit was raised to 30, the disc requirement was quietly dropped; and it remained forgotten when the ordinary limit rose to 40 in 1963. When I asked the department why, it produced (after some prodding) a masterly reply: 'It was no longer serving a useful purpose.' The useful purpose, of course, is to tell the world what a lorry's limit is.

The nature of the modern lorry is an encouragement to speeding. The safety-minded lorry-driver Harry Coburn has already been quoted: 'You've got to be doing about forty-five to get into top gear—it's as simple as that.' He was speaking of the big artics with gearboxes for anything up to eighteen forward speeds. When their specifications are set out in hauliers' journals their maximum speeds are frequently well over the motorway limit: 67 for a Seddon Atkinson, 70 for a Leyland Buffalo, even 75 for a Ford Transcontinental. An article on optimum gearing in *Commercial Motor* gave examples of cruising speeds of 65 and even 72; and there is never a hint of 'but this is illegal'.

Once a lorry-driver has gone up through the gears and is cruising down the motorway at over 60, he is irritated by anything that might make him change down. That is why motorists so often have the frightening experience of finding a big lorry tailgating them. It is more frightening still for the motorist who knows how long the lorry's stopping distance is. It also explains why, when there is a multiple pile-up on the motorway, lorries are almost invariably involved. A further disturbing fact was brought out by a study by the Road Research Laboratory of close-following behaviour on the M4 and M5. Automatic camera recordings showed that whereas motorists increased their safety margin as speed went up, lorry-drivers did the opposite. At 60 m.p.h. in lane two, the report shows, nearly half the close-following lorries were leaving a gap of less than two seconds. In view of the lorries' great stopping distance, this gave 'some cause for concern', the report said mildly (Sumner and Baguley, 1978).

The figures given above for the cost of a traffic fatality or injury are, the department says, 'minimum estimates'. In addition to medical and social security costs they include lost output and 'pain, grief and suffering'. The latter makes up about half the total in the case of death or serious injury, yet is less than what some other countries reckon (or than what courts award: in 1980 a man crippled in a road accident got

£300,000 damages). When reckoning the cost of an accident and not an individual casualty, further items must be added: police, administration and damage to vehicles and other property. The toll of 1979 (below average for accident numbers) works out like this:

	Accidents	Cost per accident	Total cost
Fatal	5,824	£112,700	£656,364,800
Serious	66,927	6,020	402,900,540
Slight	182,216	810	147,594,960
			£1,206,860,300

In addition the statisticians take account of an estimated 1,500,000 damage-only accidents reported to insurance companies, reckoned in 1979 at £350 each, making a total of £1,731,860,300. The cost of each year's unreported damage-only accidents is beyond calculation. A further figure not in the statistics is for injury accidents not reported to the police, for reasons not hard to guess. On the basis of parallel studies done at hospitals in Birmingham and in Sweden, it is accepted that such injuries are under-recorded by 30 per cent. The cost of such accidents would appear to add about £160 million to the 1979 total. Even if one refrains from putting a figure to the unreported damage-only accidents, great though their economic cost is, the total comes to nearly £1,892 million, or £2,243 million in 1980 terms.

How much of this can rightly be attributed to lorries? The department's statistics do not make calculations easy. The latest full set available at the time of writing, for 1978, shows that 1,063 'goods vehicles over 1½ tons unladen' were involved in fatal accidents and 17,732 in injury accidents, but it does not show the precise number of accidents (for in some accidents, two or more such vehicles are involved) or the numbers of deaths or injuries in them. However, a Road Research Laboratory report (Williams, 1980) shows that in 1977 goods vehicles were involved in 906 fatal accidents (nearly 15 per cent of the total), 4,803 serious accidents (7 per cent) and 11,167 slight accidents (5.8 per cent). Williams manages, incidentally, to give separate figures for 'over 3 tons unladen': still a pretty broad category, but its fatal accident rate, in proportion to vehicle numbers, is 2½ times that for the lorries of 1½ to 3 tons.

The official cost of the accidents involving lorries was, in 1980 prices, £165,000,000. If they were involved in a further 30 per cent of unrecorded accidents, that adds £13,500,000, but I shall assume a lower figure and bring the total to only £175 million. Then there are damage-only accidents. If they are reckoned simply in proportion to the number of lorries, and only at the average price, they add £20,800,000. One can say £196 million in all.

Now comes the question of responsibility. It would be a very pro-lorry assumption to say that all the pedestrians, cyclists, motorcyclists and occupants of other vehicles killed or injured in these accidents were 50 per cent to blame for their fate. Not only do the greater width, length, instability and other inherent qualities of the lorry involve it in accidents; its 'mass, size and rigidity', to quote Riley/Bates again, also promote a high proportion of casualties to the costly serious/ fatal level. It is a telling fact that when pedestrians are hit by a lorry of over three tons, the death-to-injury ration is 1:3, but it is only 1:10 when they are hit by a car; for cyclists the ratios are 1:4 and 1:22 (Williams, 1980). Besides, whenever lorries are involved, accident costs are likely to be above the average in each category. It seems not unkind to put the lorries' total cost responsibility at 75/25, which makes their figure £147 million. I shall return to this figure in Chapter 7.

In the department's background paper for Armitage it said its policy is 'to achieve a further progressive improvement in the safety of heavy goods vehicles by matching standards of performance to advances in technology'. It is an uninspiring promise: many advances in technology exist but the department has not compelled their use. And although it knows that heavier lorries would add to safety problems, it still presses for them. It fails, too, to crack down on dangerous rule-bending.

This chapter began with the pains and perils that arise from fatigue. Fifty or sixty hours in a noisy cab can cause another affliction: deafness. In the course of a letter to the *New Statesman* in June 1980 a lorry-driver, H. C. Mullin, said this: '. . . I explained that I could not hear without the use of two powerful hearing-aids (many lorry-drivers are similarly afflicted).' It is a little worrying.

5

Decibels and bad vibrations

The transport department began making promises in the sixties about 'civilising' the heavy lorry. Though commendable, this was a mere statement of its clear duty, for the protection and enhancement of a public good such as 'the quality of life' is a prime example of a governmental function. Freedom from preventable noise, fumes, blight or fear is a good that is not freely bought and sold in the market (even high-salaried officials who buy homes in tranquil streets cannot wholly escape). So long as governments do not compel the creators of noise or other forms of pollution to mend their ways, none of the vast public cost—unquantifiable but real—appears in the offenders' balance-sheets or in their charges to their customers. 'Let the customer decide' is an unsound philosophy until this is put right.

As soon as there is talk of 'civilising', the offenders assert, misleadingly, that costs would be put up; and go instantly to the government to say how difficult and expensive it would be to do anything. The official reply ought to be: But we would simply be redistributing the costs and benefits fairly throughout the community. During the golden age of the motor industry, this has seldom been said forcefully in any country; but in the past ten years there has been, elsewhere, at least a shift of emphasis. This is partly a matter of who is responsible for instigating any actual civilising measures. In the US, this task is in the hands of the Environmental Protection Agency; in West Germany, of the interior ministry; in the Netherlands, of the ministry of public health and environment . . . and in Britain, it is in the hands of the transport department.

Other countries believe that if one agency can argue against another on public issues, the public will benefit, but the British civil service abhors the 'adversary relationship', whether between departments or within departments. There has certainly been no danger of adversary problems in Marsham

Street. In the triple nineteen-storey towers that Transport shares with Environment, the civil servants of the two departments also share what they like to call 'a common citizenship'. Environment does not goad Transport. And within Transport, nobody goads the freight directorate, 'the sponsor directorate of the road-haulage industry', because a kindly senior civil servant decided that it should have command of the civilising of lorries. When John Horam became William Rodgers's junior minister in the department in 1977, and thought he would try to do something about the lorries, and consulted his Civil Service Yearbook, and found that 'lorries and the environment' came under the freight directorate, he thought to himself, That is wrong. With Rodgers's approval, he proposed the creation of a separate environment directorate. Difficulties were made. The freight directorate came up with a subtle objection: If you do this, it will imply a criticism of freight directorate; it will be saying we have not done enough about the environment. The ministers still pressed, but 'negative power' ruled: by the time of the 1979 election the change had not been made. With the arrival of Norman Fowler, freight directorate could stop worrying.

The two previous chapters have shown how gently these guardians of the environment have treated the industry over licensing, enforcement and accident control. They were responsible as well for two further lines of action, at least as relevant to the promised civilising: to require the vehicles themselves to be less unpleasant, and to limit where the more offensive ones could go. This chapter will deal with the first of these, and chiefly the question of noise.

A defender of the civil servants cannot attempt to argue that little has been achieved because noise has not been on the agenda for long. In the relatively tranquil days of 1960, noise was already such a cause of complaint that an official inquiry was ordered (its conclusions will be noted later on). In 1962, when there were fewer than 11 million vehicles on the roads, against nearly 18½ million in 1980, and fewer than 20,000 lorries over 8 tons unladen, against more than 115,000, an official inner London survey showed that traffic noise disturbed 36 per cent of people within their homes. No sceptical official could well argue that noise had been made an issue by a fussy, sensitive few. Yet nothing of any account happened—

except, of course, for a great growth in traffic, and especially of the big lorries, the worst noise-makers. A time for new promises came in 1970, when the protests over proposals for still bigger lorries brought the declaration from John Peyton, transport minister, that the time had come to curb 'a growing and undoubted nuisance'. An appearance of concern even became prudent for the lorry industry and for its allies within the department. One ready official way of responding to calls for action is to insist that there must first be research: otherwise how is one to know whether the proposed action (a restraint on the economically virtuous ton-mile creators) is cost-effective? After all, one is being confronted with un-scientific things—emotions, activists, politicians worried into sounding environmentalist. Do most people *really* not like lorries? One must quantify.

The early seventies were a good time for social survey consultants. In 1972 a firm called Social and Community Planning Research drew up questionnaires and interviewed a random sample of 5,686 people in 150 places, urban and rural, to find out how much they were bothered by traffic. The results were not published fully, for some reason, until 1978 (Morton-Williams et al, 1978). Road traffic was far and away the greatest noise nuisance: 89 per cent heard it at home, and 23 per cent were bothered by it. Although 83 per cent heard aircraft, only 13 per cent were bothered; and 35 per cent heard trains but only 2 per cent were bothered. When asked what particular traffic noises bothered them, 22 per cent said lorries—exceeded only by motorcycles. Whenever at least one vehicle in twenty was a lorry, 53 per cent experienced vibration as well, and 27 per cent were 'quite' or 'very' bothered. When people were asked what it was about traffic that bothered them most outside the house as well as in it, the order of disturbance was: pedestrian danger, noise, fumes, dust and dirt, vibration, parking.

One conclusion these consultants came to was that people did not like a lot of traffic: 'The most annoyed group were those whose eighteen-hour traffic flow (6 a.m.–midnight) was ten thousand or more vehicles . . . people living on busy main roads carrying through traffic.' A more useful conclusion was that the 'bothered' percentages were very likely an under-statement: 'People tend to take very much for granted what they find around them outside the home . . . They do not feel that they can exert much influence on what happens.'

The fact that although traffic noise is the predominant nuisance, people make fewer formal complaints about it than about other nuisances has brought this comment from a noise researcher, John Langdon of the Building Research Establishment: 'This may be because of the difficulty of identifying any particular offender, or inability to conceive of any appropriate authority with whom to pursue the complaint.' Langdon conducted a noise survey in 1972. Of 2,933 people interviewed at home in fifty-three residential streets in Greater London, 48 per cent were bothered by traffic noise; and lorries and buses were what they mentioned four times as often as cars. His survey brought out the special annoyingness of lorries in towns. Wherever there was a lot of stop-and-go traffic, he found that the annoyance people expressed was much greater than the measured decibel level would have suggested *when there was a high proportion of lorries.* His report said: 'It may well be that the difference between the noise from heavy and light vehicles, most noticeable in non-free-flow conditions, is even further increased when the noise is heard indoors.' He emphasised 'the importance of heavy vehicles . . . as major sources of nuisance'. A contributing factor, he thought, might be 'the felt incompatibility of such vehicles in close proximity to the dwelling' (Langdon, 1977).

Lorries were at the heart of yet another survey carried out in 1972. A team of thirty-three people from a consortium of consultants (Llewelyn-Davies/Forestier-Walker/Bor), plus a professor of transport economics, were engaged by the transport department to investigate a question that is still at the centre of the freight argument: If a given volume of freight is sent in lorries instead of trains, or in trains instead of lorries, what are the relative costs and benefits to society? What are the gains and losses that do not show in the balance-sheets of the freight transporters or of their customers? The survey, the consultants were told, 'could assist the government in considering strategic options for British Rail'—a cautious way of saying it could influence decisions on how much to invest in roads and in railways.

The consultants conducted three case-studies. They calculated the effects of using lorries instead of trains to carry nearly two million tons of coal a year from seven collieries near Nottingham, and to carry 3,600,000 tons of steel, iron and scrap in the Sheffield–Rotherham area; and the effects of using trains instead of lorries to carry 387,000 tons of steel from Sheffield to the West Midlands. The results are contained in four thick volumes entitled 'Freight Transport and the Environment' which have never been published, but which the department kindly lent me. The verdict was that rail was a clear environmental winner.

The effects considered were noise, vibration, air pollution, visual intrusion, vehicle and pedestrian delays, accidents and extra road maintenance. The consultants could not put a price on all items, but insofar as they could, they concluded that sending the Nottingham coal by road, using 1,000 lorry trips a day instead of 21 train trips, would cost a net £553,000 a year (more than £1,700,000 in 1980 prices); and the Sheffield switch to road (2,420 extra lorry trips, 24 fewer trains) would cost £785,000. By contrast, the Sheffield switch to rail (a minor one—4 extra trains, 145 fewer lorries) would produce a £40,500 benefit.

Answers given to the consultants' questionnaires by people in pit villages near Nottingham belied the notion that environmental concern is a middle-class thing. In Linby village 49 per cent were disturbed/very disturbed by traffic noise and 46 per cent by vibration; 66 per cent said large lorries should be restricted/very much restricted. When they and other villagers were shown a list of twenty-six nuisances and asked to name the five that most concerned them, the ones most often named, in descending order, were large vehicles, traffic noise, bad post-office service, poor shops, traffic vibrations.

In all three case-studies, the lorry option exposed far more households to unwanted effects (in the Nottingham area the estimate was that 18,000 households would have more noise and 1,600 less; in Sheffield, 19,000 against 600). Furthermore, when trains ran near people's houses the noise seldom bothered them much. In Sheffield, 'of people interviewed in houses overlooking the line at a distance of approximately twenty metres, only four out of thirty-six were disturbed by train noise. No one appeared to be disturbed by vibration from trains.' The consultants concluded: 'For whatever reasons, people living along a railway are less disturbed by trains than people living along a road are disturbed by cars, lorries, buses, etc. . . . The social cost of transfers from rail to road is bound to be greater than the social cost of transfers from road to rail.'

The consultants proposed further research to put money values on the environmental effects of traffic ('a house price study could be particularly relevant'), and said methods ought to be developed for making 'predictions of the environmental climate' on a broad scale. (Similar ideas were emerging elsewhere. The report for 1974 of the European Conference of Ministers of Transport, to which Britain belongs, said: 'Planning used to be based primarily on economic criteria, whereas now priority has to go to *social* criteria . . . Techniques for taking social effects into account will have to be improved.') However, few people in the department wanted attention drawn to the negative effects of a more-freight-by-road policy. Not even a summary of the consultants' pro-rail conclusions was issued so that the public might take note of them. And the department decided against trying to do any environmental quantifying.

In 1976 another set of consultants, Martin & Vorhees, did a survey to try to discover what it was that made people feel strongly about lorries. This was not for the department, but part of a larger transport study for West Yorkshire metropolitan county. The responses of 773 residents interviewed at ten sites, mainly on busy roads, were unsurprising but worth being formally recorded. First, people disliked *big* lorries. When lorries with three axles or more made up more than a fifth of the traffic stream, protests began. If noise levels were high, especially with morning and late evening peaks, there was usually a 'high emotional response'. Reactions against lorries were particularly strong if residents perceived 'a deterioration in the quality and status of their area' or if lorries were 'dissonant with people's expectations about an area'. The consultants concluded that lorries are 'objects of fear and perhaps one of the most obvious dangers to one's domestic/ local environment'. At a site on the A58 north-east of Leeds, when residents were asked, 'If you could change one thing to improve the area, what would it be?', forty-four out of seventy-seven said, 'Get rid of lorries.'

The coming of the Armitage inquiry inspired the department to ask Social and Community Planning Research, the firm that had done a big survey in 1972, to do yet another 'with the object of finding out more about the extent and severity of lorry nuisance nationally and the characteristics of lorry traffic which cause nuisance'. In July 1980 the department gave Sir Arthur Armitage some interim results derived from interviews in 1,000 households. Some examples:

—'Possibly one in five of the population consider the number of lorries in their road to be unreasonable . . . The greater the amount of lorry traffic, the more likely it is to be considered unreasonable.'

—'Many more people appear to suffer nuisance from lorries as pedestrians or car occupants than as residents. About 40 per cent of car occupants . . . said they were very much or quite a lot bothered by lorries.'

—When people were shown photographs of three big, three medium and three small lorries and asked to give them nuisance ratings for noise, vibration, fumes and danger to pedestrians, 'larger lorries were perceived as creating more nuisance than smaller ones on all four counts'. Similarly, 83 per cent said a four-axle articulated lorry was 'a lot of nuisance', 42 per cent a three-axle lorry, and only from 5 to 13 per cent a selection of two-axle lorries.

The department has also learned from the survey that people are not blind: 'Estimates of the amount of lorry traffic passing their homes ("a great deal", "quite a lot", "not very much", etc.) seem in general to be closely related to the numbers of lorries actually counted.'

Given the vulnerability of Britain's heavily urbanised population, and given the department's belief in the virtues of an ever-growing number of big lorries, one might have expected Britain to have led the way, too, in palliative measures.

There was a time of promise in 1960: a committee under Sir Alan Wilson was appointed to inquire into noise abatement, and Ernest Marples asked it to give priority to traffic noise. Vehicle-makers and other industrialists were on the committee, so its conclusions cannot be thought impractical. It recommended as an interim measure—'what is immediately technically possible'—that the maximum noise of all new lorries should be limited to 85 decibels. Decibels will be explained in a moment; the first point to be made is that by the start of the eighties, when the number of big noise-makers had enormously multiplied, the permitted maximum was still far higher than that.

Marples began by proposing almost what the committee urged: 86 decibels. He retreated, however, in the face of the lorry-makers, who when they profess to want to make less offensive machines are like the young St Augustine saying, 'Give me chastity and continency, but not yet.' Years passed. Barbara Castle ordered that from 1970 the maximum for new lorries would be 89 decibels. The extent of the decline from Wilson's proposal can be understood only if it is noted that decibels, which measure sound pressure, are recorded on a logarithmic scale, and that to the human ear an increase from 80 decibels to 90 means a *doubling* of the noise.

Barbara Castle also announced an effective-sounding measure: she gave police and departmental officials power to check offending vehicles with meters at the roadside. A firm named Dawe Instruments set to work making the meters. But it sold very few, and even those few were scarcely used. The difficulty was that the metering had to be done with great care to stand up in court: on level ground, away from noise-reflecting walls and when a second noisy vehicle was not passing. The police united in not taking on the trouble. A Dawe Instruments executive said years later: 'We caught a cold on it.'

Other countries have shown that enforcement of noise laws works if special squads of police are assigned to it. Zurich, Lausanne and other Swiss towns have 'noise brigades' of five to ten men, who also police excessive noise from other sources. France has since 1973 had teams of mobile police equipped to meter vehicle fumes as well as noise; in 1978 eighty-six of these teams fined 85,000 vehicle-owners and compelled them to report with faults rectified. In the US, San Francisco and Colorado Springs are two among a number of cities with noise squads with similar powers. In Britain, the environment/transport department told MPs in 1972 that measures were coming to meter the noise of lorries both at the roadside and (avoiding all difficulties) at annual inspections. Testing stations actually began preparing to instal noise-checking equipment; but the scheme was quietly dropped.

Soon the Common Market became an excellent ally of those who said 'but not yet'. In 1971 John Peyton had announced that from 1974 new lorries of less than 200 horsepower would have to come down to 86 decibels, though bigger ones could stay at 89. This was hardly drastic, for the lorry-makers had told Wilson ten years earlier that 85 could be achieved without expensive redesign—chiefly by means of insulation panels. However, even this measure never took effect. A perfect justification for inaction emerged: Britain was joining the Common Market. Among the freedoms that an acceder to the community gives up is the freedom to require vehicles within its borders to be quieter than the maximums agreed by a horsetrading committee in Brussels. The reason is that the community is founded on an economic philosophy that has produced rules, and secretariats, devoted to the virtues of freely-flowing goods (freely-flowing within the community, that is; products from outside are rather a different matter). Regulations controlling the noisiness or other unpleasant qualities of machines are not the creation of an enthusiastic Brussels environment directorate (there is such a directorate, but it is small and little-regarded) but of Directorate-General XI (Internal Market). Within DG XI they come under Directorate A/Movement of Goods/ Removal of Technical Barriers of an Industrial Nature/ Standardisation. This is ideal for the lobbyists in the Brussels office of the Committee of Common Market Vehicle Constructors. In committee bargaining, the 'barriers to trade' arguments of the countries with car and lorry factories have always been able to override any sensitive member that wanted a big decibel reduction. In 1970 the old six-nation Market had put its lorry noise maximum at 92 decibels (91 plus one-decibel tolerance), a level noticeably louder than Britain's 89. So with Britain's entry in 1973, its level went up.

Noise was not forgotten, however, in Directorate A of DG XI. Talks began in 1973. Proposals were made that by autumn 1976 the limits for new lorries should be: up to 200 horsepower, 87; above that, 89 (again, including the one-decibel tolerance). Lorry-makers in Britain and on the continent got ready to meet this minimal change. Indeed, a further reduction was expected to follow shortly, and at least one British diesel-engine maker, Perkins, invested a lot of money in a noise-abatement package. But then came more delays. New limits were also being discussed for cars and buses, so anyone who wished for delay had plenty of time-consuming permutations to argue about. Germany, having far fewer big lorries than Britain, was more eager for a sharp reduction in bus noise. British officials from Marsham Street pleaded for more time for their lorry-makers. They got it. Not until early 1977 was agreement reached on the 87/89 limits for lorries; and they were to mean nothing for years. The directive said that each country could, if it wished, apply them to new models from April 1980 and to all lorries coming from the factory after September 1982. They were merely barred from doing it *sooner*. What did Marsham Street do? 'For administrative reasons' it ordained that the reductions would not apply to any lorries coming on the road before 1 April 1983, *ten years* after the talks had begun.

Meanwhile the Japanese limit was brought down in 1979 to 86 (noticeably quieter than 89); the Swiss was at 88 and coming down to 86 in 1982 (in 1979 the Swiss lorry-maker, Saurer, was already in mass production at 86.5); and the US limit was also 86 for 1982.

With the weak 1977 decision came a promise: the Council of Ministers set a target of 80 decibels for all vehicles by 1985 and it asked Directorate A to be quick with some proposals. Eighty would mean that juggernauts had to be as quiet as many cars, so urgency was necessary if the manufacturers were to be stirred into the necessary technical action. No lorry-maker could be expected to go ahead without a mandatory date. Noise-abatement added a little to a lorry's weight and price, and in a competitive world few hauliers would pay for that unless they were compelled to. But there was no urgency. When an official of Directorate A was asked two years later if anything had been achieved, he said, 'Nothing, unfortunately.' Neither the British government nor any other had been pressing. 'It is up to the public to push the authorities,' he said. 'So long as the authorities are strongly defending the interests of the manufacturers, there is nothing the Brussels commission can do.'

How was the public to do its pushing? In Britain a useful-seeming body, the Noise Advisory Council, had been created in 1970. This quango was meant to be a source of expert advice and a channel for public opinion on the action needed against all noise sources—aircraft, traffic, factories. However, departments rarely set up bodies that are likely to be troublesome to them. The civil servants who decided its structure made a junior environment minister its chairman, provided it with government office space and put men of their department in charge of it. Industries that would be affected by the fight against noise have all along been strongly represented. At the period under discussion, its 'surface transport working group' had the following members: chief engineer of the National Freight Corporation (thousands of lorries), a man from a subsidiary of Guest, Keen & Nettlefold (big user of lorries), the director of the Motor Industry Research Association (financed by the industry), a university research fellow in industrial science (a field heavily dependent on friendly grants from industry), and one man each from British Rail and the Civic Trust.

In 1974 the council did say this: 'Public opinion must be continually stimulated to recognise the importance of noise and the possibilities of its alleviation.' The public got far less stimulation from the council and its minders, however, than from the painful fact that noise was steadily getting worse. If people were stimulated to look up Noise Advisory Council in the London telephone directory in the hope of talking about alleviation, they found that it was not listed. Its office was not excessively disturbed by ringing bells. At the time when Directorate A was doing 'nothing, unfortunately', the officials who spoke for the council made clear that the council was not being stimulated to complain. 'We don't think the council would tend to press too frequently for too much,' one of them said. 'Having achieved something, we cannot return to the well right away.' He said the council had wanted the 1977 agreement to bring all lorries down to 87, but it did not make an issue of it: 'If we had pressed, we might have lost the whole lot.' It is a daunting thought: the Noise Advisory Council causing Brussels to do nothing whatever.

The council did, however, go so far as to make public, though not at all noisily, a complaint to William Rodgers that his 1977 transport White Paper contained only 'generalised undeveloped references' to transport noise, 'the most serious and widespread noise nuisance in the UK'.. It wanted 'no delay' by Britain in working to achieve an EEC level of 80 by 1985. And it raised a question about a prototype lorry then being developed under government auspices, which the White Paper said would be 'about as quiet as present-day cars'. If it proved capable of being mass-produced at an acceptable price, the White Paper said, 'the government will encourage the manufacturers to include much quieter performance as a feature of their future range of models'. The council asked drily 'what form the encouragement . . . will take'—was not a Brussels regulation the only way?

The quiet lorry project was another outcome of the flurry of environmental interest at the start of the seventies. In 1970 an official working group of scientists told the transport department that at least 9,600,000 people were already living in homes exposed to traffic noise above the 'acceptable' level, and if nothing were done the number could well be thirty million by 1980. It raised the possibility of a wonderful reduction of the number afflicted: by 1980 the noise of all new vehicles could be halved in two five-year phases, bringing lorries down to 80 decibels. For lorries, 'several years research would be required', followed by design and development (Road Research Laboratory, 1970). With this in mind, the Road Research Laboratory was put in charge of a quiet lorry programme in 1971. One participating firm, Leyland, dropped out after a few years; but near the end of 1978 a machine was at last unveiled at the laboratory. John Horam and Sir Peter Baldwin, it was announced, would be there to give their blessing; but on the day 'it clashed with something else at the last moment'. They thus missed facing any questions of the 'Now what?' type about the fine, though belated, piece of Rolls Royce/Foden technology on show: a 320 h.p. tractive unit (suitable, significantly, for a 40-ton artic) emitting only 80 decibels. This was achieved by redesigning the engine, cooling system, gearbox and silencer, and by adding glass-fibre panelling. The weight penalty was about a quarter of a ton—not much in the grand total. With a quick decision, Rolls engineers said, it could be coming off the production line in 1981.

There was, of course, no quick decision; and little evidence, even, of enthusiasm from the transport department, let alone from hauliers or lorry-makers. In 1980 the lorry's operating costs were being tested by lending it to an Oxfordshire haulier. He was delighted at the privilege, and passing lorry-drivers were insisting on climbing into it and savouring its interior quietness, which was also like that of a family car. When Sir Arthur Armitage asked the department about the lorry's running costs, it produced a pessimistic estimate of a 1.3 per cent penalty. But the calculation erred in several points. For example, it assumed an extra manufacturing cost of 8 to 10 per cent, whereas the makers expect that in mass production the extra might be 3 to 4 per cent; and it assumed higher fuel consumption owing to the extra weight, whereas the quiet lorry's superior fan system actually brings a net fuel saving. In the US a quiet prototype has been found to reduce costs—even though its maintenance costs are high, something the British lorry avoids. In 1980 German, Dutch and Swiss makers were also working on quiet lorries. One day there would be a market for them.

Before returning to the decisive factor—political will, or public stimulation—a question must be answered: What is 'acceptable' noise? What should be the limit to the noise that the community imposes on the people who live, work, shop, or perhaps even bravely wish to walk with pleasure in a street? Once again one must go back to the hopeful days of Sir Alan Wilson's inquiry. The fixing of permissible street noise levels begins from how the average person reacts. Noise is a problem only because people dislike it, are wakened by it, have their normal pursuits disrupted by it and are sometimes made ill or deafened by it. Traffic noise is measured with meters adjusted to what is called an A-weighted decibel scale, which ignores the lower vibrations (a pro-lorry scale, as will be explained later). By the time of the Wilson inquiry, much international work had been done to decide the 'acceptable' level of day-by-day noise at the façades of dwellings. Wilson concluded that at the worst, in daytime in a busy urban setting, people inside their houses should not be exposed for more than 10 per cent of the time to more than 50dB(A), to use the acoustician's shorthand; which means about 65db(A) outside the windows. The reasoning was that noise above 50 begins to interfere with conversation and listening to radio or television. The significance of this in terms of vehicles and community cost was well summarised by a member of the 1970 working group, M. E. Burt—a senior man at the Road Research Laboratory at a time when environmental thinkers there were not yet under restraint. In a study entitled *Roads and the Environment* he said: 'The only way of producing a significant and general effect is to quieten the vehicles. But the question is how much to quieten them?' He suggested a criterion: 'The majority of the population (say 80 to 90 per cent) when at home in rooms fronting on to the road should be able most (say 90 per cent) of the time during the day to conduct a conversation with ordinary windows open.' If nothing were done to quieten vehicles (which is indeed what happened), he calculated that by 1980 only 39 per cent of the population would enjoy that minimum tranquillity.

Burt considered whether, nevertheless, compulsory quiet-ening of vehicles would be economically justified. An alter-native was to double-glaze people's windows. First of all, Burt made a point of principle: 'The vehicles make the noise and should therefore be the means of reducing it.' He questioned whether people 'should be forced to protect themselves in their own homes', and said: 'In summer one should surely be able to sit in one's home with ordinary single-glazed windows and keep them open.' And what of people in their gardens or walking in the street? 'Insulating buildings does nothing for them.' He went on to make a cost/benefit calculation. Assum-ing that a house with 90dB(A) at its façade became un-inhabitable, he worked out a range of figures for loss of house value. The total existing disbenefit for fifteen million urban houses at an average value (1970) of £5,000 came to £6,750 million, giving an annual value of £675 million at a 10 per cent interest rate. Though his calculation might be questioned, he said the annual cost was clearly hundreds of millions, and that was only for 'loss of amenity for homes in urban areas'. By contrast, halving the noise of all lorries had been calculated by the working group (which included auto-motive specialists) to add £50 million a year to operating costs, and for all other vehicles it might be another £200 million.

Burt presented a further economic argument for quick action. Even though the phasing out of noisy vehicles would take some time, the lives of roads and buildings were much longer. 'If it is practical and economic substantially to reduce traffic noise at source, a decision to this effect by about 1975 will obviate the need to incorporate features in buildings which would outlast the nuisance.' Instead, what has hap-pened? Council housing provides a good example. When it is built on noisy roads, 7 per cent is officially added to the cost for insulation and other noise-baffling features, and double that if the dwellings face south and thus present a more sensitive façade to the road. In the national accounts this cost is not, of course, debited to roads; nor is all such extra outlay from private pockets. Large sums have, however, been added to the road bill by the requirement, since 1973, that if a house is put into the 'unacceptable' noise category by a new road or an improvement such as dualling within three hundred metres of it, insulation must be provided.

This palliative was conceded under the Land Compensation Act after the outcry raised by sufferers from some of the early urban motorways. The environment department saw to it that the outlay would be kept within strict bounds. By that time a noise-exposure standard had been generally agreed: that it was unacceptable for the noise at house fronts to exceed 65dB(A) for more than 10 per cent of the time during the hours from 6 a.m. to midnight. Before drafting the Act, the department proposed, on the basis of a new but misleading household survey, that houses should qualify for insulation grants only when they exceeded a much noisier 70dB(A). Representatives of the Greater London Council and other authorities objected. A compromise of 68 was agreed. Even so, the liability to pay grants was only about two-thirds of what it would have been if people had qualified at 65dB(A), an official study shows (Davies and Dawson, 1980). Furthermore, only a tiny proportion of households at 68-plus actually got grants. If the 68 limit is exceeded simply as a result of traffic arising from some road-widening or motorway-building a short distance away, or of a lorry-routing scheme, or of the general (officially blessed) growth of traffic, sufferers do not qualify. This creates great injustices. Many cities have residential roads that have been exposed for years to noise levels double, and sometimes even treble, the 68 standard.

Proposals by local authorities that more sufferers should be made eligible have been spurned. The government's fear of the cost is understandable. In 1975 the consultants Martin & Vorhees found that in West Yorkshire, a region of more than two million people, 52,900 dwellings with 7½ per cent of the population were exposed to traffic noise above 71dB(A), a level sharply above the 'acceptable'. Merely to insulate this limited number would then have cost £26,244,000. As West Yorkshire's entire roadbuilding budget for the period 1975–91 was expected to be no more than £70 million, and the £26 million would have to come out of that, the consultants said wisely: 'Some compromise . . . can therefore be seen as inevitable.'

A national estimate was produced in 1979 by the Noise Advisory Council. It reckoned that 2,300,000 homes were above the 68 level, and to insulate them would cost (1978 prices) £1,610 million. A member of the council, Eric Epson, told me: 'These are houses whose conditions we consider to be sub-standard. They should be brought up to a reasonable standard—it's not good, but reasonable. We hope at least that a scheme might be started to help the very worst houses over a period of years.'

Large though the £1,610 million figure was, it would have been much larger if the official estimate of the number of sufferers had not been revised downwards. A figure of 2,300,000 dwellings means about 6,000,000 people; yet in 1970, it will be remembered, the estimate had been at least 9,600,000 people. The official explanation of the fall, despite a great increase in traffic noise, was that the earlier estimate was extrapolated, unsoundly, from a noise survey in London, which is noisier than other places. Nevertheless, the percentage of the population now officially above the acceptable level in Britain is smaller, surprisingly, than in France, Germany, Belgium, Denmark and even Switzerland. Even if the estimate of 2,300,000 dwellings is correct, it must be repeated that they are beyond the limit of the acceptable. The report setting out the prevailing estimates, 'Forecasts of Exposure to Traffic Noise in Residential Areas' (D. G. Harland, Transport and Road Research Laboratory, 1976, unpublished) says that surveys in 1972 showed that roads 'were judged to be noisy' even when the much lower level of 60 decibels was exceeded more than 10 per cent of the time, and the number of people living on such roads 'will increase to 20 million by the turn of the century'.

There is no immediate hope, however, of even 'the very worst houses' being made eligible for help. The present limited aid comes dearer than the transport department would like. The department has been vague about the cost, but it did tell an inquiring MP that by April 1980 'well in excess of 22,000 dwellings' beside motorways and trunk roads had been given double-glazing at a cost in 1980 terms of up to £1,000 each. That alone makes about £22 million. The department had no figures for other roads, but the total there must have been much greater. So the money spent merely to quieten the *inside* of a tiny percentage of houses would have paid for a good deal of lorry-quietening. The economics is odd.

Although lorries are recognised as a large contributor to the suffering, official methods understate their guilt. John Langdon's finding has already been mentioned: that stop-and-go town traffic with a high percentage of lorries in it causes, decibel for decibel, more annoyance. One cause of this is the diesel engine's low-frequency vibration which, though largely unrecorded in the dB(A) metering, easily penetrates windows and walls; and as its wavelength happens to match the size of many domestic rooms, they reverberate like soundboxes. Objects rattle on shelves and floors vibrate under people's feet. And double-glazing is no barrier to it. Engine redesign would reduce it; but because of this low-frequency element, a lorry that passes the 80dB(A) test will never be as tolerable as an 80dB(A) car. Furthermore, when new car and lorry types are tested for decibels, they all do the same 30 m.p.h. drive-past. This too favours lorries, for at the lower speeds common in congested urban settings, where people are most exposed, the noise of petrol engines is abated far more than that of diesel engines.

A curious aspect of the long-drawn-out failure to quieten lorries is that it ought to have raised protests from ardent roadbuilders, as all the millions needed for noise insulation grants, and also for noise-abatement barriers or cuttings, meant fewer miles of roads. (In 1979 the estimated cost of a three-mile, four-lane road in Greenwich, with cuttings and noise-baffling walls and earth mounds, was £55 million. This road was to relieve part of the A2, where many thousands of juggernauts a day put the noise level up to nearly three times the 'acceptable'.) However, no road lobbyists were heard campaigning for quiet lorries. It was left to the dispirited public and to such men as the local authorities' environmental health officers, who grew weary of pressing for rational action. 'We've been thumping the table about this for a long time,' a West Yorkshire official told me. About the millions going for insulation, he made a simple point that would be echoed in almost any county hall: 'It's all very well isolating people in their little brick boxes. What about the environment around those little boxes? People have to leave their homes.' Another point repeatedly made, by engine design specialists as well as by those who spent years doing household noise surveys, was that no more research was needed. John Langdon of the Building Research Establishment told me: 'They're all busy paying researchers money. That is a lot cheaper than actually doing anything. We know all we need to know to take effective action. It's a question of *will* rather than knowledge.'

In 1980 an attempt to mobilise willpower internationally was made by the environment directorate of the 24-nation Organisation for Economic Cooperation and Development at a Paris conference. The delegates were told that in OECD countries—Western Europe, the US, Canada, Australia, New Zealand, Japan—more than a hundred million people were already living above the acceptable level. If vehicles were not soon made much quieter, noise impact would increase by a third in Europe by the year 2000. Delegations from West Germany and the Netherlands led those campaigning for an attempt to be made, despite lost time, to achieve the long-promised EEC reduction to 80 decibels for all vehicles by 1985 or as soon as possible thereafter. (It is significant that in both countries there is a government Noise Abatement Office, or rather, in their languages, noise-*fighting* office, a thing as yet unknown in Marsham Street.) Dr Rood van Noort, head of the Dutch noise-fighters, reported on a plan that was being introduced in the Netherlands to stimulate the use of quieter vehicles even before the next reduction was agreed. Every new vehicle would be taxed according to its noise output, with the amount possibly doubling with each three-decibel increase. The revenue would go to pay for a ten-year pro-gramme to help the sufferers by means of noise barriers and soundproofing. Van Noort made the point that the more quickly vehicles were quietened, the less would have to be spent—and of course the less would be levied in tax. In 1980, as a preliminary step, vehicle-users began contributing to the work of van Noort's sixty-man office through a special fuel tax. In Germany the chief noise-fighter, Dr Ansgar Vogel, was drafting regulations for an alternative way of stimulating the manufacture of quieter lorries while waiting for action in Brussels: by barring vehicles above a certain decibel level from large urban areas, especially at night, thereby creating a market for quiet ones. His philosophy is: Give the manu-facturer the opportunity to make money with products friendly to the environment.

These schemes arise from a desire to break out of the EEC straitjacket; but of course van Noort and Vogel were still fighting for an 80-decibel international limit. At Paris they did not notice any table-thumping for speedy action being done by Britain's eleven-man delegation, chiefly civil servants led by a junior environment minister. Vehicle-makers behind the scenes were saying how costly a severe reduction would be. The best the Dutch and Germans could achieve was a declaration that the limit should come down to 80 before 1990. They called it a step forward and hoped that at Brussels it would help them to attain an agreement for 80 decibels by, at the worst, 1987.

What would the British be saying there? The head of the transport department's vehicle directorate, J. W. Furness, whose visitors at Marsham Street are chiefly from the motor industry, made the following statement to Armitage about the 80-decibel objective: 'We have put this to our partners in Europe as a proposal for about the 1990s. There is considerable doubt whether we can achieve it in practice. We might achieve something near that, 82 or 83.' Even if, despite the vehicle men's wishes, 80 were enforced by 1990, the quiet lorries would then replace the noisy ones only at the rate of about 10 per cent a year; and meanwhile the heaviest, noisiest ones would have been increasing in number. Only after five years might there be some noticeable reduction in noise levels. But for millions of people enduring officially unacceptable noise, there would be no real respite until the year 2000.

Back in 1972, when only ten unproductive years had followed Sir Alan Wilson's report, but when environmental promises were thought politically wise, the transport minister, John Peyton, said in the Commons as part of his reply to a motion against heavier lorries: 'We have embarked upon a substantial research programme aimed at the radical reduction, if not elimination, of the atrocious noise made by heavy vehicles.' That was the quiet lorry programme. In 1980 there was only one drawback about the fine noise-reducing technology that resulted: it was not on the assembly-line. And something else whose basis was laid at about the same time, the Noise Advisory Council, seemed to be equally in limbo. 'We're twenty-five good souls giving our time unpaid,' one member said to me plaintively, 'but we haven't had a full meeting for a year.'

A surprising statement in the transport department's evidence to Armitage was: 'The fumes of diesel engines are not toxic.' Unlike petrol fumes, it is true, they contain no lead. But according to the department's own statistics, diesel-engined vehicles in 1978 emitted the following quantities of harmful pollutants: carbon monoxide, 241,000 tonnes; hydrocarbons, 39,000; aldehydes, 3,000; oxides of nitrogen, 176,000; sulphur dioxide, 35,000; particulates, 35,000. Of the latter three, diesel vehicles produce 36, 64 and 55½ per cent respectively of the annual total. The department itself went on to say two paragraphs later, 'Some of the particulates may be carcinogenic.' Some of the hydrocarbons, of the polycyclic type, certainly are. The environment department, in a separate submission, managed to tell Armitage so. It added that diesel engines emit about twice as much of these per gallon as petrol engines, and that in Greater London lorries accounted for about 15 per cent of the total emitted. It also said that intensive research was being done in the US (by the Environmental Protection Agency) into the 'carcinogenic potential' of diesel, but there was 'not a great deal of concern in the UK'.

Armitage was likely to get soothing guidance on the question, for one of his advisory assessors, Professor Patrick Lawther, has been widely accused of minimising the possible dangers of exhaust gases. In the US, meanwhile, stricter limits were being imposed on diesel emissions.

A further troubling quality of the heavy lorry is its impact on buildings. What happens when a lorry fails to negotiate a corner or plunges off the road is clear enough. The question here is of the insidious damage from vibration, whether airborne or groundborne. Inquiries reveal a disturbing history of official evasiveness.

The official view on airborne (low-frequency) vibrations is that they cannot damage buildings until they reach an intensity beyond human tolerance. Groundborne vibrations are another matter. Even when they are barely perceptible, according to an early Road Research Laboratory study (Whiffin and Leonard, 1971), they can be harmful to 'ruins and ancient monuments'. This study does not, unfortunately, mention a type of building of more direct concern to many people: old houses, which are structurally much more vulnerable than modern ones. It does say that when groundborne vibrations are strong enough to annoy householders, they can also cause 'architectural' damage, such as cracking of plaster, even to ordinary modern houses, and when they reach the point of being 'unpleasant' they can cause structural damage as well.

This would naturally occur sooner in old houses; and they are often beside arterial routes.

This 1971 survey, being an early-seventies product, showed a good deal of concern. It made a number of recommendations in which the phrases 'more research is needed' and 'little is known' recur. It said the increase in the number of very heavy axle-loads (which, of course, has much exceeded the expectations of 1971) 'will increase the chance of triggering action and the possibility of more rapid fatigue damage in buildings', and it proposed research to devise lorry suspensions that would reduce the impact.

Lorry designers in fact know very well how to make suspensions that are less damaging to both roads and buildings, but these cost more and need careful maintenance, so most lorry operators go for 'relatively simple but rugged mechanical spring units', in the words of a later Road Research report, *Loads and Vibrations Caused by Eight Commercial Vehicles with Gross Weights Exceeding 32 Tons* (Leonard et al, 1974). This report has some odd aspects. It gives the results of tests with lorries ranging up to 44 tons, and one cannily-worded sentence in its conclusions has since been often quoted by advocates of heavier lorries: 'Vehicles with gross weights as high as forty-four tons need not generate larger dynamic loads or vibrations than are produced by some existing thirty-two-ton vehicles.' This is like saying that a well-trained alsatian need not endanger children more than a smaller but ill-trained mongrel. On another page the report makes clear that a 44-tonner 'need not' be more damaging only because it could be given a gentler suspension; but then so could the 32-tonners. The report further reveals that the eight lorries, supplied by private firms, were such a mixture of types that no valid conclusions could be drawn about relative damaging effects. As for further research into better suspensions, by 1980 the laboratory was still evaluating three types.

The 1971 survey said that traffic vibration from 'road surfaces of good riding quality' is 'normally' acceptable for both buildings and people, but it called for research into 'the degrees of surface irregularity' that cause damaging vibration. As the heavy lorry axle-loads that break up the road surface and cause the most vibration were well known to be increasing, this would seem to have been an urgent matter. Again, little has happened. In 1978 the laboratory reported on tests

done in a house near Uxbridge where there was no irregularity
at all: free-flowing traffic, road level, surface 'smooth and
even'. 'Clearly further work is required,' the report said, and
promised some: 'Measurements of noise and structural vibration in houses adjacent to bumpy roads, steep hills and where
congested flow conditions exist will be combined with data
obtained . . . where there have been complaints of vibration'
(Martin et al, 1978). By 1980 this had not been done—and
there was no intention of doing it.

A further line of research suggested in the 1971 survey was
into 'the compacting effect of traffic vibrations on the
materials beneath the foundations' of buildings, particularly
'the older types', as well as 'vibrations generated in various
types of soil'. The importance of this was that there was
already evidence that long-continuing vibrations, even if they
were not at all acute, could shake down old rubble-based
foundations and thus cause subsidence damage. Here again
the transport department has played an odd role. In 1976 a
scientist at Plymouth Polytechnic, Dr Howard Ward, began
work on what was to have been a four-year study for the Road
Research Laboratory, with particular attention to this problem. He told me in 1977: 'I am quite surprised that people
haven't taken this problem seriously.' In two years he hoped
to have enough data, from measurements at a wide range of
sites, to show what was a safe limit for vibration exposure, so
that lorries could be banned near vulnerable structures. 'It
would be silly,' he said, 'to increase lorry weights until we
have more information.' After I quoted some of his words in
The Sunday Times, he was rebuked by the Road Research
Laboratory and told, 'You shouldn't say things like that.'

When Dr Ward was only half-way through his study, he left
for a new post in Hong Kong. Later in 1979 I asked the
environment department what research was being done into
vibration damage to historic buildings, and was told in a letter
from its historic areas conservation division that 'a lengthy
study . . . now nearing completion . . . is being carried out'—
by whom? By Ward, it said, at Plymouth Polytechnic. I
replied pointing out that Ward's study was dormant; that the
Road Research Laboratory now said it was concerned only
with vibration effects on *people,* as buildings were the
concern of the Building Research Establishment; and that this
establishment was doing no such research. I said: 'It would be

unfortunate if the impression was given that no official research was being done for fear of the evidence that might emerge.' The silence that followed was long even by Marsham Street standards. After fifty-eight days I got a brief note merely passing on a copy of a Commons reply saying what I already knew, that no such research was planned.

Ward submitted a report at the end of 1979 on his preliminary work. He told the Civic Trust: 'Most of the energy in the ground vibrations occurs in the bandwidth 0–50 Hz, with the peak occurring around 20 Hz . . . It will be the groundborne vibrations that are going to be more significant [than airborne] . . . These vibrations contain the energy in the lower-frequency bandwidth [and] are likely to be the source of damage to structures . . . In any case far more work will have to be done.'

There is other evidence of departmental foot-dragging. Early in 1979 the Civic Trust had persuaded scientists of the Road Research Laboratory to undertake vibration measurements in a number of old houses beside busy roads. From a long list of eager volunteers the trust proposed seven, ranging from a YHA hostel, dating from the fifteenth century, on the A130 at Saffron Walden, to a former inn beside the A16 at Stamford. The hostel's owners had reported that lorries frequently hit the kerb outside, and during six years a cellar wall had moved inward more than six inches. A laboratory team spent just half an hour there and another half-hour at a partly medieval house beside the A131 near Braintree—and the method they used was suitable for analysing not vibration damage but effects on people. The trust was told that the measurements confirmed the laboratory's view that airborne annoyance to people was what mattered. The impression gained by the trust was that the scientists who originally agreed to the exercise were under a cloud: that orders had come down from Marsham Street forbidding measurement of groundborne vibration.

The trust took the question up with Dr Martin Holdgate's directorate of research operations at Marsham Street. It was hard to get a simple answer, but after eight months the directorate said this: 'There is little that research can offer in quantifying any effects that traffic vibration might have on historic buildings. The main reason for this is to be found in the great variety and construction [*sic*] of such buildings.' Instead of fact-finding it suggested 'remedial action for each site-specific problem'. The Civic Trust, in recounting this story to the Armitage inquiry, comments that this implies there are 'a limited number of sites where there may be problems', and says: 'If this suggestion is to be taken seriously, the full armoury of "remedial actions" needs to be set out . . . and a price estimated. Knowing the cost would concentrate attention on ways of reducing the vibration-producing characteristics of lorries and curbing the growth of road freight.'

Perhaps inspired by this, Armitage asked the transport department to tell him more about vibration—'its effect on people and buildings', current research, 'costs and effects of possible measures', and so forth. The department's slim reply was comical in its uninformativeness—comical, or insolent. A third of it consisted of verbatim extracts from the Construction and Use Regulations for tyres and springs, covering everything from road rollers to 'vehicles first used before 1.1.1932'. Armitage also learned that groundborne vibration 'originates with the variations in the contact forces between the wheels of a vehicle and the road surface'. The reply did say that lorry vibration 'can be reduced by improved suspension and tyres' and it revived the 1978 promise of research on 'the effect of surface discontinuity on ground vibration generation', though giving no date. It said *nothing whatever* about ground-borne damage to buildings.

A later departmental paper conceded just a possibility. 'Groundborne vibration from heavy vehicles is unlikely to be significant except where the axles hit an irregularity'; the department did not 'expect' heavier lorries to cause 'significantly more'. (This much-liked word 'significant' had been used earlier in a departmental letter to the Civic Trust, which commented tartly to Armitage: 'It is indeed significant if owners of buildings are having to spend money on repairs and maintenance . . . The cost to the nation could be very high.') Yet another paper for Armitage was especially soothing: it said good road maintenance and 'continuing improvements' to lorry suspensions had 'almost certainly' reduced groundborne vibration, and lorries should be 'less likely' to cause vibration damage in future.

In fact, heavier lorries mean more damage. The department had plenty of evidence in its files if it had wished to read it. In 1970 the Royal Institute of British Architects, alarmed at the

threat of heavier lorries, had made detailed representations to
the department. One point was: 'The fact that the load per axle
is to be retained at ten tons is irrelevant since pressures are
redistributed below ground. Five to seven feet down—probably
at foundation level—a pair of axles each carrying ten tons will
exert a pressure of twenty tons. Thus the increase in weight
limits could not be offset by distribution over several axles.
Twenty feet down the whole load on the vehicle would be
operative as a vibrating source, and it would be this which
would affect buildings, not individual axle-loadings.' Two
years later, pressure in the EEC for 40-tonners brought a new
protest to John Peyton from the RIBA. 'There is now clear
evidence to link structural failure in buildings, especially in
old towns and villages, with the passage of heavy lorries,' it
said; and it asked every architect with supporting evidence to
send it to Peyton. One who did was William Allen, a vibration
specialist and former chief architect to the Building Research
Establishment. He repeated the point about the deep-down
impact and sent examples from his own practice. In an
interview he said: 'A great many of our buildings date from
the eighteenth century backwards and in those days they just
did not know how to put down proper foundations. Consequently these old buildings are literally being shaken to
pieces. This is the sort of damage you do not see until it is too
late.'

The department could have supplemented its files from
other sources. In 1975 the surveyor to St Paul's, Bernard
Feilden, reported that the cathedral showed more defects
from subsidence on its south side, where heavy traffic passed
close by, than on the north. A mass of similar evidence has
been accumulated by J. H. Crockett, a consultant for twenty-
five years in this work. He surveyed all English cathedrals and
a number of important churches and found with dramatic
regularity that whenever they had traffic passing on one side,
that was the side that showed damage. Detailed recordings
made over many years have convinced him that traffic
vibration need not be acute to cause damaging subsidence or
other structural harm: an accumulation over the years can do
it. A heavy flow of big lorries of course accelerates the
process. The paired axles of an articulated lorry's trailer are
especially bad because their linked suspensions cause a
rebound effect with sharper, multiplied impacts. In addition,

the airborne low-frequency noise of lorries causes strong vibrations at the tops of buildings. The combination of ground and air impact, Crockett fears, can trigger off damage.

If it had wished, too, the department could even have sent someone from Marsham Street to visit a few of the houses proposed by the Civic Trust's volunteers. He could have gone, for example, to a seventeenth-century cottage near Kenilworth Castle, standing three feet from the A452, where its owner, Mrs Pat Fulham, could have pointed to the gable ends she had had to have repaired, and to the big cracks that had since developed in her façade. She could have told him, like thousands of people elsewhere, about her foiled efforts to get lorry traffic diverted away or to win a repair grant for 'a building of special architectural or historical interest'. (She says: 'If they can't stop the traffic why can't I have a grant to repair the damage? Why should I have to pay for their mismanagement?') Or the department's man could have gone to the A34 near Blenheim Palace, where John Turner, chairman of the Woodstock Society, would have shown him eighteenth-century houses whose façades had had to be completely re-built because they were bulging dangerously, and others now cracking which before long would need the same expensive treatment. Turner would have pointed out that these were sturdy houses on solid foundations; after more than two hundred years the trouble had begun when big lorries multiplied.

The Civic Trust told Armitage: 'Ignorance is used as a reason for not compensating those who bear the cost and also for taking no steps to reduce the cost.' It is hardly surprising that the research directorate called off its scientists. Why do research that confirmed the lorry's guilt and demonstrated that the department owed people large sums?

6

Sensitive streets

In the same debate of 1972 in which John Peyton promised action against 'atrocious noise' he also said this: 'If vehicles do grow at all in weight or size, this should be only for the most powerful reasons and subject to strict limitations as to routes. The rule that a vehicle should be free to go almost literally wherever it can burst a passage is both brutal and archaic and should be discarded.' The environment secretary, Geoffrey Rippon, said in his mellower style: 'We cannot indefinitely allow these lorries, of whatever weight or size . . . to chunter through our towns and villages along roads totally unsuited to them.'

In 1980 the director-general of the Road Haulage Association, George Newman, told Armitage that no lorry would travel on unsuitable roads if it were not necessary, and declared: 'The road network is the lorry network.' But now there was little likelihood of a counter-view coming from Peyton's and Rippon's successors in Marsham Street, Norman Fowler and Michael Heseltine.

The transport department had long ago digested and eliminated the unpalatable notion of national lorry routing. The idea was outlined in 1974 in a departmental paper on which hauliers and others were asked to comment. Peyton's immediate successor, Fred Mulley, spoke of growing concern about big lorries using 'quite unsuitable' routes and said the department and local authorities were 'actively seeking to alleviate' the problem. (These 'actively's' chime with 'urgent's' down the years.) The paper proposed a national system of possibly 3,500 miles of primary routes which lorries over 24 tons (of which there were then 70,000, half as many as now) would be directed to use. These lorries could have distinctive markings, and all road junctions could have signs saying what category of lorry could proceed. The big lorries could be allowed off designated routes to make deliveries at certain hours. They might be required to display information about where they had come from and where they were going. The paper was drafted, perhaps reluctantly, by the freight direct-orate's Gerry Flanagan, the man I have quoted as saying, 'We don't *want* to transfer freight from road to rail.'

The scheme served to illuminate the dilemma inherent in ever-growing road haulage. The hauliers said a national network would have to include far more than 3,500 miles; but people living along primary routes and already well supplied with lorries protested that it would be unjust to channel yet more their way. This point was dramatised when the Greater London Council actually produced a map of proposed lorry routes and asked everyone to comment. So many thousands of residents said heatedly, 'We've got an intolerable number already" that the GLC quickly dropped the plan. In 1977 the transport White Paper announced the abandonment of the national scheme, with an explanation that failed to obscure the dilemma. The consultations had shown, it said, that 'heavy lorries generally use the better routes', and that 'there are serious environmental objections to encouraging lorries to use roads which are not adequate for them'. Would not those designated roads have been the 'better routes'?

The department was left with little to offer. It made the wise assertion that heavy lorries have least impact on people's lives when they are 'on good roads away from residential areas'. Yes, and Concorde has least impact in mid-Atlantic. The supreme virtue of the lorry constantly emphasised by both department and hauliers is that it goes door-to-door. The 'good roads' argument was (and is) used by the department to justify more building of both motorways and bypasses. It was less sure about what to do when the multiplying juggernauts, encouraged by those roads, hit the towns and cities at either end of their fast, high-profit, 'efficient' motorway runs. Lorry problems in cities 'are not usually to be solved by new roads', the White Paper conceded. Back in 1970 the Royal Institute of British Architects had said to the department: 'There must be some point ... beyond which large goods vehicles are not permitted to go. As with freight traffic on the railways, there needs to be established in our motorway and primary road network a "route availability" system leading to distributor depots—the equivalent of the railways' goods depots—adjacent to, but not too close to, the heart of the towns and cities.'

By 1977 the department was toying with the idea; what was achieved by 1980 will be considered in Chapter 8.

The department had one other civilising measure at its disposal, though it was not of its own creation. This was the Heavy Commercial Vehicles Act 1973, the child of a Tory MP, Hugh Dykes, and therefore known as the Dykes Act. Dykes's original idea was that the department would oversee a national map, with red zones (bans over a certain weight) and amber zones (restrictions). The lorry lobby went to work, and the red/amber national plan faded away. Instead, the Act asked each county authority to develop a 'lorry plan' and, more important, the counties were given clear powers to bar lorries of three tons and up from roads for amenity reasons. The steps the department took to encourage the use of these powers scarcely looked 'active' or 'urgent'. Authorities in England and Wales were told that they must report a proposal for *at least one* lorry ban by the start of 1977, and Scottish authorities a year later. Some authorities had begun making ambitious plans in 1973, but then cool 'advice notes' began to come from the department. Officials from London or from the department's regional offices spoke to local traffic planners in this style: 'Play it down. Just publish one order to comply with the requirement. Think of the cost—those new signs you will have to put up—the cost to the hauliers—now is not the time—'

The hauliers: that was it. 'The haulage industry mounted a massive campaign against the Act and in fact told the government that it would not carry out its provisions,' the London Amenity and Transport Association told Armitage. The hauliers were frightened, for if some people began enjoying the benefit of 'no entry except for access' bans, the rest would be wanting them too. Where would it end? It was all very well for hauliers to show environmental concern in the hope of being allowed 40-ton lorries (as the department counselled), but they did not want to pay a real price. As local proposals slowly emerged, the Road Haulage Association and especially the Freight Transport Association spent a good deal of time arranging to make them as mild as possible if they could not block them. In 1977 the FTA told its members it was having meetings with county officials to ensure that they did not 'choose the options which could lead to further restrictions'. Hugh Featherstone, FTA director-general, was sending 'regular newsletters' to local authorities to influence their lorry policy. By the end of 1978 the FTA reported that most authorities had 'achieved a sensible balance between environmental benefit and distribution costs'.

One county that the FTA thought definitely not sensible was Berkshire. After long campaigning by people in Windsor about big lorries using the town as a rat-run between the M3 and M4 (those 'good roads'), the county proposed a Windsor Cordon: on twelve approach roads, points would be fixed past which no lorry over 5 tons unladen (about 16 gross) would be able to go unless a luminous windscreen sticker showed that it had been given access rights. At a general conference on lorry routing in 1977, the FTA's director of planning, Richard Turner, pleaded for minimal restrictions everywhere—and got a warm reply from a Windsor official. People from roads blighted by lorries had 'consistently filled the public gallery at both district council and county council meetings', the official said. 'Their protests have been vocal and well presented.' So they were getting the Windsor Cordon. 'How can you defend your statement on the necessity for your industry to use larger vehicles in the interest of economy,' he said to Turner, 'when clearly the experience in my area is that, resulting from the explosion in vehicle size over the last few years, public opinion is forcing practically all commercial vehicles off certain roads?'

Concerted pleas and protests from the FTA, RHA and National Farmers' Union failed to dissuade Berkshire from establishing the Windsor Cordon. They challenged the cordon in the High Court, and lost. They went on to appeal; and the FTA explained why in its monthly journal, Freight: 'Lorry control at local level has reached a watershed. No longer are lorry bans confined to short stretches of road or zones in perhaps residential areas. They are taking on a major strategic significance . . . The concept that delays in the road programme can be offset by strategic lorry bans concentrating all the lorry traffic on other already heavily overburdened routes is totally wrong . . . Weakness on these issues . . . could have quickly led to a rash of similar schemes as other hardpressed communities jumped on the bandwagon.' However, in 1980 the watershed *was* passed: the appeal failed. From then on the metaphor-loving FTA had to concentrate on dissuading other councils from jumping on the bandwagon and spreading the rash.

The lorry associations' task was complicated by their knowledge that they must not seem unfeeling. In the late seventies William Rodgers had tried to persuade them to be more cooperative for their own good. The freight directorate under-secretary of that day, John Dole, went so far as to say at the RHA's annual conference: 'Essential as they are, lorries are the devil to live with. They wake us, shake us and break us—if we are unlucky enough to get in the way.' He said the government was determined to civilise the lorry. The department and the hauliers must cooperate closely 'to find the least uncomfortable and the least expensive remedy . . . There must be a series of careful measures . . .'

The hauliers tried to yield nothing and yet sound civilised. It was difficult. Jack Male, RHA chairman in 1977, complained about people who liked to attack the lorry from every angle: 'They accuse it of being noisy, of being dangerous, of causing pollution, of causing damage to roads and to buildings old and new, of causing congestion, of travelling too slow.' A few sentences later in the same speech he effectively granted all these points by saying this: 'We acknowledge that there is considerable scope for improvement in vehicle design and operating practice which could reduce noise, air pollution, accident involvement, vibration, road wear and delays caused to other road-users.'

The following year an RHA vice-chairman, Ken Rogers, was more subtle: 'Commercial road haulage has been maligned for many years now by the use of that emotive word "juggernaut" . . . Why is it no-one *loves* the lorry or talks about the *jolly* juggernaut? Is it because of size, noise, appearance, diesel fumes or what? . . . What many people seem to miss is that the vast majority of road hauliers are themselves conservationists. We too wish to preserve the beauty and heritage of our country. We have no wish to drive heavy goods vehicles through picturesque villages or through the centres of cities . . . We will be delighted to work together with the conservation bodies and perhaps jointly we can bring pressure to bear upon the authorities to help with the provision of new bypasses and motorways.' He became fond of this line. A year later he was saying, 'We hauliers are also environmentalists' at an RHA dinner in Devon. A toast to the association was proposed by the county chairman, and Rogers said the RHA was anxious to continue to be part of the council's 'consultative network' when dealing with 'all those emotive problems raised by ill-informed, anti-lorry lobbyists'.

Little talk of being an environmentalist was heard from the RHA's 1979–80 chairman, John Silbermann. When the Conservatives had been in power for six months, he said hauliers could help Britain win its economic war: 'But we must be free to do so. Every unnecessary constraint must be removed. Every impediment must be discarded. We can no longer afford the luxuries of an excess of "environmentalism" . . . Our watchword should no longer be "controls first—profit second" but "profit first—controls second".' Perhaps he had dismissed the idea of wooing the public after a chastening experience at Brighton that autumn. The RHA laid on a costly exhibition of the delights of road haulage which it had hoped would attract up to fifty thousand people. Thirty thousand catalogues were printed, but most had to be scrapped: attendance was about eight thousand.

'Profit first—controls second': the slogan is surprising only because it declares openly what hauliers had always seen as the truth. No doubt 1979 seemed a good time to go to the attack. (The Sunday Times had just revealed a confidential paper prepared by a special policy adviser to Margaret Thatcher which recommended as one objective, 'Reduce oversensitivity to environmental considerations.') Nobody in Marsham Street was likely to be reminding Norman Fowler of the words that had been injected (not by someone in freight directorate) into William Rodgers's White Paper: 'A less noisy, less polluted environment is as much a part of the standard of living in its broadest sense as lower prices in the shops.'

A quiet, safe, unpolluted street is an economic good. If it is blighted that is an economic cost. The trouble is that no system exists for ensuring that governments always make the polluters, whoever they may be, accountable for the unpriced costs they impose. Factories are made to spend money to swallow the smoke from their chimneys: everybody can point to them, everybody knows where to go. Pollution on wheels is another matter. The polluters are here and gone, their victims are dispersed over thousands of miles. In the words of an American economist, Mancur Olson, who specialises in this question, the victims are 'a large unorganised group that cannot bargain with the generator of the diseconomy'. In such cases, he says, when *laissez-faire* prevails, the damage done by the polluter can be 'tens or even hundreds of times greater than the savings the generator of externalities derives from them' (Olson, 1977). And yet it is easy for unthinking governments to ignore the damage. As another specialist in the field, Professor David Pearce of Aberdeen, puts it: 'The problem with environmental goods . . . is that their actual price appears to be zero simply because there is no market' (Pearce, 1976). Here, then, it is especially important for government departments to be performing their role of imposing justice on the polluter through a combination of regulations and taxes.

The Civic Trust suggested to Armitage two reasons why officials in Marsham Street had failed in this role: 'The freight industry is organised to bring its point of view to bear in a way which environmental interest groups have never been able to match,' and 'The more remote one is from a local environmental problem the less significant it appears to be . . . Because numbers cannot be put to most environmental effects they tend to get discounted by people not directly experiencing them.' Then comes a fine understatement: 'Central government has in practice therefore not regarded environmental factors as major determinants of freight policies.'

The hauliers, carrying on a form of heavy engineering on the public roads, have as a result been in the happy position of being able to sell their product, goods movement, below its real cost. It is no wonder that heavy lorries have multiplied. In the language of economists, there has been a misallocation of resources; and that is a further public ill that governments in theory exist to prevent. The lorry operators' associations are frightened of this argument taking hold in the public mind. Year after year they confuse the issue by insisting that if they are made to spend money to civilise their lorries or the way they are operated, the benefit will be small and the increase in shop prices will be large. At the FTA's 1979 conference its planning officer, Richard Turner, got on thin ice when he replied to a claim by Hugh Dykes, MP, there as a guest speaker, that if lorry controls meant higher prices, the public were willing to pay. Turner argued that the price of local environmental gains was paid by the public at large through the cost imposed on hauliers; and he asked whether the price

of cornflakes was higher in Windsor, now it was defended by
its cordon, than elsewhere. His question can be stood on its
head: If nothing is done about lorries, why should people in
lorry-plagued streets pay as dear for their cornflakes as those
in quiet streets? And go further: Why should not the haulage
industry be required to spend money to soften, at the very
least, the impact of all its operations, so that if prices go up
fractionally, all users of goods contribute to the betterment?

At that FTA conference, Dykes tried to persuade the lorry
men to consider public feeling: 'Sensible and pragmatic road
hauliers will recognise the strains and pressures . . . The
public is inherently hostile to juggernauts. This is understandable and must be accepted. Equally, if the public sees a
responsible attitude by road hauliers, latent hostility will be
dampened and contained.' There was no sign of new thinking,
however. The distribution chief of United Biscuits, Alan
West, complained that the Dykes Act gave local authorities
power to enforce bans 'simply to make life more pleasant for
the populace of the area concerned'—how irrational!—'and
without any regard for practicality or economics'.

Among the 1,800 submissions sent to him, Armitage found
plenty of evidence from 'areas concerned' which had not yet
been able to escape such 'generators of externalities' as United
Biscuits. One was an example—in no way unusual—of an old
village on a lesser A-road: Mayfield, East Sussex, on the
A267, which is described in the county structure plan as a
'major distributor', though in the village the road narrows to
nineteen feet. More and more lorries roll through—especially
roll-on/roll-off juggernauts using the port of Newhaven. As
Armitage was considering the 'consequences' of the growth in
road freight, the Mayfield and Five Ashes Society told him a
few: 'A detrimental effect on health . . . noise . . . sleep is
disturbed . . . impossible to have windows open . . . daily skir-
mishes, slight unreported accidents and near misses . . .
vehicles frequently damaged . . . many residents are very
nervous, particularly since one serious accident . . . a lorry
wing-mirror hitting a pedestrian on the head while she was
walking on the narrow pavement, which has resulted in
permanent serious disability . . . the stress caused, especially
to the elderly and mothers with young children, by walking on
narrow pavements with large vehicles travelling at 30 m.p.h.

and more within inches...a frightening experience...
fewer visitors and tourists coming to the village ... numerous
complaints about the noise and speed of heavy vehicles ...
actual destruction of property ... worry of damage by vibrations ... already a glass plate has been shattered, tiles slip,
beams in the older houses move.' The society's chairman,
Margaret Brown, in a letter to me added some words she
might have sent to Armitage: 'Historic villages will be a mass
of rubble populated by a mass of crippled neurotics afraid to
step out of their crumbling doorways if something doesn't
stop the increase of heavy vehicles racing through them.'

A glimpse of life in an old market town was given to
Armitage in the more formal words of a town hall official. The
environment department attached to its submission some
paragraphs from Kington (Hereford & Worcester) supporting
the town's wish for a bypass: 'Although the traffic volume is
not excessive numerically, the A44 which negotiates Kington's
centre has a profound and deleterious effect on the shopping
streets. The narrow streets and pavements are unable to
cope with numbers of heavy goods vehicles. Quite ordinary
loads, by today's standards, have failed to negotiate the town
and have caused delays of many hours ... Goods vehicles
inch past each other perilously close to historic buildings,
mounting pavements and crossing basement areas. Shoppers
eschew Kington, unable to face conflict with noise, vibration,
heavy fumes and immediate physical danger ... The need for
the bypass is vital; upon it depends the safety of Kington's
inhabitants and the historic town centre's very fabric.'

Perhaps the department was willing to make public that
town's woes because it was soon to have its bypass, at a cost
of about £2½ million. None was promised for Mayfield nor
for hundreds of other places.

And then there was the unbypassable problem, for the mass
of the population, of lorries in cities. The key words used by
officials who have tried to work out what to do are 'sensitive'
and 'insensitive'. If as many lorries as possible are barred from
sensitive roads and channelled on to insensitive roads, there
will be an increase in the happiness of the greatest number to
gladden the shade of Jeremy Bentham. In particular, the
prevailing decibel level on already lorry-battered roads can be
calculated to go up only a point or so, whereas on roads freed
of lorries it will go down sharply. However, there are

difficulties, as three researchers at the University of Aston, Birmingham, reported at a Road Research Laboratory seminar. After working out a possible 'strategic route' system in an area of Birmingham comprising 67,500 households, and totting up the quantifiable net gains, they said: 'There are, of course, environmental disbenefits . . . These are quite considerable and would certainly be perceived by those who live or shop on strategic routes. It seems unlikely, therefore, that it would be politically feasible to introduce a lorry network in a short space of time . . . There are, perhaps, two ways in which the impact . . . might be relieved; by providing remedial works for buildings along these roads or by combining a lorry quietening policy with the strategic network' (Transport and Road Research Laboratory, 1977). There was a drawback to lorry quietening (aside from its mirage-like nature): 'Lorry traffic has many other impacts . . . air pollution, danger, visual intrusion, etc.' Remedial works would include double-glazing, pedestrian crossings and 'land use controls to ensure that any new development is for activities which are insensitive to traffic or is at least designed to protect occupants from the environment of heavily trafficked streets'.

There, many years after Buchanan, is an urban 'design for living'. At the seminar, an official from Marsham Street, D. Bishop, made the meaning even clearer by talking of 'the designation of a network of major roads from which environmentally sensitive land uses would be slowly removed'. (High streets, we have ways to stop you being sensitive.) Pedestrians, shops, offices, flats—all would be 'removed' to make way for a lorry take-over, and finally all these lengths of townscape would presumably be lined with windowless factory walls. Nobody stood up to object.

Since then no new official solutions have emerged. Marsham Street is bankrupt of ideas, except for one: the number of heavy lorries must not be reduced, but must increase. Those inconveniently sensitive creatures, people, suffer and retreat into their shells—and often into the back half of their shells, as the borough of Reading pointed out to Armitage: 'Many people in residential roads in Reading have ceased to live and sleep in the fronts of their houses. Multiplied all over the country this must constitute a substantial housing loss.'

The department has coolly handed the local authorities an impossible task: to deal with the mess. The United Biscuits man quoted earlier, Alan West, said most authorities 'content themselves and their local pressure groups with pedestrian precincts, the odd weight restriction and increasing numbers of width restrictions'. This was often true; not, however, because demands for action were becoming fewer, but because it was hard for an authority to find a road it could label insensitive. Some of the difficulties in the counties were made clear by Michael Hardy, Hertfordshire county surveyor, at a highway engineers' conference in 1979. First of all, the Dykes Act had required counties to produce 'lorry plans', but how could each do that in isolation? 'Very few comprehensive plans emerged because there was and still is no national policy or framework for ensuring that lorries do use the most suitable and least environmentally sensitive routes.' Then, how does an authority decide when a road has a serious enough lorry problem to justify a control? People on minor roads in Hertfordshire with as few as 360, or 260 or even only 60 lorries in a ten-hour day had been demanding action. 'Whilst the police are understandably most reluctant to agree to take on the burden of enforcement for very small environmental gains . . . there is pressure to introduce bans . . . on the grounds that some improvement would be better than none.'

Hardy and his assistant, Peter Fells, were far from being hostile to hauliers, but they did want some changes in the law to produce at least a less incoherent national system of lorry controls. Transport department officials were telling them in 1979: 'You have all the powers you need.' Their reply was: 'You have given us a rotten way of enforcing the law.' The growth of a variety of local bans, they said, had caused puzzlement and frustration among the best-intentioned lorry-drivers. In evidence to Armitage they suggested what amounts to a revival of the national network idea, with rules to permit easy policing of drivers who ignore bans. Here are some of their proposals:

Drivers of lorries over 16 tons (and eventually of lower weights) would be issued annually with an atlas showing the roads they must use on long journeys—motorways and primary routes—and specifying where they were to leave them for their destinations.

Drivers would be issued with a card for each journey stipulating where they were to load and unload, and the route to be followed (this is done in France and elsewhere).

Signposts would be adapted to give the necessary route information.

The meaning of the loose word 'access' would be made precisely enforceable.

When wearing his Institution of Highway Engineers hat, Hardy presented to Armitage the complement to these proposals: a plan for improvements to the lorry network in his proposed 'road hierarchy'—at a cost of £2,800 million (1978 prices). His network system, he said, could not take effect fully until this work had been done, and that might be well into the nineties.

So it all held out no great hope. And even if more efficient control methods were introduced and the police welcomed the task, and even if a national network were shown to be practicable, and even if people on the chosen primary routes would stand for the added misery, it would amount to a series of local palliatives and would leave the 'sensitive' problem within cities unsolved. The quest returns in the end to the need for comprehensive action. The Civic Trust told Armitage that central government should take on the task 'of anticipating the environmental effects of policies and developments that influence the movement of freight, and of proposing policies that reduce road freight movement'. Government intervention was urged, too, by the Association of County Councils (which opposes heavier lorries): 'It is a matter of considerable concern that there is no government policy on how to reduce the effect of the road haulage industry on the environment. No concerted attempt appears to have been made to control the way in which the industry can externalise many of its costs . . . and generally operate as though it owed no responsibility to the public . . . There is, we would suggest, a need to create a dialogue between the industry and public-sector interests.' And the association proposed that Norman Fowler should have representatives of lorry operators and local authorities, and Marsham Street officials, 'get round the table to find solutions'.

A meeting of minds at any such conference seemed unlikely. The FTA became so concerned about the quantity of 'anti-lorry' ideas put to Armitage that it held a news conference, even before Armitage had begun writing his report, to denounce them en masse. The FTA president, Malcolm Banks, traffic manager of Littlewoods, said all such notions as freight transfers to rail and water, higher taxation, lorry bans and compulsory freight transhipment centres 'were no solution at all and would be disastrous'. What could be done? 'The real answer is to build roads and bypasses and segregate lorries from people.' As for other measures, 'we cannot afford them'. He did not seem likely to understand talk of externalities, even coming from the Association of County Councils— or this further remark from the association: 'Society will have to decide at some stage how great a cost to the quality of life it is prepared to bear in the interests of economic improvement.' Let alone this from the borough of Reading: 'The council believes that the public in general would accept higher costs of goods rather than further deterioration of the environment through more, larger and heavier lorries.'

If lorry operators are to be made to pay their real environmental costs, how shall it be done? First, like erring factories, they must be made to spend money to meet stricter regulations requiring their vehicles and their manner of operation to be less offensive. In addition, they must pay special levies, both as compensation to the community for the costs they impose and as an incentive to lessen their impact. This thought reached Armitage by way of the Association of County Councils: 'Serious consideration should be given by the government to the use of fiscal incentives to stimulate the introduction and use of "humanised" lorries.'

The very thought of this makes the operators fume. When the FTA director-general, Hugh Featherstone, gave oral evidence to Armitage, he called it absurd, and said: 'Would this do anything to alleviate the hardship? There is no point otherwise. It wouldn't help the people who suffer. It won't help poor Mrs Bloggs who sits in a house in the high street with heavy lorries thundering past.' In fact it could help her in a number of ways. One has already been mentioned in the previous chapter; the scheme that the Dutch have been developing to tax vehicles according to their noise, and use the money to help sufferers. This is especially fitting when, thanks to the helpful complexities of international red tape, lorry-makers have been able to postpone interminably any improvement by means of regulation. Two men who helped to inspire the Dutch action are Ariel Alexandre and Jean-Philippe Barde, officials of the Organisation for Economic

Cooperation and Development. They have put their case like this: 'A market economy that is dominated by satisfiable needs fulfils the wants and aspirations of only some of the people . . . Since goods and services are traded for money, the same should be done with unwanted commodities. In the case of highway noise, let the polluters be taxed on the noise that they cause and let the victims be paid suitable compensation' (Alexandre and Barde, 1976). In the same article they say: 'The noise standards currently in force tend to be an incentive to maintain the status quo . . . a brake on innovation.' This is equally true of other aspects of the lorry—its suspension, for example, designed down to the permitted minimum.

The possibility that lorries might be categorised by means of a 'nuisance index' was developed at the Road Research Laboratory in the early seventies. Public attitudes to the noise, vibration, fumes and danger of lorries were collated, lorries of less than 3½ tons were given a figure of one, and bigger ones were given nuisance factors according to weight, ranging up to nearly eleven for those over 28 tons. The object then was to give rankings to 'the cost-effectiveness of alternative controls' but such an index could also be used for calculating levies. A system by which a nuisance index could also be an incentive for improvement is suggested by the transport consultant Stephen Plowden: 'At the time a new model was tested for compliance with the Construction and Use Regulations . . . it would also be rated on this scale. Local regulations, determining whether and under what conditions vehicles should be permitted on particular roads . . . would be related to the scale' (Plowden, 1980). Towns would have power to ban lorries with a high nuisance figure, and charge others entry taxes on a sliding scale—giving operators an incentive to use such vehicles as the Creusen electric lorries (payload up to five tons) that have been running in the Netherlands for years.

The transport department let the idea of a nuisance index fade out of sight, perhaps because it was not happy about the elevenfold score attributed to the biggest lorries. In 1980 a paper presented at a London conference on transport research by a senior Road Research Laboratory man, L. H. Watkins, spoke of directing research 'more into the realm of applied psychology, both in studying people's attitudes to the problem and in providing ways of satisfying their aspirations'. He was speaking of roads and traffic in general; but his words are in tune with a thought often wistfully expressed by departmental officials, to this effect: 'If only lorries could be painted red, with windows, to make them look like London buses, people would stop hating them.' People are unreasonable and must somehow be cajoled or tricked into liking nasty things. This applied psychology approach has for some time been in the mind of a senior environmental consultant, Roy Waller, with Atkins Research, a firm of consulting engineers. He put it to me like this: 'We do not know how to minimise the subjective "size" of the vehicle at the same time as maximising load-carrying capacity.' He wanted the department to have him do a study to find out which of the various "parameters" of a juggernaut—noise, size, configuration, and so forth—created the most dislike; the aim being, as he put it in 1979, 'to get the biggest load we can on the roads with the smallest environmental impact'. But the department had not engaged him: perhaps the laboratory was doing the work itself.

To return to the subject of levies: the revenue from them could be used, during the long period when they were bringing kinder vehicles into the traffic stream, to help sufferers in various ways. In addition to the noise-baffling measures planned in the Netherlands, there could be funds, for example, to enable local authorities to afford substantial rate reductions for households or shops on roads with high nuisance indexes, instead of the meagre and erratic reductions now conceded. There could be compensation for buildings damaged by lorry vibration or direct impact (and the department could rise above its policy of wilful ignorance). There could even be spare money in the department's hands to permit more aid to the railways and canals, thus encouraging the opposite of 'getting the biggest load we can on the roads'. And of course the levies themselves, by making the hauliers pay more of their true costs, would create fairer competition between the freight-carriers.

The idea that taxes on lorries should be increased as a way of reducing their numbers was offered up in passing by the Geddes report of 1965 and was clearly recommended by Christopher Foster's 1978 report on the licensing system. He quoted environmentalists as saying that limitation of numbers was 'the only effective way to deal with the problem' and that 'there is now or will be sooner or later an unacceptable level of heavy goods traffic'. He urged the department to assess 'the existing level of nuisance . . . both quantifiable and unquantifiable'. Quantifiable costs would include property damage and the lost value of unused front rooms: 'At present it is simply not known how many houses throughout the country are affected in this way.' He also wanted a study to decide why 'the proportion of freight travelling by road varies considerably from one country to another'. And he wanted estimates made of the likely environmental impact of lorries in thirty years' time, to give 'some indication of the levels at which any excise imposition or other controls over the industry need to be pitched'. As I have said earlier, he assented to the department's rejection of quantity licensing (formal limits on the number of long-distance lorries), but then he said this: 'Increased excise duties, if used selectively, could not only ensure that the haulage industry maximised its existing vehicle use but also that its activities were directed away from environmentally sensitive areas.' This was his conclusion: 'Heavier duties . . . will by increasing the cost of road transport encourage the use of other transport and economise on the use of road transport, ensuring higher load factors and the rationalisation of depots and distribution centres . . . We would strongly recommend . . . that the level of duty should be based on a rational appraisal of the relationship between environmental capacity and traffic levels.'

The RHA and FTA objected strongly to these proposals. So too did the freight directorate. In 1980 the proposals were still languishing under the pigeonhole treatment. When Foster reported, the department had in any case become evasive about adding a social/environmental element to the taxes paid by lorries. In 1976 its consultation document, under the socially conscious eye of the late Anthony Crosland, had said that lorries 'should meet the full resource and environmental costs which they impose on the community'. A year later William Rodgers's White Paper softened this to: 'There are arguments for charging lorries more than their public costs in recognition of the noise, vibration and pollution they cause . . . Such costs cannot however be measured in any objective way, and a tax based on them would be no substitute for constructive policies to help people who suffer from the impact of lorries.' (A clever example there for aspiring civil servants: no substitute for constructive policies. You simultaneously rubbish the idea and imply that you have constructive policies.) 'The government . . . will take social and environmental considerations into account . . . in deciding by how much road taxation should exceed the directly ascertainable public costs of roads.' Vague enough, but 'by how much' does at least amount to an undertaking that lorries shall meet more than their ascertainable road costs. Of those costs there was also a promise 'that all classes of lorry shall eventually meet in full the costs attributed to them'. Nothing happened about social/environmental costs. The hollowness even of the basic road-cost promise will be displayed in the next chapter.

7

High damage, low taxes

Commercial road-users enjoy a business privilege: an essential part of their capital equipment is provided and maintained not by them but by the government. They pay tax, of course, to the road-provider. The question is: Are the operators of every class of lorry paying enough to meet their share of the road bill? The answer is no. For years the most damaging ones have been underpaying. They have in effect had a vast subsidy.

By the transport department's own calculation (one which, as I shall show, is remarkably kind to the operators) the subsidy to a 32-ton lorry doing on average mileage worked out like this in 1980–81:

Cost to the road system		£4,494
Licence	£1,188	
Tax on diesel	£2,513	£3,701
Tax shortfall		£793

The department tends to be imprecise about lorry numbers, but if its estimate for that year of 85,400 32-tonners is right, they alone were receiving a subsidy from the taxpayer (by the department's kind calculation) of £67,722,000; and 40,000 other big lorries were also underpayers.

In due course I shall compute some new and sounder figures for the big lorries' indebtedness. First, however, it is necessary to explore some of the mysteries of axle-loads, damaging powers and road track costs. Large sums depend on the way the costs are allocated among various classes of vehicle. And much more is at stake besides, for when still heavier lorries are being debated, full facts are needed for a sound decision on the economic pros and cons. Yet few people outside the department (or within it, for that matter) are well-informed on these matters. Neither ministers, MPs nor county councillors have been able to trouble officials with searching inquiries. The department has found it easy to perpetuate a tax system irrationally favourable to the heaviest lorries. The interest of the ordinary citizen in the many hundreds of millions of pounds eased from the lorry operators' shoulders over the years is obvious enough. He must also be concerned about the official stimulus thus given to the most damaging lorries; about the resulting break-up of highways; and about the questionable economic claims made by the lorry industry and by its official friends in London and Brussels. To seek out the facts, and so enable MPs, the public and perhaps even permanent secretaries to ask overdue questions, will therefore be a valuable exercise, and one that will have its amusing moments.

The first great question is: Has the damaging power of the big lorries' axle-loads been reliably assessed? This is essential to ensure that roads are both built and repaired to last a reasonable time, and that the cost is shared fairly; and it is also at the heart of the economic argument.

Anybody can understand that heavily-laden lorry wheels pound the road far harder than lighter ones, let alone car wheels. The first thorough study to put some figures on the difference was carried out in 1958–60 by the American Association of State Highway Officials. Nearly 150 vehicles with axle-loads ranging from one ton upwards were driven a total of seventeen million miles over a variety of test tracks in Illinois incorporating more than 800 different types of road structure. The chief purpose was to give the states accurate guidance on the weight limits and the highway design standards that would give the best balance between truckers' operating costs and outlay on roads. For people concerned with vehicle taxation, close analysis of the figures showed that modest axle-loads, up to about six tons on a pair of wheels, did not do much damage, but thereafter the toll went up very sharply. As a rough rule of thumb, experts concluded that road damage increased in proportion to the fourth power of the axle-load. For example, what was called a 'standard axle' of 18,000 lb (eight tons) was found to do not three times the road damage of a 6,000 lb axle, but $18,000^4 \div 6,000^4$, which mathematicians will find is *81 times* as much.

This rule of thumb was laid down in the early sixties, at a time when there were relatively few lorries with axle-loads above the 'standard axle' level of eight tons. The British transport department did not work seriously on the relative cost responsibility of various lorries until the mid-seventies. It adopted the fourth-power calculation, and it was soon dignified as 'the fourth-power law'. But by then evidence was emerging in Britain and elsewhere to indicate that the fourth power, dramatic though its effect was, was too modest for the axle-loads of nine and ten tons (and often more with illegal overloading) that were becoming common with the ever-growing fleet of top-weight juggernauts. In 1976 the department's *Transport Policy* document reported evidence suggesting that the heaviest axle-loads should be raised to the power of 4½, 5, 6 or even higher to show their true relative damaging effect. However, the document surprisingly declared nevertheless that 'the use of a fourth-power relationship . . . is justified in the present state of knowledge'. A year later the Road Research Laboratory's highway design specialist, Norman Lister, produced a paper presented at a Paris symosium. This paper was also to have been printed as one of the laboratory's regular reports, but publication was cancelled. Fortunately, however, it was printed in Paris (Lister, 1977). One can therefore learn what emerged when Lister did a computer analysis of what happens when different axle-loads are repeated at random and over roads of varying strengths. Only on strong pavements (such as a newly-built trunk road) did a power of four prove to be 'a reasonable approximation', says Lister. Unhappily, he tabulates results for eight-ton and thirteen-ton axles but not for Britain's ten-ton axles. However, he calculates that on weak pavements a mere eight-ton axle merits a power of up to 6; and that the damage done by a thirteen-ton axle ranges up to a power of 8.3. For the ten-ton axle it is clearly well above the fourth power. Indeed, Lister says: 'In all cases exponents are greater than four for wheel loads at and above present legal limits.'

By failing to ascribe a greater damaging power to the highest axle-loads, the department appears once again to have been kind to the juggernauts. If a lorry has just one axle of ten tons and its others are six, eight, eight (a common configuration for a 32-tonner), ascribing a fifth-power instead of a fourth-power effect to that ten-ton axle will show the damaging effect of that lorry to be 5.6 times what the department reckons it to be. Such a reckoning would of course increase the tax liability of all such lorries. It would also be a strong argument for *reducing* the present ten-ton limit; and for condemning the EEC proposal for drive axles of a very damaging 11.55 tonnes. Not surprisingly, a close scrutiny of the question has been resisted by interested officials. In Marsham Street, one may recall, Joseph Peeler wrote, 'It would be undesirable to allow the inquiry to get into the complex technicalities of axle weights'; and in Brussels the European Parliament's transport committee was advised in 1979, 'It would not be appropriate to explore this area in any detail.'

Some things cannot be kept under wraps. Roads break up in public. Drivers seethe in public on motorways choked by vast labours of reconstruction. This expensive chaos has three chief causes: a gross underestimate by the transport department of the growth in numbers of the top-weight lorries, the very ones it was encouraging and cosseting; the underrating of these lorries' damaging power; and the department's failure to crack down on overloading.

Roads *could* be built to carry brutal lorries with twenty-ton axle-loads. Hauliers would be happy but the road cost would be prohibitive. Any road/vehicle system must be a compromise. When the American highway officials did their painstaking tests, they could not hope to persuade the trucking industry to reduce its axle-loads to, say, a gentle seven tons, but they did produce a national recommendation of an axle-load maximum of 20,000 lb—just under nine tons. Only a dozen American states now exceed this and it is the limit for all US federal highways, as well as for most of Canada. Trucks with the same payload as Britain's big artics must spread the impact over five axles. The result is that freight is carried on their roads *far less damagingly per hundred tons of payload*. In Britain, the axle-load rules favour the haulier. This is even more true of the twelve-tonne axles of Italy, France, Belgium and Luxembourg (sometimes even thirteen tonnes in the last three), but those countries at least have proportionately far fewer big lorries.

The economic principle is not news to the department. Norman Lister of the Road Research Laboratory opened the paper he gave in Paris with a clear statement of it: 'Heavy lorries benefit a community only if the advantage they give of carrying freight more cheaply than lighter vehicles is not outweighed by the extra cost of repairing any additional deterioration they cause to the highway network, and by any extra environmental disadvantage' (Lister, 1977). And yet when more and more miles of motorway broke up from the late seventies onwards, often less than halfway through their twenty-year 'design life', the department tried to soothe the public by presenting the havoc as a success story. The line was that the millions of axle-loads for which the roads had been designed had passed over them in a shorter period than expected, which demonstrated how good they had been for lorries. In early 1980, when Sir Arthur Armitage asked men of the Institution of Highway Engineers about the break-up, their emphasis was somewhat different. Professor Tom Williams, then president of the institution, said that in the previous decade 'value for money became paramount' and 'design methods were too precise'. In other words, the department had cut things too fine.

No engineer drew Armitage's attention to the fact that the very rapidity of the break-up meant that much of the repairing had to be done in an exceedingly costly way. Ideally, highway engineers keep a close eye on all roads and give them a surface overlay before they suffer deep-down damage. 'The preferred approach is to overlay . . . before major deterioration of the pavement surface becomes apparent,' as Norman Lister told a highway-maintenance conference (Lister, 1980). On the motorways the department generally failed to do so. Year after year long stretches therefore had to be completely rebuilt to a depth of two feet or more, at nearly eight times the cost of an overlay. Reconstruction also takes much longer, as Lister pointed out, 'and consequently incurs much greater traffic delays'. The cost of the delays is high. After all, if time-saving is the magic thing that justifies all roadbuilding, time-wasting must go in the debit balance. The department admits this. It told Armitage that the cost of delays during motorway repairs amounts to another 40 per cent on top of the cost of the work; it now comes to about £30 million a year. The department did not say, however, that this should be added to the motorway-bashing lorries' taxable track costs. Nor did it raise a further question: If the original sum spent on roadbuilding had a cost/benefit justification based on a twenty-year promise of unimpeded vehicle-miles which have in fact suffered such an unseemly hiccup, how does the cost/benefit work out in reality? Has the return on some stretches of the M1, M5 or M6 become negative?

The most urgent message of the motorway break-up was that it conveyed a challenge to the department's juggernaut policy. It had encouraged more and more freight to be carried in a highly damaging way, and the public was paying. The department became sensitive about anything that might draw attention to the fact; and especially so when the Armitage inquiry was under way and nothing must suggest that bigger juggernauts were less than wonderful. Here the department provides some light relief.

Year after year, automatic weight-recorders sunk into the road surface at thirty points on various motorways and A-roads were demonstrating a rapid rise in the proportion of heavy axles (nine, ten tons and more) in the traffic stream. A scientist at the Road Research Laboratory, E. W. H. Currer, analysed these data and in 1979 prepared a report, *Commercial Traffic: Its Estimated Damaging Effect, 1945–2005.* An inquiring member of an amenity society was told by Currer in October 1979 that it was about to be published. Sixteen hundred copies were in fact ready printed, with a laboratory number, LR910. But when someone high up in Marsham Street saw an advance copy he decided that LR910 was too revealing for the public or for curious journalists. At the last minute the laboratory was ordered, presumably with the knowledge of the permanent secretary, Sir Peter Baldwin, to withhold the report. However, its existence and its sudden unavailability became known. An MP put down a question, and I wrote about the suppression in *The Sunday Times.* The question was scarcely on the order-paper before the department had a prudent rethink. Within two or three days LR910 became available. The episode is a telling example of the power officials have over information—except when by chance a beam of light is thrown on them.

By its ridiculous attempt to muffle awkward facts the department performed a service, for it drew the attention of the public (and of Armitage) to a report that might not otherwise have won much space in the press. E. W. H. Currer presents a great many figures, graphs and histograms but does not spell out their meaning for non-engineers, let alone point to their significance for policy-makers. However, one can deduce why his dry presentation was enough to raise tremors.

Axle-loads, those highly political things, are at the heart of it. When highway engineers are designing a road to last, they hope, twenty years without serious resurfacing, they must have forecasts of the number of lorries that will run over it in that period. But the number is not all. What matters much more is a sound forecast of how many millions of axle-loads there will be through the whole spectrum of weights. From this the engineers can calculate the 'damage factor' of the expected lorries.

The whole process need not be shown here. It is enough to say that in 1970 the highway planners concluded that even on the busiest motorways and trunk roads there would continue to be so many moderate-sized lorries for the next twenty years that the average damage factor per lorry (full, half-laden and empty) would be only 1.08 eight-ton 'standard axles'. They issued Road Note 29 instructing roadbuilders accordingly. They were badly wrong. And that is what LR910 showed. The vast increase during the seventies of lorries at and near 32 tons and the declining use of less damaging lorries brought the damage factor to *twice* what the roadbuilders had been told to plan for.

Some of Currer's figures from the automatic weight-recorders help to explain why the lanes-closed cones went up before time on the motorways. On the southbound slow lane of the M6 at Great Barr, Birmingham, in the five-year period 1973 to 1977 there was hardly any increase in the number of lorry axles going by (from 5,304,000 to 5,408,000) but there was such an increase in heavy axles that their *damage factor* went up by 87 per cent. The trend was almost as bad as elsewhere. This was precisely the period during which lorries of over 28 tons proliferated and became responsible for well over half the nation's ton-mileage. The nature of the lorries was causing the premature break-up. About the same tonnage of goods was being moved, but in a much more damaging way.

It was not Currer's role, of course, to say, 'Perhaps we should have less damaging lorries.' Knowing departmental policy, he had to work on the assumption that the damage factor would rise still further, so he recommended that engineers designing a motorway to last to the end of the century should assume a damage factor nearly three times higher than in Road Note 29. Currer also presented a table 'for the estimation of the remaining lives of existing roads and for the design of pavement-strengthening measures'. Here was disturbing news for county engineers already cutting road spending to a minimum. Even on modest roads carrying fewer than 250 lorries a day in each direction, Currer said, the axle-damage factor in 1990 would be twice what it was in 1970, and by 2005 more than threefold. For motorways and trunk roads the forecast was a trebling by 1990 and more than a quadrupling by 2005.

What might be the cost? When LR910 raised Commons questions, the department estimated that the revised figures meant that roads would cost 5 per cent more to build (which seems low, even though a few extra centimetres of bitumen makes a big difference), and that in the period 1980–90 roads would cost 25 per cent more to repair. On motorways and trunk roads alone, every year about 100 miles would be under repair.

It hardly seemed a policy to benefit the public. The department's failure to tax the most damaging lorries adequately can now be seen as all the more extraordinary.

Its method of allocating road track costs among various vehicles combines science, statistics, guesswork and arbitrary decisions, and produces a great many figures to three or four decimal places which give a false impression of exceeding accuracy. A study of the method can begin by showing how the department allocated the cost in 1980–81 of building, maintaining, administering and policing the roads among the chief classes of road user, and what each class paid in tax (£ million, 1980 prices):

	Costs attributed	Excise and fuel tax
15,335,000 cars and taxis	1,402	3,300
77,000 buses and coaches	77	114
1,253,000 light vans	93	305
63,000 goods vehicles up to 3½t gross	7	20
516,000 over 3½t gross	790	820

Taxes on vehicles have served for many generations as a resource for the Exchequer, so there is nothing questionable

in their yielding much more than the road costs attributed to
them. What is remarkable is that the smaller, less damaging
and more inoffensive a commercial vehicle is, the harder it is
hit. Light vans pay at the rate of 3.3 to 1, the next class of vans
and lorries nearly 3 to 1, but the bigger lorries just over 1 to 1.

If one looks next in detail at those 516,000 lorries, ranging
from 3½ to 32 tons, one finds that the failure of the civil
servants to achieve even an appearance of equity becomes
still more blatant. Those that were taking least out of the road
were handsomely meeting their costs; for example, according
to figures published by the department, three-axle 16-tonners
were 2 to 1 in credit. But the 32-tonners and several other
types were seriously underpaying, even after having benefited
from all the kindnesses that the civil servants could calculate
in their favour. Here are the underpayers as stated by the
department ('per vehicle' figures for average mileages):

	Per vehicle	Total
85,400 32-tonners	£793	£67,722,000
500 31-tonners	628	314,000
13,700 30-tonners	416	5,699,200
100 29-tonners	116	11,600
25,800 3-axle 24-tonners	104	2,683,000
400 3-axle 23-tonners	115	46,000
		£76,476,000

The first lesson of these figures is that these 125,900 lorries
were being cross-subsidised by the less objectionable ones.
And this was not a sudden freak of transport life. Officials in
Marsham Street have known at least since 1973 that the
lorries with the worst damage factor were underpaying. One
might have expected an alert and tidy-minded under-secretary
to have said years ago: 'Look here, some of these chaps are
meeting their costs two and three times over and others are
getting away with murder. Can't have that. It must be one
reason why so many hauliers are phasing out middling lorries
and buying enormous ones. Misallocation of resources.
Besides, it's unjust. If I were running a small or medium lorry,
I'd be protesting.' The most that was done, though, was to
impose a few belated tax increases that barely kept pace with
inflation and did not cure the inequity.

The failure of the department to manage matters in the

public interest goes still deeper. The calculation of cost responsibilities was kind from the start to the bigger lorries; but when the figures nevertheless showed them to be under-paying, ways were found to make them look less culpable. Here an important point must be established. If a departmental recalculation shifts millions of pounds of 'costs attributed' away from the big lorries and reduces their apparent guilt, that does not make cars or vans liable for more tax, because they remain overwhelmingly in credit. The shift is a great help to the guilty ones but nobody else need notice it.

The allocation of annual road costs among everyone from pedestrians upwards is an exercise originally devised for the purpose of making the big lorries pay fairly. Its complexity gives civil servants opportunities to make subtly weighted decisions. This is especially true of road maintenance costs (which now almost equal the cost of new roadbuilding). Some maintenance items, such as drainage and grasscutting, are allocated simply according to the average mileage run by the various classes of vehicle. At the other extreme, the cost of resurfacing and full reconstruction is allocated according to the damaging power of the vehicles, with the result that about 95 per cent of it is is assigned to lorries. It is in allocating the items in between that administrative decisions can favour the heavy lorry.

Here is a small example of what can be done. When the system was worked out in the early seventies, the cost of a variety of items—gritting, traffic signs, lighting, and the maintenance of bridges, culverts, retaining walls and earth-works—was allocated not by axle-loads or gross weight but by an intermediate measure, 'passenger car units' (PCUs). An average lorry was declared equal, in traffic terms, to two cars, and a 32-tonner amounted, with dubious precision, to 2.912 cars; a surprisingly modest figure, but at least it made the cost of those items fall a little more heavily on the bigger lorries. In 1977 the Road Haulage Association, not content with the kindnesses lorries already enjoyed, began pressing for further concessions: its chairman, Jack Male, announced ' a resumption of the argument on track costs'. In 1978 the civil servants dropped the PCU reckoning. Every item concerned, amounting to more than £300 million, was put on a simple vehicle-mile basis. The effect was to shift about £20 million of the annual cost responsibility off lorries, and thus to reduce the explicit tax guilt of the heavy ones. It is true that such items as signs and lighting might reasonably be shared out according to vehicle-miles. This is certainly not true of bridges, retaining walls or earthworks. The impact of big lorries on bridges is discussed later in this chapter; and as for retaining walls, some counties, such as West Yorkshire, find that the increase in heavy lorries has brought a growing number of failures. It is surprising that these items were not in fact allocated from the start according to gross weight. In the state of Oregon, a leader for years in road-cost studies, half the cost of bridge maintenance is allocated solely to lorries. To relieve them of any extra responsibility at all is astonishing.

That was not the only good news for the hauliers in 1978. Despite inflation, the total costs attributed to lorries fell by £85 million. Of this, £20 million has just been explained, and a further £10 million was put down to a departmental estimate that lorry mileage was down (in fact it proved to be up). Where had the remaining £55 million gone? I can only quote the department's explanation: 'The remaining £55 million was accounted for by applying a straightforward pro rata criterion according to the importance of the costs of a particular vehicle class in relation to the costs of all vehicles.' The only translation I can suggest is: 'We found that lorry costs still looked highish so we shifted the ratios to suit ourselves.' But I may be wrong.

As I have explained, costs can be painlessly shifted, on paper, from lorries to other road-users. In this exercise, pedestrians are useful too. In 1980–81, for example, before the civil servants even began allocating the year's £1,040 million maintenance bill among vehicle-users, they deducted £163,200,000 as being attributable to pedestrians: a remarkable 14 per cent for road-users who otherwise do not count for much in the department. How could this be? Here is the department's reckoning:

50 per cent of all sweeping and cleaning	£36,400,000
50 per cent of all street lighting	£84,200,000
35 per cent of footway, cycle-track, kerb, fence and barrier maintenance	£42,600,000

These percentages, like all the other allocations on which so much money depends, are based, says the department, 'on expert advice from highway engineers and research scientists'.

However, a more informal glimpse of the method was given by an official whom I questioned: 'We don't know how to allocate to pedestrians, so we say, Let's be arbitrary and allocate fifty-fifty.' After that one feels free to offer one's own arbitrary figures. One could comment at random, however, that street-sweepers might question the first item; that most money for lighting goes to roads with heavy traffic, which suggests that traffic is the chief decider; and that barriers exist, at great inconvenience to pedestrians, to speed the flow of vehicles, and it is vehicles that damage them. And here one finds some more departmental burden-shifting: before 1978, none of the maintenance cost of fences and barriers was put on pedestrians.

The arbitrariness goes further. Pedestrians spend little time on most trunk roads and are banned from motorways; yet half the cost of sweeping and cleaning *all* roads, and even half the cost of motorway patrols, has all along been allocated to them. By 1979–80 even this was not enough: half the cost of trunk road and motorway lighting was allocated to them as well. Even if one grants the department the trunk road part of its arithmetic, that leaves about £6 million of motorway spending attributed to pedestrians. The department has not even shown the courage to stand by this oddity. In 1980 an MP asked Norman Fowler 'how much of the cost of lighting, sweeping, cleaning and patrolling motorways is attributed to pedestrians and cyclists . . . and if this practice will cease'. The answer that some civil servant provided for Fowler was (to be parliamentary) misleading. It was: 'None.'

Road damage has been pushing up the maintenance bill so much (despite constant pressure on county engineers to trim where possible) that new construction has been squeezed. Even so, it was allotted £1,085 million in 1980–81. How much of the cost of new roads should be attributed to lorries? Yet again they have enjoyed kindnesses.

A road built to serve wide, long, heavy vehicles as well as cars and vans needs a stronger structure, wider lanes, gentler gradients, robuster bridges and higher overhead clearances. The way to reckon how much this adds to the cost is to estimate what would be saved if a cars-only motorway were built. In 1968 the department put the notional saving at 17½ per cent. This low figure was achieved, however, by making some doubtful assumptions—for example, that the lanes would still be the full twelve feet wide and the hard shoulders would not be reduced. In Oregon, that state skilled in track costs, it is reckoned that the notional motorway could have lanes a foot narrower, and hard shoulders two feet narrower. The 1968 calculation was made, moreover, when the costly extra strength needed to take big lorries was being badly underestimated. However, the extra cost of building for lorries was in the end actually put by the department at only 15 per cent. In Oregon, the percentage ranges from 28 to 35. When the department's figure was questioned in 1976 by British Rail, it quoted British road construction firms as putting the lorry-derived increment at between 25 and 100 per cent, 'depending upon terrain, traffic composition, etc.'. But the department is unmoved. In 1980 Fowler refused to change the figure even to take account of its own estimate that the rise in the damage factor of the lorry fleet has added 5 per cent to the cost of roadbuilding.

The kindness to heavy lorries continues even in the treatment of the remaining 85 per cent of the road construction bill. This has to be allocated among *all* road-users according to the value they get out of the road. The department divides the cost-responsibility according to passenger car units—the measure mentioned earlier. Each vehicle's PCU value is meant to express its effect in the traffic stream: whether it takes more space than a car, has slower acceleration, a wider turning-circle, and so forth. Back in 1968, when there were far fewer big lorries, a commonly accepted PCU value for an average lorry was three. However, the department's track-cost study of that date opted for two—a figure that was kind to lorries even then. When the department returned to the subject in the seventies, the proliferation of big lorries had made the figure two even more questionable, and yet it was sanctified. How did this happen? A departmental official told me: 'We had to produce a system quickly. We plumped for two because it was in the 1968 report. One had to choose a figure.' On such decision-making do large sums turn.

In the department's track-cost papers one finds a 5-ton lorry given a PCU value of 1.184, a 16-tonner 1.888, a 32-tonner 2.912. Such precise figures seem worthy of respect. They are not. Having arbitrarily given the whole range of lorries an average PCU value of two, the department assigns that value to the lorry at the mid-point in the range and makes the rest fall arithmetically into place with their impressive decimal places.

What if one 'plumped' for a modest average of three, which the department itself could hardly challenge? Then the PCU value for a 32-tonner becomes 4.66. Millions annually are added to the share of capital costs allocated to the already guilty 32-tonners. The official quoted above said to me: 'If we're not far out on this, it doesn't make much difference.' It *does* make a difference to all lorries not already wholesomely in credit.

Furthermore, a PCU average of three and a 32-ton value of 4.66 are indeed modest. Consider: a 32-tonner, occupying more than 400 square feet (nearly six times a family car), and occupying each mile of its road space for a longer time, and needing to preserve a much greater braking distance ahead of it, and frequently reducing traffic flow, by its mere presence, from two lanes to one—a lorry doing all these things must surely rank as the equivalent of rather more than five passenger cars. Some more convincing figures were presented at a Paris conference on urban transport by Gabriel Bouladon, a transport specialist until recently with the respected Battelle Institute of Geneva. On the basis of French and German studies, Bouladon gave a lorry with a four-tonne payload (about seven tons gross) a PCU value of 2.6, and one carrying more than twenty tonnes payload, such as a 32-tonner, a value of ten (Bouladon, 1979). If this were accepted, the 32-ton lorries' share of 1980–81 roadbuilding costs would go up by about £100 million, vastly increasing their deficit; and scores of thousands of other lorries would swell the total of under-payments.

A final question will sound dangerous to lorry men: If the roads still being built are officially justified almost wholly as 'industrial routes' or to relieve towns of lorry nuisance, should not this fact alone require that far more than 15 per cent of their cost is attributed solely to lorries? When I put this to a senior departmental economist, his reply appeared to accept the point: 'We might have to change the proportion.' This ought to be pursued.

It is now time to attempt a reckoning of the tax debt of the more damaging lorries. The first step is to see what it has been merely according to the department's kindly methods.

In the year 1975–6, when preparing its *Transport Policy* consultation document, the department calculated track costs and tax yields for all lorry types. It was news to nobody that road expenditure had been going up for years, in real terms and also through inflation. Yet lorry operators had been happy to see the tax on diesel stand at 22½p a gallon since 1970 and the lorry excise duty remain unchanged from 1967 until 1975, when it went up by a third. Even with that excise increase, lorries with heavy axle-loads were dramatically underpaying in 1975–6. Some people in the department did not want the public to learn this sensitive news. They tried to keep it out of *Transport Policy* (a document ostensibly for informing the public). As a compromise, a small table was printed showing eight of the lorry types that were not meeting their road costs; but nothing so vulgarly informative as actual sums of money was shown, only ratios such as 0.6:1.

I asked for the figures from which the ratios were derived. After the usual weeks of delay that follow a request for a fact that the department is not eager to publicise, it produced them. The most striking to emerge was that even according to the department's methods, a 32-ton artic doing an average mileage was in 1975–6 meeting only £2,065 of its £3,779 track costs, and thus being subsidised by £1,714 a year. As there were then reckoned to be 41,500 of these, their annual subsidy came to £71,131,000. More than 150,000 other lorries were also falling short, bringing the total subsidy enjoyed by underpayers to more than £150 million. When I published these comprehensible facts in *The Sunday Times*, they were naturally read with more zest by the public at large than by haulage men. Other newspapers showed an interest in the story, but the department's press office fobbed them off with a wet-blanket response: 'There's nothing really new in that. It's in the consultation document.'

How was it that taxation had been allowed to fall so far behind reality? One senior official told me in 1979 that the department 'didn't adjust quickly enough' to the rising road bill, and another said the department had not done a revenue/cost breakdown for the years preceding 1975: 'There was nobody actually looking at it.' This suggests a surprising laxness following the stimulating regime of Barbara Castle, which had produced a proposal (aborted) for an extra tax on the heaviest lorries even though they were then still more than meeting their track costs. The fact was, though, that someone had been 'looking at it' before 1975, for when Sir Arthur Armitage asked for track-cost statistics, one year for which the department produced figures (and for fifty-seven types of lorry) was 1972–3. They showed that 32-ton lorries were already failing by £4½ million to meet the costs then attributed to them, and other damaging lorries were borderline. In truth their cost liability was much greater than the figures showed, for the department had calculated the damage of axle-loads by an obsolete third-power rule. Even so, the figures were ample warning that someone ought to be 'looking at it' the following year. But with an officious lack of zeal, the department did nothing for three years, by which time the huge deficits shown in the previous paragraph had arisen.

Armitage had almost as much difficulty as mere journalists in getting useful facts from the department. He was given revenue/cost figures of a range of lorries for 1975–6 and for the period 1977–80, but if he wanted to see what the deficits came to in millions he had to be knowing enough to look in a quite separate paper for the numbers of lorries in each class, and work the million' out for himself. In that paper the numbers were puzzlingly different from those the department had previously given: for example, there were now said to have been not 41,500 32-tonners in 1975, but 60,000. As for 1976–7, there was virtually a blank—oddly, for in that year I had been able to obtain a selection of revenue/cost sums.

The gaps and uncertainties meant that any calculation of the officially admitted subsidy to the underpaying lorries could only be approximate. But here is the sort of presentation that the department could have made for the enlightenment of Armitage and the public (parentheses where guesswork is necessary):

	Underpayment by 32-ton lorries	Underpayment by others	Total underpayments in 1980 prices
1972–3	£ (20,000,000)	£ (12,000,000)	£ (98,350,000)
1973–4	(33,000,000)	(20,000,000)	(149,300,000)
1974–5	(45,000,000)	(30,000,000)	(181,900,000)
1975–6	71,131,000	79,684,000	294,693,000
1976–7	(80,000,000)	(50,000,000)	(217,960,000)
1977–8	51,336,000	27,462,000	114,040,000

(continued from previous page)

1978–9	35,632,800	4,130,000	53,138,000
1979–80	41,731,200	6,105,000	56,376,000
1980–81	67,722,000	8,754,000	76,476,000
			£1,242,233,000

The 1972 figures allow for the effect of the fourth-power rule. All the attempts to fill the department's gaps are consciously on the low side; and even where the department did supply figures, they lack some categories of underpayers; so the grand total is certainly less than the reality. If the department can produce a convincing alternative I shall be happy to see it.

During those nine years, British Rail was given the following subsidies for its freight operations: 1975, £66,300,000; 1976, £35,200,000; 1977, £2,700,000; 1978, £100,000; 1979 and 1980, nil. In 1980 prices, these total £192,583,000. British Rail could perhaps have been more emphatic when it said in its evidence to Armitage: 'Economic analysis leads to the conclusion that demand for maximum-weight vehicles has been over-stimulated . . . This anomalous position . . . should be rectified.' Most of the underpaying lorries were, after all, its long-distance competitors. Moreover, the grand total does not yet include anything to correct the department's false kindnesses or its failure to charge anything for the lorries' public impact.

I have already quoted the department's declaration that in addition to road costs, vehicles should pay enough to cover their social costs. The 1976 document *Transport Policy* even recognised that it was a matter of economic efficiency: 'It is in the interests of a more efficient overall allocation of resources that all those who impose costs on other members of the community (whether by causing noise, pollution, congestion, etc.) should be charged for so doing.' As I have explained, the taxes paid on cars, vans and small lorries so much exceed their road costs that a further allocation for social costs would leave them still comfortably in credit. It is the operators of big lorries—the very ones that do most harm—who fear a social levy because it would increase their tax guilt.

What might the levy come to? I shall attempt an estimate.

Accidents

In Chapter 4 I gave an official figure of £1,727,646,000 for the 1979 cost of traffic accidents. It is impressive to see how the department can make such a sum disappear.

It first deducts everything covered by vehicle-users' insurance. Then it produces estimates, which it confesses are arbitrary, that vehicle-users themselves bear half the cost of lost output and varying proportions of the pain-and-grief costs that weigh so heavily in fatal and serious casualties. These estimates are unconvincing. For example, in accidents causing serious injury (including thousands of lasting cripplings and disfigurings each year) the pain, grief and suffering borne by people other than vehicle-users—relatives, friends and other members of the community—is said to amount to only 20 per cent of the whole. What makes this even more dubious is the fact that a third of the people seriously injured are not vehicle users at all, but pedestrians and cyclists.

One way or another, the department calculated in 1976 that only a quarter of the total accident bill (then £875 million) fell on the community at large and 'should be included in the total of road costs' (*Transport Policy*). It went on to make a pro-lorry assumption that 'each driver is equally responsible for accident involvement and for the costs that result'; and it attributed only £25 million of the 1976 total to lorries. Then came its climactic achievement: it decided to charge the lorries nothing at all.

Its explanation was that 'the total cost estimate is more tentative, and the allocation to vehicle classes made with less justification' than in the case of direct road costs. When Sir Arthur Armitage asked the department about this, it merely repeated the old argument. The justification that a track-cost official had put to me was: 'We don't know who is responsible for accidents. We don't know the responsibility of pedestrians and cyclists. I can't see how we would make much progress until we decided responsibility.'

So were they working on it?

'No. I don't think it's a problem that needs to be solved. It's a small sum.'

In this as in so much else, they were taking care to be puzzled when it suited them. The 'we don't know who is responsible' line is unconvincing. How does such a sensitive department dare to charge each motorist the same arbitrary licence fee?

And when it wishes to shift large sums of road-track costs on to pedestrians, it has no qualms about saying: 'Let's be arbitrary.' In any case, it has given itself a 'responsibility' precedent with police costs: they are allocated according to each vehicle type's annual mileage. When accident statistics are at last fully recorded according to lorries' gross weight, acceptable allocations should be no problem.

The department's scrupulous paralysis is all the more surprising when one finds that accident costs are counted, and in full, when they work in favour of something the department wants to do. Whenever it is promoting the construction or improvement of a road, the scheme is justified in part by summing the cost of the accidents which, it is claimed, the scheme will prevent in years to come. Heads they win . . .

In Chapter 4 I produced a lorry accident cost figure of £147 million. I shall round it down to a moderate £140 million.

Noise

That traffic noise does impose large costs on the community was made clear in Chapter 5. Even if psychological and physiological suffering is hard to quantify, economists can recognise other indicators, such as the cost of double-glazing or unused front rooms; or, taking another approach, the cost of quietening lorries. In 1976 the department proposed a figure, which it confessed 'may in fact be seriously under-estimated', of £42 million for lorry noise (1975 prices), or £83 million now. Underestimated indeed. Merely to double-glaze the minimal 2,300,000 homes suggested by the Noise Advisory Council, to make life tolerable *inside* them only, would cost £220 million a year if spread over ten years. I propose £300 million as a moderate total noise bill for lorries.

Ground vibration

Until the department does its duty and studies the effects on buildings, one can only say that hidden damage is shortening the lives of millions of buildings, and that many thousands are either visibly declining or having large sums spent on them to save them from death. There is also the damage done to under-street mains and other installations. The department told Armitage: 'Traffic is doubtless a contributory factor . . . but there is as yet no evidence to suggest that heavy vehicles alone are a major cause of such damage.' How clever that 'alone' is! And again there is 'the problem of determining how the proportion of costs . . . should be distributed'. For vibration, say £150 million.

Fumes

The department's 1975–6 estimate was £16 million, derived from a 1970 official estimate that air pollution from all motor vehicles in the UK cost £37 million. An estimate in striking contrast was made in 1973 in the US by the Council for Environmental Quality: between twelve and fourteen thousand million dollars for vehicle pollution. For Britain, with one-eighth the number of vehicles, a parallel figure in 1973 would have been about £800 million, not allowing for the fact that a much more concentrated population suffers more from pollution. In 1980 that would be £2,300 million, of which one-tenth might be attributable to goods vehicles. If one scorned the American estimate and plumped instead for £150 million, would not that seem moderate?

Congestion

In 1976 the department performed another service for lorries by finding itself unable to include in their public costs— 'however desirable this may seem'—a sum for the congestion they cause to other road-users. The argument was that vehicles impose congestion costs on one another, and therefore should not pay the state for doing so. Others have thought differently. A study which the department followed on other points (Pryke and Dodgson, 1975) attributed to lorries a minimum chargeable congestion cost for 1972 of £61 million to £66 million (say £200 million in 1980). Two Road Research Laboratory men, G. Margason and P. J. Corcoran, presented a calculation at a Paris symposium (Organisation for Economic Cooperation and Development, 1977) that the delay caused to other traffic by a lorry under 16 tons cost £150 to £300 a year, and that by bigger lorries £200 to £400. I have already quoted the figure given by Gabriel Bouladon at another OECD conference that a top-weight lorry's effect on traffic was the equivalent of ten cars. If one hazarded an average figure (1980) for all lorries of only £300 (having knocked something off for the congestion that cars cause them), one would have a total of over £150 million. In addition there is the cost, mentioned earlier, of traffic delays caused by road repairs—work attributable almost entirely to lorries—which on motorways and trunk and principal roads alone the department estimates at nearly £40 million in 1980 prices.

(Congestion, though ignored by the department as a social cost, is used even more than accidents as a quantifiable justification for roadbuilding. Indeed, 80 per cent of the cost/benefit argument for a scheme is that existing roads are or will be congested.)

Intrusion, severance, fear

It is hard to put a price on the disrupting effects heavy lorries have on people's neighbourhoods, but the cost is real. It is well expressed in the evidence to Armitage of the Council for the Protection of Rural England: 'The greatest impact these vehicles have on individuals is caused by their sheer physical size. The reaction is one of fear, particularly . . . in streets with narrow pavements or in lanes. It is fear for the safety of children or of pedestrians and cyclists. It is fear that a vehicle may not be able to brake in time or that it may crush pedestrians as it overrides the pavement . . . This fear extends even to people indoors who are afraid that their houses may be struck or be damaged by vibration . . . There is the damage done to the landscape by road improvements which turn a winding country road into a fast road by the removal of bends, hedgerows and hedgerow trees, so altering the character of the countryside . . .' What might the price be? An annual £1 a head may seem excessively modest, but it makes £50 million.

The following total now emerges for the annual social/environmental costs that lorries ought to meet:

Accidents	£140 million
Noise	300
Vibration	150
Fumes	150
Congestion	200
Intrusion, etc.	50
	£990 million

A further sum must be estimated for all the department's kindly under-calculations of track costs. I hazard £300 million.

The taxable annual costs of the 516,000 lorries of over 3½ tons gross now add up like this:

Road costs attributed by the department	£ 790 million
Track-cost rectifications	300
Social/environmental	990
	£2,080 million

If their tax yield was, as the department calculated, £820 million in 1980–81, their total shortfall was £1,260 million.

This result naturally has its greatest impact on those lorries whose tax payments are officially already marginal or in deficit; and especially on the 32-tonners. If their share of the additional costs were calculated simply according to their mileage, that would be too easy on them. Another option, still a mild one, is to share the extra according to the department's passenger-car-unit ratings. The 32-tonners then owe an extra £492 million, or £5,760 extra each; and the underpayment per lorry in 1980–81 rises from £793 to £6,553. The effect of such a tax rise on a haulier's business would be striking. According to cost tables in *Motor Transport,* to make a decent profit in 1980 on a 32-tonner doing 50,000 miles a year a haulier had to charge 93p a mile. The full tax would require him to put that up by 14 per cent. That might well affect the 'allocation of resources'; in human terms, the number of juggernauts.

I designedly said 'if' the lorries' tax yield was £820 million, for many thousands of lorry operators manage to ease their already light tax burden by evasion. When up to 9 per cent of car-owners have been able to get away without paying for a flat-rate tax disc, according to a departmental survey, it is not surprising that lorries subject to a scale of seventy-six rates can tax-dodge far more easily. Knowledgeable men are needed to check them; but the enforcement staff has been both chronically undermanned and sadly disunified. In 1977 the department calculated that between 10 and 13 per cent of commercial vehicles, from vans upwards, were running untaxed. It is reasonable to assume that the evasion rate was higher among the 516,000 lorries than among the 1,300,000 smaller vehicles, but an evasion rate of only 13 per cent would mean that the 516,000 evaded £37 million in 1980. And that is only part of the story.

When an operator buys his disc, he produces a weighbridge certificate. Here is where the cheating can start. The tax goes up with each quarter-ton, so weight-shedding is a useful art. Official allowances are generous enough: spare wheel and tools removed, weight of water and fuel deducted; but crafty men strip off other things too. And artics give special opportunities for a more serious kind of tax-paring. A tractive unit that is to be operated with a heavy trailer, perhaps for refrigerated meat, can be taken to the weighbridge with a skeleton trailer, known as a skel (which may be borrowed for the weighing-in of a whole series of artics). Or an operator may produce a certificate merely for his tractive unit and save perhaps £900 a year.

Strong evidence about the frequency of these and other tricks began emerging in the mid-seventies when officials of Kent County Council's consumer protection service, doing roadside overloading checks, were so concerned at the frequency of dodgy lorry tax discs that they took to recording them and sending the information to the vehicle licensing centre at Swansea. With public spirit as their only incentive they were soon reporting evasions amounting to hundreds of thousands of pounds a year—spotted just as a sideline of their occasional weight checks.

When I reported this in *The Sunday Times* and said the Kent officials felt that tax-checking 'seems to be casually done' by the transport department's traffic examiners, a curious thing happened. An assistant secretary in freight directorate wrote to me to complain that this appeared to be 'an unjustified slur'. He did so because of a protest from the traffic examiners' office at Eastbourne. In my reply I cited what the Kent officials had found on two recent days: 146 lorries checked, 15 untaxed, 41 undertaxed (one with a disc borrowed from a Jaguar)—a sample suggesting 10 per cent straight evasion and a further 28 per cent cheating. I pointed out that in the past year in the entire south-east licensing area (Kent, Sussex, Hampshire and parts of Dorset, Berkshire and Surrey), the department's own examiners had achieved only fifty-three convictions for such offences. I affirmed that the Kent officials felt strongly that the examiners were not acting with sufficient thoroughness. With great flexibility, the assistant secretary withdrew his 'unjustified slur' phrase—saying, surprisingly, that he was 'now satisfied' that the Kent officials were *not* criticising the examiners. As for the fifty-three convictions, he said the examiners passed most tax offences to Swansea for action, but there, unfortunately, the 'priority task' was to 'overcome the teething troubles' in Swansea's computer. He produced no figures to show whether the examiners in their vast area had won more money for the Exchequer than the Kent men in their volunteer work.

The assistant secretary also said that traffic examiners 'check tax discs as a matter of course' but 'cannot do all the jobs all the time'. If they spent more time on tax offences 'they would have that much less time for . . . offences with a more direct road safety implication'. This was 'even more true of vehicle examiners' (I had asked why discs could not be checked during the annual vehicle test). On this point, the Foster report on licensing recommended that a test certificate should not be issued unless a valid excise licence were produced; but nothing has been done.

In 1978, after a national survey of car tax evasion, the department promised a similar survey of lorries. When asked two years later whether this was being done, Norman Fowler said it was not: it would be 'expensive and time-consuming'. As the fines and 'mitigated penalties' collected from all operators of goods vehicles, including vans, came in 1979 to scarcely £500,000, a little more spending on enforcement would seem likely to be cost-effective. Instead, the enforcers were still understaffed and convictions were at an even lower rate than three years earlier.

The department has been no more zealous in bringing about a promised change in the tax system that would put payments more nearly in line with damaging power. Excise duty would be levied not according to unladen weight, but gross weight, and vehicles that spread their weight less damagingly over more axles would pay less. An operator would thus have some incentive to use a 32-tonner, for example, with five axles instead of the present highly damaging four. In 1977 William Rodgers said: 'The necessary changes . . . are under way.' The new system would be introduced, said the department in a subtly chosen phrase, 'not before 1979'. All sorts of years are not before 1979. When 1979 had passed, the date became 1983. No clear explanation was given for the slippage; but perhaps a clue can be found in the fact that the change would shift some of the tax burden from the overtaxed lighter lorries to the hitherto kindly-treated heavy ones. The department itself said there would be 'a substantial increase' in the tax payable by a big four-axle artic; the new system 'will provide operators with an incentive to acquire less damaging vehicles, thereby promoting economic usage of the roads. And it will help to ensure a fairer basis of competition between road and rail.'

When the department asked in 1979 for public comments on the proposed change, it spoke of the social costs of lorries as only 'a factor to be taken into account'. This continuing vagueness brought the following proposals from the London Amenity and Transport Association: 'Lorries should be classified on a scale which takes account of their nuisance-causing characteristics. Each new model . . . should be allotted a number of points on this scale . . . Urban areas, and some country areas too, would be graded according to their sensitivity . . . Vehicles of above a certain rating would not be allowed into the more sensitive areas at all.'

The association added a complaint about the way the department treated responses to its consultation papers: 'Our representations rarely seem to have any effect, but as they go unanswered, we have no idea whether this is because they have been considered and rejected, and if so on what grounds; considered but not understood; or not considered at all.' It still has no idea: there was no reply.

The achievement of a rational balance between the cost of moving goods and the cost of road damage and social impact is now, in theory, an EEC objective. Yet the 'harmonisation' proposals of Directorate-General VII have been subjected to as little independent scrutiny as the calculations of Marsham Street. DG VII says that its proposed lorry types, ranging from a four-axle 35-tonner to a six-axle 44-tonner, would in some cases be more damaging per 100 tons payload than Britain's maximum lorry, and in others less damaging. On balance, it claims, they would offer good payloads for moderate damage. Its figures were largely based on material provided by a 'working group' of committed men: thirty-four representing lorry-makers, nine the International Road Union, one the Road Haulage Association and three DG VII itself. When the European Environmental Bureau offered a counter-view,

John Edsberg of DG VII tried to muffle it, as I have mentioned in Chapter 1. As for the bureau's detailed questioning of his payload/damage claims, he told the bureau: 'It would probably be better to leave it out altogether.' (After an appeal by the bureau to the EEC commissioner for transport, and some minor amendments by the bureau, Edsberg accepted the paper.) The bureau's chief points on damage were:

—that DG VII said that 'for the present . . . moderate axle weights are being proposed', but these included a very damaging drive axle (11 tonnes + 5 per cent tolerance = 11.55 tonnes) which was 'a definite shift in favour of lorry operators'.

—that while DG VII calculated damage by a fourth-power rule, it said this would 'probably be reviewed in the next few years'. Uncertainty 'should encourage caution', the bureau said, and pressed for a full study first.

—that even on DG VII's own assumptions, its biggest four-axle lorry would be 39 per cent more damaging than Britain's far-from-gentle one, for a payload increase of only 14 per cent.

—that countries now using twelve- or thirteen-tonne axles would not be required by DG VII to come down in weight within their borders: 'Thus the proposal is not a true compromise . . . nor is the objective of creating a common market for lorry manufacturers being achieved.'

DG VII's dubious 11.55-tonne axle was proposed partly to placate the French and others who rejected a 10-tonne maximum; and partly because a 40-tonne artic would be too unstable with only 10 tonnes of the total on its drive axle. (The simple alternative is to have a three-axle tractive unit, but hauliers resist the extra weight and cost.) On a fourth-power reckoning, the 11.55 axle does 78 per cent more damage than a 10-tonne; on a fifth-power reckoning, 105 per cent more.

Marsham Street, like Brussels, tended to play down the flaws in the proposals. When Sir Arthur Armitage asked the transport department to say what the effect on Britain might be, it gave an estimate that the advent of a mixture of the heavier lorries might enable the same tonnage to be carried with 9 per cent less damage. But then it conceded that this calculation looked optimistic. The answer will vary according to which lorries the hauliers go for. If a 'worst case' occurred and they switched singlemindedly to DG VII's four-axle 35-tonners, the department said, damage would increase by 19 per cent. (All the department's estimates, cling, of course, to a fourth-power reckoning, and even avoid counting the damaging effect of the 5 per cent tolerance.) Certainly vast numbers of 35-tonners would be unleashed on British roads, for the operators who have prematurely bought many thousands of lorries built to run at over 32 tons are longing to do so.

The department also told Armitage that it saw no reason why higher gross weights should mean more illegal overloading of axles. In fact such overloads would become commoner. They are most often caused by bad positioning of the load on the trailer. Some useful information on the point emerged in a Road Research Laboratory report (Corcoran, Glover and Shane 1980). It showed that the department's estimate of a possible reduction in road damage depended on all loads being ideally positioned. With existing lorries, placing loads only one metre forward of the optimum position increases road damage by 31 per cent. If *much heavier* loads were mispositioned, the axle-load effect would be greater on many of the proposed vehicles. And indeed the report says that for this reason 'road damage could increase'.

Many uncertainties also cloud the calculation of possible cost savings to operators, this report makes clear. Once lorries pass the 24-tonne size, savings from further weight increases are in any case small, it says, and they depend on the lorries' being fully loaded (a point considered further in the next chapter). The EEC lorries, *if fully loaded,* might bring annual savings of nearly £150 million (1980 prices)—but perhaps much less. Furthermore, for a complete cost/benefit assessment 'it will be necessary to estimate the absolute change in road and bridge construction and maintenance costs and to evaluate as far as possible the effects of heavier vehicles on road safety, environmental disturbance and traffic delays'.

Further hints about unanswered questions reached Armitage from the County Surveyors' Society, a body that seldom raises doubts about juggernauts. It said research was needed to determine the damaging effect of closely-spaced tri-axles (which most of the heavier lorries' trailers would have), and especially the deep-down 'bulbs of pressure' they exert on road foundations. It also pointed out that the original American road-damage tests were carried out at only 30 m.p.h., whereas the extra dynamic effect of high speeds 'could be of the order of 100 per cent, particularly under downhill vehicle speeds' and 'there is some evidence of premature failure due to this cause'. Research, it said, 'is urgently required'.

None of these things was mentioned to Armitage by the transport department. On one aspect of the EEC proposals, however, it did reveal concern: their effect on British bridges. A bridge collapse is, after all, a more precise event than road damage and leaves little scope for evasiveness.

'Bridges both modern and old would be subjected to the risk of exposure to loads for which they have not been designed,' the department said. In particular it was concerned about the proposed heavy drive axle and closely-spaced 24-tonne trailer tri-axle. 'If no steps were taken to safeguard our bridges, the effect of the directive would be extremely serious.' Aside from the risk of collapse, 'repeated overloading would speed up the rate of deterioration of bridge structures, with costly consequences' and the heavier axles 'could have an adverse effect on . . . culverts, subways, sewers and sub-stations'. If the very damaging EEC 35-tonner were widely adopted, 'it would be necessary to assume axle overloading as a normal condition' (a statement overturning what the department had said earlier).

These statements came after a firm of consulting engineers, Husband & Company, had delivered a report to the department in March 1980. The report itself was not passed to Armitage until four months later; and was not passed at all to people much concerned with bridge safety, such as county surveyors, the county and metropolitan authorities or the Institution of Highway Engineers: they had to hear of it by chance and apply for copies. These people knew that an expensive exercise called Operation Bridgeguard had already had to be carried out after Britain's lorry limit went up to 32 tons in 1964: all bridges built before 1922 had been checked, some had been given weight limits and thousands had been strengthened—but only in a money-saving way that did not bring them up to the standard laid down for new bridges. The Husband & Company report gives a good deal of computer-backed analysis of bending moments and shear forces acceptable on various spans. Here are some of its chief points:

—Short-span bridges built before 1922 (more than two-fifths of the kingdom's 155,000 bridges) would be particularly vulnerable. The 24-tonne tri-axle would put an excessive load on all bridges classed 'full strength' under Bridgeguard; on some spans an excess of 38 per cent.

—Even on modern bridges, shear forces would be exceeded, especially on long spans.

—Higher axle-loads would reduce the life of stone or brick arched bridges and 'seriously reduce the anticipated fatigue life' of metal ones, especially those with long spans.

—A Bridgeguard-style assessment of metal bridge decks and girders would be needed, as metal fatigue damage is assumed to increase according to a third-power rule (which makes an 11.55-tonne axle 50 per cent more damaging than a 10-ton).

—Modern long spans were designed to give a good safety margin with five 22-ton lorries in one lane—something that used to be thought unlikely, moderate though it now seems—and they 'can easily be overloaded by a build-up of heavy traffic'. They are probably 'deficient in live load capacity'. (Five 44-tonne lorries nose-to-tail on such a bridge would represent a disturbing 'worst case', to use the engineers' phrase.)

Husband & Company also drew attention to the fact that the present growth of mere 32-tonners is a cause of concern. Some modern long spans need checking to see if they are strong enough for queues of them; the twin axles of their trailers can exceed the official Bridgeguard 'full strength' rating; and they are shortening the life or older bridges.

What might be the cost of a vast bridge-renewal programme? Husband & Company estimated that a minimum of 1,400 bridges on trunk and principal roads and 6,500 on lesser roads would have to be strengthened or replaced, at a cost (1980) of £1,358 million. In addition, to check and strengthen 'the special family of long bridges' to ensure their safety for existing juggernauts, let alone bigger ones, 'could be a major undertaking' costing £120 million. The total bill 'could be significantly higher'. And there would be the further cost of traffic chaos during rebuilding (on the main roads alone, the department said, this 'might well be in the order of £50 million').

When the department sent Armitage the Husband report, it provided a commentary that softened the message. For a start, it failed to mention the long bridges. As for the 6,500 bridges on lesser roads, 'the right solution in most cases might be to impose a weight restriction rather than to reconstruct the bridge'. Such a solution, however, would cut across the EEC's (and hauliers') aim to have 'harmonised' lorries circulating freely; though it would be good news to people on such roads. The department went on to say that 44-tonne lorries could be designed without the excessive drive axle and closely-spaced tri-axle, and that this would eliminate 'the need for any additional expenditure on UK bridges'. These statements are problematic. First, the EEC is committed to the 11.55 axle; and if the tri-axle is more widely spaced it has trouble going round corners and imposes more strain on the road surface. More important, the department ignores Husband & Company's revelation that longer spans are already in trouble and that lorries above 32 tons, whatever their axles, could make things worse.

If one takes the Husband minimum cost estimate of £1,478 million and adds £150 million for traffic delays from bridge-works on all roads, and then spreads the total over ten years, that gives £163 million a year. In addition there is the general increase in bridge maintenance which Husband & Company pointed to but did not quantify. A remarkable picture emerges: any cost savings the EEC lorries might offer operators would be more than nullified by the bridge bill alone.

DG VII and the transport department have avoided saying anything about American views on the desirable balance between haulage costs and road costs. Some telling evidence was presented to Armitage, however, by the Council for Environmental Conservation: transcripts of statements made to a congressional sub-committee in 1977 and 1979 by the American Association of State Highway and Transportation Officials (Aashto), as it is now known. It would see the DG VII proposals as outrageous. They are far above its recommended maximums, followed by the Federal Government and by the majority of the states and of Canadian provinces. Aashto has concluded that the best balance can be struck between getting the most out of the roads and giving them 'a reasonable life expectancy' if the maximum for a single axle is 20,000 lb and for a trailer tandem 34,000. Weights above that would 'jeopardise our investment in highways', Aashto told the congressmen. Putting all weights into pounds produces the following contrast:

	America's optimum	Britain's limits	The EEC's proposals
Single axle	20,000	22,400	24,245
Tandem	34,000	42,590	39,680

With the EEC's proposed 5 per cent tolerance, its figures rise to 25,458 and 41,658. The damaging power of the British axle is 1½ times, and of the EEC axle twice, that of the American; and the British tandem's is 146 per cent more than that of the American. Some states have kept their axle limit to 18,000 lb (8 tons). A modest increase to 20,000 (8.9 tons) 'can result in an average loss of the remaining highway life between 25 and 40 per cent', said Aashto. 'To increase it to 22,000 pounds, as some are advocating, can result in a loss of pavement life of close to 60 per cent.' Britain's axles are not gentle.

Some good non-academic real-life evidence was presented from the state of Virginia. Big coal truckers were allowed to operate, in three counties only, with single axles of 24,000 lb (well under the EEC's 11 tonnes) and tandems of 45,000. Records kept over sixteen years showed that on well-built primary roads maintenance costs were 60 per cent up and on lesser roads they were double, compared with counties keeping to the 20,000/34,000 limit.

The gross weight limit, federally and in many states, is 35.7 tons—but spread over five axles, and thus much less damaging, ton for ton of payload, than Britain's 32. Some states have kept to an even gentler five-axle 32.7 tons. The EEC's proposed four-axle 35 would be greeted with derision.

The Aashto evidence made a point that would apply equally to many British roads: that highway authorities in the Appalachians and southern states were 'more conservative' about weights because their highways 'are of older vintage, are more circuitous . . . have rolling grades' and 'go through towns and cities at frequent intervals'.

The fuel-saving and economic advantages claimed by American truckers pressing for a weight increase were questioned by Aashto; but even if they were justified, it said, they would be outweighed by added maintenance costs. It made a point that has been ignored in Europe: 'In determining overall energy consumption, consideration must be given to the energy needed to perform the additional maintenance.' This should include 'energy expended in producing or mining the necessary materials'. This extra maintenance energy 'could exceed the energy saved by permitting increased weight limits'.

More interesting still, Aashto asked a series of questions that would never be heard from highway engineers in Britain: 'Would the increased weight divert freight from railroads and barge lines due to the increased competitive advantage of trucks? . . . Is consideration being given to the most fuel-efficient manner of transporting freight? Is the potential for intermodal shipments, including trailers and containers on railroad flat-cars and on ships and barges, being fully utilised? Will increased truck weights and sizes have an adverse effect on highway safety?' And in speaking of road-rail cooperation, Aashto uttered words that would have perturbed the best minds of Marsham Street: 'The country needs an integrated transportation policy.'

8

Off the rails

A question that the transport department must be made to face
is: Has its unswerving enthusiasm for unharassed, undertaxed,
cost-externalising road transport been good for Britain? And
furthermore: As the golden age of oil fades, will the juggernaut heritage be regretted? Of course the department is modest
about claiming credit for the fact that Britain leads the
industrial world in the growth of road freight and the decline
of rail and water freight. I have already quoted its statement to
Armitage: 'Most changes and developments in the freight
transport industry have been unconnected with any steps
taken by government.' The department's *laissez-faire* line was
that the industrial and other customers of freight operators by
road, rail and water 'have a great variety of requirements . . .
which together determine the pattern of demand for freight
services'. One almost expects the department to become
invisible; but at another point in the same background paper it
did bring itself to speak of one contribution it had made: the
motorway and trunk road programme had 'facilitated the
growth of road freight'. That all the encouragements given to
big lorries also facilitated the growth was of course not
mentioned.

What the department has achieved in the past dozen years is
not the movement of an actual greater tonnage of goods, for
that has stayed about the same or even declined. No, the
amazing 98,000 million annual tonne-kilometres merely
demonstrate the fact that the goods are on average being
shifted 50 per cent further, which is not an economic good in
itself. 'Cheap transport' has meant that firms have almost
been able to ignore its cost in their decision-making. 'Local
factories serving local markets have been replaced by larger
factories serving a national or even international market,' the
department told Armitage (though not adding that this hardly

supported its frequent assertion that motorways pushed into the regions create jobs there).

A Road Research Laboratory study, *Developments in Freight Transport* (Corcoran, Hitchcock and McMahon, 1980), specially produced for the benefit of Armitage, usefully sums up the combined effect of motorways and bigger lorries: they make it possible 'to complete return journeys in one day which would previously have required an overnight stop'. This study is not at all critical of what has happened, so some of the points it makes are all the more telling. Distribution depots, like factories, have become fewer and larger: 'Road improvements tend to encourage the trend towards fewer depots and greater delivery distances . . . One of the objectives of distribution management is to minimise inventory costs; this can often result in an increase in the use of transport and transport costs.' In manufacturing, 'The attainment of economies of scale versus increased demand for freight transport will weigh heavily in most industries, since transport costs are a relatively low proportion of total costs . . . Rationalisation and mergers have tended to lead to concentration of production away from congested inner city sites . . . Increased freight transport is the result' (not to mention inner city decline). And then comes a further worrying end-result of all this department-blessed transport so cheap that it hardly deserved a thought. After talking to numerous industrialists, the researchers report: 'Indeed, some interviewees were of the opinion that their industries had possibly become too concentrated. Many expressed fears about the industrial relations problems associated with large concerns . . . It is felt that very large factories tend to have labour-relations problems due to their size . . . Fears were also expressed about vulnerability to transport problems . . . However, where an industry may feel that production has become over-concentrated, a reversal is unlikely, due to the amount of investment that has taken place.'

That is the juggernaut heritage. The department intends to carry it further by increasing the mileage of motorways and trunk roads by a third and the weight of juggernauts by 35 per cent. What of the fuel to keep the exceedingly transport-dependent economy going? The department's assumption, stated in its 1980 White Paper, *Policy for Roads,* is that oil prices will go up 'between two and a half and three times in real terms between 1976 and 2001'. It shows no sign of anxiety: 'Vehicle manufacturers can be expected to introduce increasingly more efficient models. There will be a growing incentive for people to select vehicles with improved fuel performance and to economise in their use of fuel. In the longer term there may be increasing scope for turning to other energy sources.' A slightly more troubling picture was presented in 1978 by John Mitchell, a senior British Petroleum economist, at a Road Research Laboratory symposium. He made the point that oil does not 'run out' but becomes increasingly expensive to extract, once peak production is passed. And he said: 'At some point maybe within the next five years, maybe within the next ten, the rate of production then current will be 10 per cent or so of the remaining reserves then known . . . From that point on it will be very difficult to maintain total production . . . It is at that moment that there really will be some kind of turning-point . . . beside which what we have had so far will just look like a rehearsal . . . *Growth* in oil supply will end within a lead time early in the life of any industrial plant now being designed or housing estate or motorway now being planned' (Transport and Road Research Laboratory, 1979).

At the same symposium the then transport secretary, William Rodgers, spoke of planners over the past thirty years who had unthinkingly increased the need for transport: for example, by creating large schools requiring 'extremely difficult and expensive journeys for children' or large hospitals to which 'you have to travel a whole day by public transport for a half-hour appointment'. Planners had assumed that everyone was, and would continue to be, easily mobile. Rodgers said they must now consider 'whether we can, without constricting people's lives and opportunities, actually reduce the need for transport'. However, the tone of a speech that Rodgers's permanent secretary, Sir Peter Baldwin, gave at the close of the symposium was rather different. 'Robust' was a word in vogue in the civil service, and especially with Baldwin.

In trying to decide what to do about transport energy, he said, 'one searches for something robust'. The great growth of personal mobility was 'one of the robust features of our scene': 'Personal mobility now constitutes a large part of personal freedom. Governments . . . must respect it, and the desire for it . . . One could conceive an economy in which there was a positive choice to conserve fuels that were particularly suitable for transport even at the cost . . . involved in choosing less economic fuels for other purposes. So the government is in this in a big way.'

There were other robust features: 'One is the infrastructure for transport that we have now actually got. We can fiddle about with it at the edges. If I may say so with respect, a great deal of the argument that has gone on between road and rail has been about fiddling about at the edges.' Roads were 'the main element on which the valued asset of personal mobility depends'. As for rising oil prices (and this was long before the Iranian troubles), they provided 'one last robust element'. Baldwin's chief concern was that ordinary people's uncertainty about supplies 'may itself act as a brake upon confidence and the advance of the world economy'. One had to move tactfully: 'We have to find a way of introducing conservation of fuel into people's lives in a way which they find is no great burden to them.' There was to be no shrinking empire for Marsham Street: 'Transport has to be a premium user of fuel, as a service that will certainly have to continue as far ahead as any of us can see on a scale no smaller than now.'

Baldwin's message is that *other* oil-users must take the cuts. Road vehicles consume about a quarter of Britain's petroleum (and of that quarter, heavy lorries use about a fifth). Of course a shift from oil for heating and power generation can achieve a great deal, but other large users, such as the chemical and plastics industries, might assert that they too have robust infrastructures. The haulage industry, though, fully agrees with Baldwin. In spring 1980 John Silbermann of the Road Haulage Association said this: 'It has been computed that if all oil consumption for non-transport purposes ceased today, the industrialised world would have adequate oil in the known present reserves to last in excess of 150 years.' He called upon all transport users 'to form a most powerful lobby' to convince everyone that the only alternative to disaster was 'reducing or ceasing' the non-transport use of oil.

Those who want road-users to be the last to face the evil day have many allies. A report in 1977 by a working group of the Advisory Council on Energy Conservation concluded that it was 'unlikely that there will be significant energy savings, in the short to medium term,' from switches of freight to rail or water. The working group was headed by a National Freight Corporation man but included no British Rail man. With great tentativeness it said that 'it may be that, in the medium to longer term, there could be' such savings. However, when it reported the following year on 'long-term possibilities' it devoted itself almost entirely to substitute fuels that might maintain 'a pattern of transport demand broadly similar in amount and type to the present one'. It explicitly avoided considering 'adaptations which could actually reduce transport demand' such as a return to smaller factories and a more localised style of living. Railways got two mentions. Having concluded that electric propulsion for long-distance lorries would be difficult ('Power pick-up en route would entail expensive overhead equipment along principal roads'), it said: 'This might help to make transfer to rail for the central portion of the journey desirable.' Then it made a pro-rail point about power pick-up: 'For tracked transport most of the disadvantages of the use of electric energy . . . disappear.'

A look at how lorries operate raises a doubt as to whether they have earned the right to claim special treatment. Cheap diesel fuel through the sixties and seventies contributed to a wasteful way of moving goods. The industry knows it is vulnerable here. A few weeks after John Silbermann made his call for exclusive oil, a columnist in the weekly *Motor Transport* said the claim would be challenged: 'Engineers are continually improving the fuel efficiency of engines but transport operators have singularly failed to improve their use, in terms of loaded mileage.' The writer said it could be argued that the use of vehicles had become less efficient since the 1968 Act ended quantity licensing.

One of the industry's chief public-relations arguments for still heavier lorries is that they would use less fuel to move a given tonnage of goods. The Freight Transport Association reckons, for example, that going from 32 tons to 40 tonnes would give nearly a 5 per cent saving. Before considering that argument more closely, it will be worth noting the fuel savings that have been achieved with existing lorries by means of common sense and a few technical improvements. The room for improvement has been great because in the era of cheap fuel so little thought was given to economy. 'The ways of yesteryear were too profligate,' as D. G. Milne, BP's

chief executive, told the FTA conference in 1979. Milne gave
some straight advice: 'The biggest energy-conserver is a light
foot.'

Clear evidence of this was provided in that year by the
National Freight Corporation in a first report on its Save It
programme for its thousands of lorries. Tests with 32-ton
lorries on the motorway showed that miles per gallon went
down from 10½ at 40 m.p.h. to 7.9 at 50 and 6.75 at 60, so that
a speed limit of 40 instead of 60 would save 35 per cent. NFC
began fitting speed governors—though certainly not for 40
m.p.h. They were set at 63. *Motor Transport* said: 'Though
this is greater than motorway speed limits of 60 m.p.h., and
could encourage the driver to break the law, it does provide
him with extra power at the critical cruising speed to overtake
and avoid "bunching".' An NFC executive told me more
bluntly: 'The men wouldn't stand for a lower limit.' In any
case, fast journey times still matter more to NFC or other
hauliers than fuel saving. The chief reason for the governors
seems to be that NFC was also fitting air deflectors above the
cabs of its artics to streamline the gap between cab and trailer,
and these reduced drag so much that without governors the
drivers were likely to cruise in the seventies. At a 63
maximum, governors plus deflectors saved 9 per cent on
trunk hauls and paid for themselves in eighteen months. A
further 6 per cent could be saved, NFC said, by means of
thermostatically-controlled engine temperatures, and 5 per
cent by keeping tyre pressures high. But all such measures
requiring cash outlay and management control are rarely
adopted among small hauliers, who are usually thinking
about how to get through the week.

In other countries, governments take the fuel (and safety)
rewards of moderate speeds seriously. In Chapter 4 I pointed
out that the motorway maximum for big artics in nearly all
continental countries is well below Britain's ill-enforced 60.
To keep drivers to the 55 m.p.h. limit in the US, some big
trucking firms use methods that the Transport and General
probably would not embrace, such as computer-aided analysis
of tachograph records, 'fines' of a couple of days' pay, and
radar-equipped detector cars for spot-checking. One firm that
uses radar says: 'Our drivers accept it. They get paid pretty
well for doing what we ask them to do.' When the fuel
efficiency of thirty-two trucks was checked on a test track, it

was shown that for each mile-an-hour reduction from high speeds down to 55 there was a 2.2 per cent fuel saving. So if the NFC governors were set at 55 there would be a 17.6 saving.

The savings achievable by technical refinements and speed control make the industry's economy claims for heavier lorries seem to deserve little weight. Besides, according to official trials, 'in fuel used per payload tonne-kilometre there is a potential small saving in some cases and not in others . . . There does not seem to be much to choose between the heavier and lighter vehicles' (Transport, Department of, January 1979). And a good deal depends on what the 'load factors' of the heavier lorries would be—the percentage of miles run part-loaded or empty. Here there are further doubts.

Men on both sides of the industry have questioned the fuel-saving claims, and for related reasons. Jack Ashwell, the transport union's national officer for lorry-drivers, said in his evidence to Armitage: 'There are too many vehicles chasing too few goods. Dead mileage is wasteful and non-productive. To contemplate increasing vehicle weights before resolving basic problems will only perpetuate the present system with larger vehicles.' (He also urged Armitage to examine the industry 'in conjunction with other modes of transport—rail and water' and favoured a national planning authority 'for an integrated transport system'.) On the employers' side, the biggest operator, NFC, upset some haulage men by saying to Armitage: 'If the 40-tonner were loaded at less than 90 per cent of its maximum payload potential, it would cost more to run per tonne-mile than a loaded 32-tonner.' But the heavier lorries would be widely used: 'Hauliers prefer to operate equipment capable of hauling any load offered . . . This would result in heavier vehicles carrying loads which could be handled by the existing 32-tonner.' And frequently running, therefore, at less than 90 per cent capacity.

The point was developed further by NFC's chief executive, Peter Thompson, at a conference of lorry fleet managers: 'We were surprised at how little rate reduction we could offer our customers as a result of increasing the potential carrying capacity of the vehicle by over 30 per cent. From an examination of the traffic that we carry currently in 32-ton vehicles, we concluded that only 20 per cent of our customers would benefit from the increased weight allowance. These figures suggest that the benefit to the UK economy from the heavier truck is not as great as many lobbies would have us believe' (Thompson, 1979). A few months later, Thompson took the argument further by producing an analysis of the way productivity (work done per vehicle) had shifted during the period 1973–8, when the numbers of medium and small lorries had declined sharply, those of 24 to 28 tons increased from 12,800 to 34,000 and those above 28 increased from 44,800 to 94,000. It did not demonstrate a gain in efficiency.

When all lorries were lumped together, there was an appearance of progress, for the swing to heavier lorries meant that a somewhat smaller total fleet was recording a bigger total of tonne-kilometers. But when the performance of the big lorries was studied separately, the picture was hardly cheerful: in the 24–28-ton category, tonne-kilometres per lorry down by 20 per cent; in over-28 category, down 17½ per cent. Thompson said: 'The effective use of the heavier vehicles has quite significantly declined . . . This has some relevance when one looks at the case for the larger truck . . . There is a good deal of evidence to show that it is less easy to fully match the larger vehicles to the loads available' (Thompson, 1980).

His analysis was supported by a Road Research Laboratory study (Cundill and Shane, 1980) that showed a decline in the average load factor of the biggest lorries between 1967 and 1976 from 0.65 to 0.5, even though the amount of mileage run empty had been reduced slightly (to 32.8 per cent). The decline in efficiency was brought to Armitage's attention by Transport 2000, the pro-rail pressure group. It said: 'By 1978 the average load of 32-ton vehicles (average tonnes lifted per loaded journey) had fallen to 15.4 tonnes. This is less than the payload capacity of most 24-tonne vehicles, and suggests that at least half the goods moved in maximum-weight vehicles could be moved in lighter vehicles, at significantly lower cost.' The big vehicles, it added, were taking work from the middleweight ones, so they too were recording a productivity decline. It all tended to cast doubt over a remark the FTA made to Armitage: 'An operator would not send a 32.5-tonne lorry where a 16-tonne lorry would do.'

'Too many vehicles chasing too few goods,' said Jack Ashwell. Then should one not have fewer vehicles? By the autumn of 1980 a growing number of recession-hit hauliers were uttering a daring thought. According to George Newman, director-general of the Road Haulage Association, at its annual conference, they were urging a return to the pre-1968 principle of quantity licensing: official control of entry to the business. But the government would never consider it, he said. Instead, he called for 'a really effective and rigorously enforced quality licensing system' that would 'eliminate fringe operators'. Soon afterwards, the RHA asked the department to crack down on the easy issue of licences. Belatedly, it wanted the restraints that had been promised but never enforced after 1968.

I have quoted Sir Peter Baldwin as saying that the road/rail argument was mainly about 'fiddling about at the edges'. The Association of County Councils is one important body that does not agree. It told Armitage: 'Whilst recognising that the scope for the transfer of goods . . . to rail, to inland water-ways and coastal shipping, etc., is limited, we consider that the government should be recommended to examine the possibilities in even greater depth than up to now, and in particular should consider what might be achieved . . . by "transferring" some of the revenue from increased taxation of heavy goods vehicles to the alternative mode . . . The subject merits more detailed study than it has received so far.'

'Even greater depth' is rather kind to the transport depart-ment. It rang no bells about 'robust infrastructure' when the railways were being Beechinged. More recently it has recog-nised that vast highway investment 'facilitated the growth of road freight' but it has not hinted at an analogy for the railways. Old men in the department have grown up with the departmental truth that the railways were 'a problem'. They cost money. They were declining. No ambitious civil servant has wished to be saddled with them: from the fifties onwards, reputations were to be sought in promoting the transport infrastructure of the future. People from outside could easily be found to reinforce this view. Richard Beeching of ICI, called in to advise, recommended reducing rail's freight-carrying to little more than bulk trainloads convenient to big firms. When Clifford Sharp, a Leicester University economist, reported to the department in 1970 on a study it had com-missioned into how 125 West Midlands firms made their freight-shipping decisions, he volunteered a postscript challenging the assumption of Barbara Castle's 1967 White Paper that 'the maximum economic use of the railways' meant the transfer of traffic from the roads. He presented an alternative hypothesis: 'That the technology of carrying goods by rail has been replaced by the superior technologies of road haulage operation, and that the maximum economic use of rail should involve a slow run-down of rail services until they eventually are confined to the carriage of a few flows of bulk traffic from collieries to power stations or from iron ore mines to iron works (and also probably the carriage of commuter passenger traffic inside large cities and conurbations).'

The following year Sharp began work on a study for the RHA and FTA aimed at helping their campaign for heavier lorries. In his report, *Living With the Lorry* (1973), he concluded that the existing split between road and rail was economically sound and any shift to rail would bring an economic cost. By 1976, when everyone had had time to digest the implications of the 1973 oil crisis, he said in a letter to me: 'My own guess is that the mileage of line required in twenty years time may be very small indeed . . . The railways can no more be saved by good management today than could the gas-mantle industry after the development of electric bulbs or the stagecoach business after the building of railway lines.' If no substitute for oil were eventually found, 'the electrification of roads (overhead) seems to be the most feasible solution'. In Marsham Street this hardly seemed extreme. An economist there told me that the railways ought to be allowed to vanish altogether. What if oil scarcity made us want them again? 'Oh, one could preserve the right-of-way and perhaps bring them back into use.'

Such was the thinking to be found in the department when it produced its consultation document of 1976, *Transport Policy*. In a passage dismissing the rail advocates' hopes, there was a burst of emotion amid the civil-service prose: 'But what of the popular belief that a dramatic environmental gain would accrue if only we shifted a large amount of long-distance freight traffic from road to rail? Alas, it is a pipe-dream.' A biased statistical argument followed, evidently drawn from an old freight directorate file, for it had been presented almost word-for-word to an MPs' sub-committee in 1972: 'In the unlikely event of a 50 per cent increase in rail freight, this would reduce total road traffic by less than 2 per cent and goods traffic by under 8 per cent.' 'Total road traffic' is hardly relevant; nor is total goods traffic, but rather that carried in top-weight long-distance lorries. The White Paper of 1977 was no more encouraging. 'Most goods traffic has to start and finish its journey by road,' it said, which 'reduces the environmental benefits that might otherwise be gained by shifting much of the present road traffic to rail.' A substantial diversion of freight to rail was declared to be not 'a sensible long-term aim'.

A slight shift toward a less hostile attitude can be detected, however, in the 'background paper' produced by the department in 1979 for Armitage. It remains firm against quantity licensing, but it does concede that rail could be 'significant' (a favoured civil-service word): 'For many traffics, rail can be competitive over fairly long distances, such as 300 kms (187 miles) or more. This is not an insignificant area of competition with road freight, as journeys over 300 kms account for 23 per cent of road freight . . . and for 31 per cent of tonne-kilometres carried by lorries over twenty-eight tonnes gross weight.' And the 'over 200 km' market gave such lorries 54 per cent of their tonne-kilometres.

In Britain, lorries were doing a large amount of work that was elsewhere being done by freight trains. The average length of haul performed by such lorries was actually greater than that of freight trains (126 km against 119). An international comparison of total surface freight in 1978 showed that the share of tonne-kilometres carried by rail was: France, 46 per cent; West Germany 37 per cent; UK less than 20 per cent. Comparisons for *long-haul* freight as the figures on page 17 show, are even more telling.

British Rail, in its evidence to Armitage, gave the following breakdown of the British inland freight market (figures in thousand million tonne-km, 1978):

Small lorries	13	11%
Heavy lorries (over 16t gross)		
—on journeys under 200 km	49	38%
—on journeys over 200 km	37	28%
Rail	20	15%
Inland waterways and pipelines	10	8%

BR said that its main competitors were those lorries in the

third category. Armitage asked: How much additional freight could BR take on? BR said that at fairly short notice it could increase tonnes carried (not tonne-km) by about eight million or 5 per cent; with the help of productivity deals and new rolling-stock it could soon handle a further eight million; and given 'appropriate investment in rolling-stock, investment in improving track capacity at bottlenecks and an appropriate increase in train crew numbers, the present volume could be increased by around 50 per cent to 250 million tonnes'. The effect on lorry traffic would be striking. Even a shift of only half that amount, BR estimated, 'would reduce the total tonne-mileage . . . of long-distance heavy lorries by 35 per cent.'

However, so long as BR was required to operate within the 'constraints laid down by government' (severe investment limits and no operating subsidy for freight), it told Armitage, 'there is not likely to be any substantial transfer of traffic'. In fact BR has for many years had to follow a policy that pushed millions of tons of freight on to the roads. It was not only that it closed down thousands of goods depots and sidings. From the sixties onwards it has been phasing out what is known as wagonload traffic: the movement of smallish consignments which in the course of their journey are disconnected from one train and shunted in a marshalling yard to join another. With what almost seems to be a masochistic devotion, it has echoed the transport department in talking of concentrating on what it 'does best': handling freight in trainload quantities, preferably direct from one siding to another. It has obeyed the edict from on high, which was 'Stop handling freight that loses money.' It has failed to insist that what it also 'does best' is to move freight at a lower cost in fuel, road damage, congestion and environmental impact, and that it should get some financial credit for that. The transport department, having given BR its orders, artfully told Armitage that BR's 'own commercial policy' is to concentrate on profitable freight flows 'and shed traffic and resources that are no longer contributing to BR's overall financial return'.

Between 1968 and 1979 the rail tonnage carried by wagon-load was reduced from 68 per cent to 14 per cent of BR's total. The increase in trainload traffic was not nearly enough to make up for the loss: *total* tonnage fell from 210 million to 70 million. Trainload operation 'enables rail to perform at its best (and therefore at its most profitable)', an unprotesting BR board member, R. B. Reid, said in 1979—but at the end of the year he had to record a freight deficit of £9 million. In 1980, recession brought the tonnage down to 150 million—and the deficit up to £75 million.

One difficulty is that most of the bulk traffic suitable for trainload, such as coal, coke, iron, steel and minerals, earns less per ton. Road hauliers have been getting more and more of the high-revenue traffic in general goods. BR carries a much smaller share of agricultural products, foodstuffs, metal products and machinery than continental railways, and especially those of France and Germany. Until the rules change, BR will be able to do little to go after this business. 'For the foreseeable future a low-risk policy must be adopted for the carriage of new traffics,' it told Armitage. The contrast of policy was brought out in a BR study comparing its perform- ance with that of nine continental railways: 'Many other railways, whilst rationalising terminals, are concentrating marshalling activities at large new yards; for them, wagon- load traffic is still the most important element in the freight business' (British Rail, 1980). This is especially true of France and Germany, which are investing in remote-control wagon movement and other devices—while in 1980 BR's freight chief, Henry Sanderson, dismissed marshalling yards as 'Victorian in concept'.

It is hard for BR to do otherwise so long as unharassed, undertaxed lorries are its competitors and its state aid is kept small. The same BR study showed that investment in BR was the lowest in Europe; and a calculation of total system costs, including capital, not met by subsidy produced the following figures: Italy, 32 per cent; Belgium, 49.6; Finland 50.2; France, 55.3; Netherlands, 55.5; Norway, 59.6; Denmark and West Germany, 61; BR, 71.2. Only Sweden (83.1) was less subsidised. In productivity, BR was found to compare well in most ways. The exception was in the overmanning of freight trains. BR shared with Italy the distinction of using twice as many men to run freight trains as the others, which have largely abolished guards and a second man on the footplate. In 1980 BR achieved a long-delayed agreement with the rail unions to undertake a three-year programme of changes in manning and in working practices—for an additional problem has been an inflexibility imposed by time-hallowed rules. The phasing-out of marshalling yards adds to the tensions of the manning negotiations. BR's hope has been to persuade the men that if they helpfully change jobs, prosperity can lie ahead. It said in 1980 that it was transforming itself 'from an outdated hangover from Victorian times to a modern competitive transport system'.

BR hopes that what is lost in the wagonload phase-out will be more than made up in new business gained with a growing service called Speedlink, which sends modern airbraked wagons on 70 m.p.h. overnight scheduled services on a limited number of trunk routes. Sections of trains can be dropped or picked up en route, but marshalling yards are avoided. The system is ideal for a rail-linked plant such as Campbell Soups of King's Lynn, which ships by Speedlink to Glasgow. A development with great implications for the future is that independent haulage firms have begun to use Speedlink instead of their own lorries for trunk hauls, leaving lorries to do the local distribution at either end. The reason is simple: subsidised though the long-distance lorries are, rising costs have begun to make rail competitive. Members of the Road Haulage Association find that BR can help them to increase their profits.

One big haulier using Speedlink is William Cory, part of the international Ocean Cory transport group. In 1979 it opened a purpose-built railhead depot at Cardiff that was expected to remove more than 200,000 tonnes of freight a year from the roads. Cory was developing similar depots at Avonmouth, Barking, Rochester and near Glasgow, and planned eventually to have sixteen in all. 'We are able to provide a fast, efficient and cost-effective alternative to road transport,' said Ocean Cory's chief. Alan Maynard, William Cory's manager, told me: 'A lot of people regret having pulled out their sidings. On the continent they have so many more.' Now the difficulty was that many British factories had been built where they could not be rail-connected—'it's so hard to reverse the damage'.

Another Speedlink user is H. Young Transport of Eastleigh, near Southampton. Its managing director, Hamilton Young, was set thinking about rail by fuel worries and the reduction of lorry drivers' hours—and also by concern over excessive empty running. As he sees it, BR is good at operating trains and he is good at collecting shipments to put on them. One or more wagons leave his Eastleigh depot every afternoon and arrive at another H. Young depot beyond Glasgow eight hours later. Instead of setting up further depots of his own, his policy is to make what are known as groupage deals with other hauliers round the country, all using Speedlink for their long hauls. 'Too many hauliers are still reckoning their expansion in terms of buying more trucks,' he said in 1980. 'I think there has to be a limit sometime to the number of trucks put on the roads.' When I asked him why he thought Britain sent so much more freight by road, he said: 'It is too easy to become a road haulage operator in this country. Many hauliers, either through inefficiency or by deliberate means, work below cost. On the continent . . . their prices are pitched at a more realistic level.'

BR also hoped to capture new business with Freightliners, the container-carrying system that was to have been the heart of the 'integrated' freight transport that Barbara Castle had hoped to see. For ten years Freightliners was under the control not of BR but of NFC, the lorry conglomerate, which in theory was constantly thinking about getting freight on to rail. In 1979, when Freightliners was transferred by William Rodgers to BR, it carried only seven million tonnes, a fraction of what had been forecast. Its managing director, Cyril Bleasdale, talked in 1980 of a possible 50 per cent increase, or even more if he got extra money for new terminals and rolling-stock. The system is especially effective in taking containers straight off ships on to rail: in 1980 it was handling 42 per cent of all deep-sea containers entering and leaving Britain, and at Southampton the figure was 70 per cent. Bleasdale was quick to emphasise the environmental advantage. At Southampton, Poole, Harwich, Felixstowe, Ipswich, Liverpool and Greenock, 'the local communities are gaining because we can load containers direct on to rail,' he said, 'and then throughout the length of the rail haul three thousand or so containers a day are not travelling along trunk roads.' A restraint on Freightliners is that so long as it is limited to depots with expensive cranes it cannot offer an 'everywhere-to-everywhere' service. In 1980 progress was being made with much simpler equipment to lift containers lorry-train/train-lorry.

Even more important, for Freightliners and for BR as a whole, will be a shift in the operating costs of long-distance lorries to put BR in the fair competitive position that the department has so long promised. This is illustrated by a statement by BR to Armitage about the distance at which Freightliners can compete when collecting a container by lorry, putting it on a train and then delivering it: 'In the early sixties the break-even distance was calculated to be less than a hundred miles. That it has more than doubled in the following fifteen years is due to the advent of the 32-ton lorry, accentuated by its inadequate contribution to road-track costs and the growth of the motorway network.' BR calculated that less wasteful manning, together with rising costs for hauliers, could bring the break-even distance down again in the next few years. If there were proper taxation of the lorries as well, it could become strongly competitive. BR told Armitage that road competition 'is the major price determinant' for much of its freight business: 'Hence the board's concern that the heavy vehicle should be seen to be paying its full cost.' Its juggernaut competitors, it said, were being cross-subsidised not only by smaller lorries but also by those doing small mileages, such as Freightliners' 600 collection-and-delivery lorries. However, as it wanted Freightliners' vehicles to be capable of handling any containers going, BR did not oppose a lorry weight increase. 'But we want to live in a world of fair competition,' Henry Sanderson told Armitage. As well as full track costs, BR wanted all lorries to cover accident and environmental costs, and with a mileage-related levy.

Some investments that would increase the freight-winning potential of BR, it told Armitage, would be in terminal facilities for Freightliners and other traffic, new rail ferries to the continent, and the Channel tunnel (this may not need government money). It also wanted more generous grants under Section 8 of the 1974 Transport Act, which allows the transport department to pay private firms half the cost of rail sidings and related equipment if the environmental benefit of taking their freight off the roads is thought to justify it. In the five years 1975–9 seventy-eight of these grants were made, totalling £21 million, with a potential of transferring sixteen million tons a year to rail. How many were refused it is impossible to say. In 1978, however, there was the instructive case of the refusal of 50 per cent grants to the Nypro chemical firm at Flixborough, to ICI on Teesside and to Shell Chemicals on Merseyside that would have enabled dangerous phenol to be delivered to Nypro in two trainloads a week instead of in sixty road tankers. The department's chief reason for refusal was that the tankers would travel most of the way by motorways, which, unlike ordinary roads, are officially not 'sensitive'. However, the briefing put in front of Rodgers's junior minister, John Horam, was evidently misleading in one important respect. Horam wrote to an inquiring MP that phenol did not give off toxic fumes but 'contact with the skin will cause burns'. This mild picture hardly tallied with the chemical handbook used by fire officers: it says phenol fumes can cause severe and possibly fatal damage to the nervous system, lungs, kidneys, liver, pancreas and spleen; and a splash of phenol on the skin measuring only eight inches by eight inches has killed a man. Publicity about the case did serve one purpose. It drew to the ministers' attention that the making of these grants had all along, by administrative edict, been in the hands of the lorry-cosseting freight directorate. It was switched to the railway directorate. Grant-making rose sharply.

One further investment much wanted by BR is an extension of its present small mileage of electrified line. To Armitage, BR presented a double fuel argument. In long-distance haulage, rail's fuel advantage over road already ranges from 2:1 up to 3.5:1; and 'rail is the only transport mode that could readily abandon oil as a fuel on a large scale'. In 1980 BR was waiting to hear whether Marsham Street would approve a large electrification programme.

When Alan Maynard of William Cory deplores the fact that so many factories established in the motorway age are not rail-linked, it is remarkable only because he is a lorry operator. What is also remarkable is that over the years BR seems to have made no fuss about getting factories sited where sidings could be put in. This certainly puzzles the continentals. An official of French Railways told me: 'In each town our *chef d'agence* keeps his ear to the ground. As soon as we know someone is going to build a factory, we make contact.' He was grieved that when New Covent Garden market was established south of the Thames on an old railway site, it was not made rail-connected. Trainloads of produce could have come in, he said, from Spain and Italy as well as France. In West Germany, every town has an incentive to see that factories are rail-linked, for the towns pay for the main link to the railway system. The German rail freight manager in London, Hartmut

Gasser, has many examples of freight flows he could have sent to Britain via the rail ferries if only there had been a siding at the destination. In Germany, Volkswagen moves everything by rail; when it established a big depot at Milton Keynes it wanted to send eight wagonloads a day there; but the development corporation did not give it a site near the railway. Then there is the case of the Vauxhall and Opel factories (both General Motors) at Luton and Risselsheim: twenty lorry-loads of components go back and forth every day because neither Vauxhall nor British Rail was concerned to do it differently. 'British Rail is not geared to ensuring that rail is used,' Gasser says.

The point was put to Armitage a number of times. Transport 2000 said: 'We ask the inquiry to recommend that use of rail or water facilities should be a condition of granting planning permission in the case of major freight generators.' The extent of the problem was shown in some detail in one of the studies made in West Yorkshire in 1977 by the consultants Martin & Vorhees. Of 450 large companies, they reported, fewer than a quarter had a rail siding or were sited where they could have one. Installation of a siding would have been commercially sound, they thought, in only thirty-three cases. A frequent counter-argument was the absence of rail links at a company's freight destinations.

Concerted action to establish far more railheads for long-haul traffic was advocated in 1980 by the Association of Metropolitan Authorities, which represents seventy-seven conurbations, cities and large towns. After a 2½-year study, it proposed a number of measures to 'exploit the potential offered by the rail network'. For example, 'a more positive approach' by the transport department, especially in approving Section 8 grants; joint development by planning authorities and British Rail of rail-linked industrial sites, perhaps with a policy of 'rail for all new bulk traffic'; a similar joint development of freight terminuses and interchanges to replace city-centre depots dating from Victorian times.

The association won a clear statement from the transport department that local authorities were themselves eligible for Section 8 grants—for an industrial estate, for example, or a municipally-backed freight depot. The association urged the department to abandon its rule that if a company appeared likely to install a siding without the help of a grant, it did not qualify for one. One odd effect of this rule has been that a grant is refused 'if planning permission has already been made conditional on the use of rail transport' (as the department itself told Armitage).

The Road Haulage Association and Freight Transport Association had taken part in the study but they rejected its conclusions—'well-meaning but a bit out of touch with the reality', said the FTA.

The reality, in the eyes of the lorry lobby and the department, was that the extreme road-dependence that had been imposed over the years was itself an argument against change. The department said to Armitage: 'It is sometimes argued that the amount of freight transport should be reduced and that the government should seek to reduce it.' 'Sometimes argued' was oddly diffident, only two years after William Rodgers's White Paper had said: 'We should aim to decrease our absolute dependence on transport.' The department told Armitage that any significant reduction would require 'a considerable change in the organisation of industry, which now uses extensive, quick and reliable transport as an integral part of its production, distribution and marketing processes'. There was, of course, no hint of such a thought as, 'We may have got the balance wrong.' The department's numerous economists have had a good deal of power when justifying the trimming of the railways or the building of 'strategic' roads, but they seem to have drawn no attention to a proposition that has long been familiar to economists in the world at large. In the words of the transport economist Kenneth Gwilliam: 'If prices in the transport sector are maintained at an artificially low level for a long period of time, there will be a tendency for industrial location to take place without regard for the true transport costs . . . and the demand for transport may therefore increase in physical terms' (Gwilliam and Mackie, 1975).

The FTA told Armitage, misleadingly, that freight 'is not self-generating'. The growth arose from 'the aspirations of a consumer-based society . . . Washing machines, refrigerators and television sets are just the tip of an iceberg which embraces [sic] an enormous growth in the range and quality of goods which the average man and his family expect to be able to buy . . . Without the lorry it would not have been possible.' The FTA's view of the trend to fewer, larger production units is equally benign: 'More freight movement, and greater expenditure on freight, has been the price of achieving greater overall economies in the total industrial process.' There has also been 'an increasing awareness of the cost of holding stock'. Supermarkets give nearly all their space to selling, not stockholding: 'This has meant that weekly deliveries have become daily deliveries, and in some of the bigger town-centre shops, daily deliveries have become hourly deliveries.' And here is one reason for more lorries on country roads: 'Animal feed storage has now moved away from its traditional port mills location (invariably rail-linked) where often there was space for two to three months' supply. Storage is now spread out in rural areas . . . carrying no more than one week's supply and relying totally on road vehicles.'

Between factory and shop, hauliers and big regional depots provide what the trade calls 'a mobile warehousing system'. Goods not in motion are seen as money locked up. In 1977, Unilever estimated that if the goods in its entire UK distribution network were tied up for one extra day that would cost £4 million.

The necessary role of lorries in getting supplies to shops provides excellent material for their advocates. This is especially true of food shops. Sainsbury's distribution chief, Len Payne (FTA's president in 1980), is fond of telling how pigs killed one day appear on his shelves next morning as pork, which if unsold is speedily transported away. He puts less emphasis on the fact that the lorries used for town deliveries to his and other supermarkets have been getting bigger. An appendix to FTA's evidence says that 'with the development of newer, larger stores . . . together with the ever-increasing evidence that larger vehicles were more economic'. Sainsbury switched to 24-ton lorries up to forty-two feet long; and other chains even go to the maximum. The side-effects are not only environmental. The 'mobile warehouse' method is good for cash flow and cost-cutting, but it kills smaller shops. The FTA said: 'Even Tesco announced at the end of 1977 that they were to close two hundred of their seven hundred stores because they were too small to be viable within Tesco's particular marketing framework. Similarly, Sainsbury's are closing twenty-four stores.' For many shoppers, this increases their absolute need for transport.

The use of top-size delivery lorries is encouraged by

suppliers' quantity discounts. The best discount goes to a capacity load for a 32-tonner: 20 or 21 tons. What would happen if lorry weights went up? Armitage was told by the Confederation of British Industry: 'We would educate our customers to order in multiples of the higher payload.' The FTA said: 'Increasingly, the largest vehicles will be used to provide a timed, one-stop consolidated delivery.'

In its evidence the FTA put the best face on the industrial shifts that have increased ton-mileage. Car component plants were 'spread to the four corners of the British Isles' as a result of regional development policies. 'Transport, frequently the lorry, links the parts together, like an extended conveyor belt' (why rail is not usually the conveyor belt is not gone into). Hoover's washing-machine factory in South Wales 'typifies transport's role in bringing jobs to the people'. That it can also take away their jobs was of course not mentioned. The FTA was as singleminded as the transport department highway-builders in ignoring a point made by Sir George Leitch's advisory committee on trunk road assessment: 'A reduction in transport cost to a depressed area may make it easier to supply other areas from the area in question, but at the same time it will make it easier to supply that area from elsewhere . . . Improved communications may do more harm than good' (Leitch et al, 1977). The effect was noted by the Scottish Association for Public Transport in its submission to Armitage. It said factories and warehouses 'are now usually centralised in the major urban markets of the south, so that distant areas including many parts of Scotland have a less frequent or dearer service than before'.

Precise instances were provided by the Road Research Laboratory study quoted earlier (Corcoran, Hitchcock and McMahon, 1980). 'Brewing is an example *par excellence* of an industry which has undergone a major upheaval . . . Between 1967 and 1977, whilst consumption increased by 31 per cent, the number of breweries declined by 41 per cent. In the period since 1973 . . . the length of haul increased by nearly one-third.' This was with a product with 'relatively high transport costs'; and here was another: 'The market for bricks has become dominated by one Midland-based company which now sells bricks even as far as Scotland . . . Local bricks produced on a smaller scale are priced out of the market except for specialised uses.' This is not bringing jobs to the people who worked in small brickworks or in old inner-city breweries. In the late sixties, Whitbread decided to phase out brewing at the London site where its fame began in 1742 and establish a vast brewery—where? Up the M1 at Luton, whence it has since been supplying London by means of juggernauts. A study done by Greater London Council officers in 1975 showed that the delivery cost to Londoners of beer from the city's remaining breweries was £8 a ton, but from the outflung, economy-of-scale brewery it was £12. If the cost of transport should double, it was calculated then, it would add 2½p to the price of a pint. However, when the time comes that transport costs outweigh economies of scale (not to mention the effect of many drinkers' resistance to the mass product), the robust infrastructure of Whitbread and other breweries will be costly to change. The cheap-transport era, though a delight to lorry men, seems likely to have awkward and costly after-effects.

When the top-weight lorries finish their speedy and profitable runs down the motorways and reach towns and cities, a few of them drop their loads at peripheral depots, from which the urban distribution is done by smaller vehicles, but this happens far more on the continent than in Britain. For most operators, the long-haul convenience easily outweighs the last few miles of congestion, and of course they do not pay for the nuisance and pain they impose on the town-dwellers. Years ago demands began to be made for municipally-sponsored transhipment depots to ensure more efficient, less obtrusive town deliveries. In 1972 the environment depart-ment announced 'a major programme of research' that would 'throw light not only on the implication of changes in transport methods (including such matters as traffic restric-tions, out-of-hours deliveries, transhipment and consolida-tion of loads) but also on the siting and planning of traffic generators (warehousing complexes, shopping areas, haulage depots, etc.)'. In 1976 the department spoke in its consultation document of the 'pressing need' to study such things, and said an 'independent' Lorries and Environment Committee was working on what was by now called transhipment. 'Indepen-dent' merely meant it was outside the department. The committee was chaired by Dan Pettit, then chairman of the National Freight Corporation; and aside from a few county

officials, chiefly engineers, it was made up of FTA and RHA
officials and representatives of big haulage firms. The department promised that when it had the committee's report it
would 'develop a new initiative in this field'. However, big
freight-movers did not want to lose their freedom to take big
lorries in and out of towns whenever it suited them. The report
was decisive only in its lack of enthusiasm. A telling comment
on the committee came at the 1979 FTA conference from Alan
West, the United Biscuits distribution chief who was quoted
on the Dykes Act in Chapter 6. He said transhipment depots
were an absurd notion that soon died, and the committee had
'put the last nail in the coffin'.

The FTA was equally dismissive in its evidence to Armitage:
the idea of communal transhipment centres was 'superficially
attractive on amenity grounds' but 'did not stand up to detailed
examination'. The transport department was scarcely more
encouraging. In the civil service way, it used words with
which it is hard to come to grips: transhipment depots were
'unlikely' to be self-financing, any advantages to lorry operators were 'likely to be outweighed' by disadvantages to
consigners, and benefits to the environment 'cannot be
guaranteed'. Its conclusion was that such depots could be
justified only 'where the removal of large lorries from an area
takes precedence over all other considerations'.

Armitage tried the department with further questions.
What was its policy 'on the desirability of the heaviest current
lorries being used in wide-scale distribution, particularly
within urban areas'? What role did it think central and local
government should play in the provision of depots? The
department avoided committing itself to any role at all. After
some irrelevancies about the Construction and Use Regulations, it said that if heavy lorries caused problems, 'it is for the
local authority concerned to consider action'. It had 'tended to
regard consolidation and transhipment depots as being essentially similar to warehousing facilities' which were provided
commercially, and warehousing 'has not given rise to any
suggestions for government intervention' (a clever example of
a logical leap there for learner-bureaucrats). Still, a local
authority 'would no doubt be able to take more active
steps . . . if it wished'. So there you are: our policy is that it is
nothing to do with us.

The FTA and the department supported their line by

quoting studies done at Chichester, Swindon and Hull, chiefly by the Road Research Laboratory, which suggested that costs would be high in relation to benefits. However, an apparent flaw in these studies has been pointed out by Stephen Plowden, who as a transport specialist with the Metra Consulting Group has done a good deal of work in this field. He says: 'The studies conducted so far have assumed that the town's delivery system would represent an *additional* link in the user's existing chain of distribution. It could instead *replace* part of that chain; instead of a manufacturer sending vehicles from his own depot to the town's depot, he could sent them there straight from his factory' (Plowden, 1980). Plowden outlines a number of ways in which a transhipment depot could benefit the distribution process as well as the public, and says there are signs that the official studies 'are being used . . . to discredit the idea of local distribution'. In particular he challenges the conclusion of the Swindon study that if the town banned all lorries over three tons unladen from its centre and had a transhipment depot, few distributors would use it unless it were heavily subsidised. His analysis need not be repeated here. It is sufficient to quote his conclusion that if towns compelled the use of small distribution vehicles (putting rail, incidentally, on a similar footing to road) there would be a 'much greater potential for savings, in both internal and external costs' than the official studies suggest. He has doubts, however, about depots run or subsidised by local authorities: 'The best course . . . is to prohibit or penalise the behaviour which causes external costs and then to leave it to freight operators themselves, who are justly proud of their flexibility, to provide suitable alternatives as a normal commercial venture.' The brutal externalities of the unfettered market would be modified by means of regulations. As a first step Plowden urges something that seems far from the transport department's mind—actual trials instead of desk studies, and financed partly by the department. 'The obvious towns to choose,' he says, 'are the medium-sized historic towns which still serve as regional centres, especially for shopping: for example, Norwich, York, Windsor, Bath, Shrewsbury, Chester.'

The department has shown no sign of ardently pursuing knowledge about the measures taken in other countries. It is aware that examples are available. Although the conclusion

of the Lorries and Environment Committee in 1976 was that
'comprehensive transhipment and consolidation is only likely
to be worth considering in very exceptional circumstances',
its report nevertheless recorded some 'relevant foreign experience'. Paris controlled lorries within a 27-square-mile central
area and had two big transhipment complexes, Sogaris on the
southern outskirts and Garonor in the north. In Holland it was
'relatively common' to have transhipment centres run co-
operatively by hauliers. Tokyo had several peripheral depots
and planned more, 'and restrictions on vehicles over 7½ tons
carrying capacity in the peak periods might be expected to
encourage use'.

Four years on, when the department offered Armitage what
it knew, it had little to add. Sogaris and Garonor were running
at a profit, and Garonor had a customs depot, bonded
warehouses, a return-load booking bureau and other facilities
for operators. But the department did not even trouble to state
the lorry size limits in force in Paris's central 'zone verte':
vehicles with surface area of 10 to 16 square metres (up to
about 21 ft long), banned 2 p.m.–8.30 p.m.; of 16 to 22.5
square metres (about 29½ ft), banned 9 a.m.–9.30 p.m. And
lorries above that size are banned from *all* Paris, 9 a.m.–8.30
p.m. The effect has been that shippers either use the transhipment depots or run direct with smaller lorries. As for Holland,
the department's report repeats that transhipment centres are
'relatively common' and adds that some are subsidised by
local authorities. If the department had inquired of the Dutch
equivalent of the FTA it would have been able to add that the
Netherlands has a national policy for 'diminishing the growth
of mobility'; that towns are imposing more and more lorry
restrictions; that many have a width limit a foot narrower than
the international maximum, thereby barring long-distance
lorries; that there are also length restrictions and, in sensitive
areas, 12-tonne gross weight limits; and that night bans on
lorries are spreading. The department's information on Sweden
came at third hand, but at least it makes clear that central
freight policy can affect what happens: 'The Swedish system
. . . divides traffic into long- and short-haul, and therefore
encourages the creation of freight interchange terminals.' On
Japan, the department said it was seeking up-to-date information; meanwhile it passed on, in four sentences, what a road
research man had learned in Tokyo in 1974, and its only

reference to lorry limits was indirect: 'Large loads were still being delivered at night, when less stringent controls were in force.' (Nowhere in its evidence did the department mention a restraint almost universal on the continent but untried in the UK: a ban on lorry movement at weekends and on public holidays.)

The department proved remarkably incurious even about what was happening in Britain. 'Garonor and British Rail are believed to be considering setting up a [freight] complex at Stourton, near Leeds,' it said, 'but the department has no further information about this.' A telephone call to Yorkshire, or to the London office of Garonor Developments, would have informed it that Garonor and BR were starting work in July 1980 on a forty-acre road/rail complex at Stourton; that another was planned at Bristol; and that BR hoped others would follow—all served by its Speedlink trains.

Could London itself not be inspired by Paris or Tokyo? In 1976 the Greater London Council studied the possibility of establishing about ten freight complexes in outer London. Besides providing warehousing, return-load booking and various other services for which hauliers would have been willing to pay, they would also have permitted transhipment for rational London distribution. Aware of the trade's reluctance, the GLC controller of planning and transportation said warily that the complexes would 'provide operators with the opportunity to adopt a flexible attitude to changing requirements, including controls . . . on heavy vehicle movements' and 'provide opportunities for increased rail use'. The first two sites considered, at Neasden and Brentford, were rail-linked. The GLC intended the Neasden depot at least to be operating before 1980; but by 1980 nothing had been achieved. It has already been made clear that lorry controls are needed to concentrate operators' minds on adopting new methods. However, in the late seventies under Conservative control the GLC policy on traffic restraint, whether of cars or lorries, moved from caution to outright hostility. In 1979 a GLC report accepted lorry operators' claims that an inner London ban on vehicles over 16 tons would add £150 million a year to their costs and would drive industry out of London. The report also produced a great many other negative arguments—for example, that such a ban would greatly increase traffic—but ignored all the possibilities of greater efficiency.

Others do not accept the operators' objections so un-critically. At a Paris conference on traffic restraints, Professor M. E. Beesley of the London Graduate School of Business Studies, who is far from being an anti-lorry man, spoke of the 'relatively mild limits' imposed on lorries in the UK. He said that the FTA had exaggerated the costs, and he suggested that the government and local authorities had been too ready to accept its calculations. An economist at the Local Government Operational Research Unit, Philip Blake, said in a submission to Armitage that hauliers claimed that restraints added intolerably to costs, 'yet precise figures to substantiate these claims are rarely, if ever, produced. The complaining resident is often told that without juggernauts he could afford to buy even less than he can now, but rarely do hauliers tell him how much the price of the juggernaut-transported goods would be affected.' Blake concluded that lorry restraint was likely to be 'extremely useful . . . at low cost to consumers'.

It is worth noting what happened in 1978 when John Horam, the junior transport minister, told the freight director-ate that he wanted outside consultants to be engaged to do a full appraisal of transhipment depots. First the civil servants objected that the exercise that became the Armitage inquiry was on the way, so the depot study could be included in that. Horam, backed by Rodgers, insisted on a separate study. The civil servants sidestepped: Let the department do it in conjunction with the Road Research Laboratory. No, said Horam: an outside inquiry. Then the civil servants moved very slowly, knowing an election was coming; and by the time Labour went out of office they had arranged nothing.

The advocates of still heavier lorries have not proposed that if given what they wanted they would in return accept stiffer controls. The FTA would certainly fight any such idea. Indeed, it has argued that lorries of 40 tons and more could actually be less unpleasant. Here is what it told Armitage:

'Heavier lorries do not mean bigger lorries.

'Environmentally the heavier lorry could pave the way for many vehicle design improvements, in particular reduced noise and road damage.

'There are no grounds for thinking that heavier lorries will not be as safe as existing ones—quite the opposite.'

The first of these statements is, at best, misleading. A lorry of 40 or 44 tonnes could indeed be built within the British 15-metre (49 ft 2½ in) limit; but the proposal is that the length should go up to 15½ metres—nearly 20 inches longer. As Chapter 3 showed, many British operators have been so eager for the extra length that they have been using it illegally (so in one sense the FTA is right).

The second statement looks puzzling, The FTA's contention is that with extra profitability, the industry could afford to develop better vehicles. This amounts to a confession that the economics of road transport have depended hitherto on cut-price vehicles. In any case, the FTA has also said, soothingly, that there would not be many of the bigger vehicles; if so, how much could they do to improve design?

The 'quite the opposite' statement seems audacious in view of the braking and stability problems revealed in Chapter 4. If the FTA's meaning is that improved technology in the heavier lorries (load-sensing and anti-jack-knife devices) would make them safer, the same technology could make lesser vehicles safer still.

I have already mentioned the FTA claim that a 40-tonne lorry would bring a 5 per cent fuel saving. Its calculation is that, if fully laden, it would carry a 27.1-tonne payload, 26 per cent more than a 32-tonner, but would use only 20 per cent more diesel. However, the FTA did not hint to Armitage what would happen if (as expected by NFC's Peter Thompson and others) the 40-tonner had a poorer load factor. It has a greedier engine and has more of its own weight to haul. The FTA's own figures show that if it came short if its maximum by less than two tonnes it would be using *more* fuel per tonne-mile.

These calculations all apply to lorries doing trunk-haulage of 1,500 miles a week. As soon as a big lorry becomes involved for much of its time in stop-and-go urban running, the operational advantage of having a single driver move a bigger payload is undermined—and this is still more marked with even bigger vehicles.

What operational savings might the EEC lorries offer overall? The suggestion of nearly £150 million a year (1980) prices) quoted on page 148 is based on the assumptions that after five years or so heavier lorries would replace two-thirds of the 32-tonners, and would run fully-loaded. The report (Corcoran, Glover, Shane, 1980) shows that the savings might be only about £55 million; less than could be achieved now with more efficient operation.

Where the heavier lorries would give certain operators a distinct bonus is on long-distance work up and down the motorways with contractual maximum loads and with containers. Here their advocates appear to be on challengeable ground in a different way. This is the type of road operation, doing a similar job to rail, which has already been taken to excess in Britain compared to other countries. By 1980, rising costs and reduced drivers' hours had begun to tilt the odds back a little in favour of rail, as the decisions of such firms as William Cory and H. Young indicate. Operators are on record as saying that they see higher maximum weights as their hope of regaining their old advantage. The transport department went so far as to say to Armitage that heavier lorries 'could be expected to generate some increased traffic and divert some traffics from the railways'. Past experience supports this forecast; for example, the shift in Freightliner competitiveness in the seventies that was mentioned earlier. An increase to 40 tonnes would allow a lorry to carry a 30 ft container loaded to a full weight of 25.4 tonnes, which otherwise must go by rail in Britain or be eased of a few tonnes. And a 44-tonner would carry a fully-laden 40 ft container weighing almost as much as as entire old-fashioned British juggernaut. BR's hoped-for expansion of container traffic could not help being harmed. The same applies to its hopes for Speedlink's capture of general merchandise trade.

Although the transport department allowed itself to mention diversion of traffic from rail, it would have been too much to expect it to present some research on the question, or to urge Armitage to pursue the point. West Germany's transport department would have done so. Being pro-rail, it takes the view that any cost-benefit calculation on heavier lorries 'would have to include the effects on other modes of transport'.

A number of opponents of the lorry lobby did, however, ask Armitage to accept that increased maximum payloads would not reduce the number of juggernauts. Once again, the Association of County Councils spoke in tune with the environmentalists: 'One of the superficially attractive arguments favouring larger lorries is that the same volume of goods will be carried by fewer vehicles . . . However, pressure for larger lorries comes essentially from those who see economic benefits, in the form of reduced transport costs. The consequence of reduced transport costs is to generate trip-making, increase journey lengths and cause social and economic changes that result in more traffic, a growth in commerical vehicles and increased energy consumption.'

The question was whether public pressures could bring about the necessary change of mind in Marsham Street. The Civic Trust said: 'Somehow a fairer balance of pressures than at present must be allowed to operate at central government level. If central government took on the task of anticipating the environmental effects of policies and developments that influence the movement of freight, and of proposing policies that reduce road freight movement, then environmental interests would have a point of access.'

Would Armitage do anything to help open the way? How would he respond to all the evidence that was at odds with the departmental view? He produced his answer in December 1980.

9

The answer they wanted

In the transport department's view, it will be remembered, the only reason for holding an inquiry was 'presentational': to help the department to persuade Parliament and public to accept heavier lorries. The leaking of Joseph Peeler's candid memorandum prevented the department from excluding sensitive environmental questions from consideration; yet in the event there was no danger 'that the main issue will be lost sight of', as Peeler had feared, or that 'the wrong answer' might emerge. He rather underrated the department's power to keep a grip on things.

If an inquiry into 'the impact of the lorry on people and their environment' had been entrusted to the usual full committee, 'people' and 'environment' would have had to be represented directly by at least two members, who would have been likely to jib at a partial report—and perhaps issue a minority one. By giving the task to one man, aided by four assessors, the department avoided any such unpleasantness. Then there was the power of evidence. Nearly every paper the department conveyed to Sir Arthur Armitage during his fifteen-month inquiry was tailored to favour the weight increase. And on nearly every point, Armitage followed the department in preference to sceptical or dissident submissions (1,800 of them) from the outside world. In deciding what he should take note of, and in writing his report, Armitage was closely helped by the inquiry secretary, a civil servant who, being from the department itself, well knew what thoughts would not be frowned on. As soon as the report was published, the secretary, Philip Wood, was given promotion.

Armitage came close to approving every detail of the EEC's harmonisation package, 11½-tonne axles and all. In recommending lorries of up to 44 tonnes, he proposed axle modifications only because the department told him that the burden on bridges would otherwise be too great. His report finds almost nothing to say against the weight increase as such; indeed, he says it would 'help' the environment. To assess the report in some detail is a necessary public act: first because its faults so directly reflect the views of the as yet unreformed department, and secondly because the report, with its gestures of environmental goodheartedness, might otherwise beguile some people into accepting it as a reasoned statement of what needs to be done.

At first sight the report raises hopes. Its three central chapters are headed 'Reducing lorry traffic; Getting lorries away from people; Improving the lorry'. This was presentationally so promising that, at first, criticism of the report was largely directed against Armitage's refusal to say that a weight increase ought to be conditional on the improvements of which he spoke. Environmental groups sent Armitage a joint protest: 'We are appalled that this recommendation was not conditional upon a prior humanisation of the heavy lorry as set out in your other recommendations . . . Your report is an open invitation to the minister to raise lorry weights while the ameliorative measures you propose may be relegated to some future time.' Closer study of those three chapters showed two of the headings to be correct only if preceded by 'Not'; and the third to be a label for a small package, already overdue, to be delivered at some uncertain date.

Armitage-cum-Wood, to be described henceforth for simplicity's sake as Armitage, is a great deviser of foggy phrases. He asks, as he had to, whether the problems created by lorries are getting worse. 'It is particularly difficult to determine . . . Subjectively they seem to be getting worse.' But then he notes the fast growth in mileage run by four-axle articulated lorries (up 42 per cent overall, and 28 per cent in built-up areas, 1973–9) and says: 'These are we believe environmentally worse than other lorries.' In many places 'the problem is insupportable. There must be improvement.' However, he has to face further troubling statistics from the department: by 1990, unless freight policy changes, the mileage of lorries over 25 tonnes (four-axle, chiefly artics) will increase by between 39 and 53 per cent, depending on whether gross domestic product rises annually by 1 per cent or 2; and by the year 2000 perhaps by 71 per cent. On the average road in the year 2000, *45 lorries in 100* would be over 25 tonnes. Improvement, then? 'There will be many places where conditions will become seriously worse'— places already suffering badly, and others that 'may not suffer unduly' at present.

So Armitage makes what seems a decisive statement: 'The public interest requires us to maintain and develop the economic benefits which heavy lorries have given us and at the same time to reduce the adverse effects which they have at present . . . We do not believe that it would be sufficient to aim to reduce the impact of lorries . . . compared to what it might otherwise have been. That would be a reduction only in a special and misleading sense. There must be an absolute reduction.'

Now here is a dilemma. How to develop the economic benefits *and* reduce the impact? Five paragraphs later there is a further declaration of policy: 'the demands of individuals and firms' should decide economic activity 'except where there are clear reasons for intervention in the public interest'. Good; but read on: 'In the case of lorries the market will best determine the proper level of demand because through it the economic costs and benefits of lorries will be brought home to those taking direct and indirect decisions about transport. If as a result lorries impose costs or nuisances on others which society is unwilling to accept, those costs and nuisances should ideally be dealt with separately and directly.' This surprising assertion of faith in the beneficent power of 'the market' leaves Armitage in a logical tangle. He himself half-concedes (though only about 14,000 words later on) that the costs imposed on others by lorry operators are not 'brought home' to them or their customers: there is 'some force', he says, in the argument that hauliers 'have no interest in reducing environmental effects and every interest in maximising their financial return'. Their externalising of costs has helped to stimulate the growth in demand which Armitage has just declared is causing suffering that must be absolutely reduced. Yet now his upholding of 'the market' brings him to the conclusion that the government should not 'set out deliberately to determine or influence the amount of lorry traffic'. So he rejects quantity licensing, the method used by other countries to limit long-distance lorry numbers.

What then can be done?

'One of the most effective ways' of reducing lorry impact,
Armitage says, is to build more roads. Already, he asserts,
roadbuilding 'has brought very large environmental gains'.
How? By allowing 'a big switch by lorries to more suitable
roads'—which ignores the growth of heavy lorry traffic in
towns and through villages. Armitage concedes that environmentalists 'believe' that more roads will encourage the use of
lorries; but what he believes is that the slowdown in roadbuilding (to a mere £800 million in 1980-81) 'has been
shortsighted and should be reversed'. Public intervention has
now become praiseworthy: 'Capital expenditure on roads
shows a high economic as well as environmental return, and
creates a permanent asset . . . Roads are after all as much a
part of the country's productive equipment as our factories
and machinery.' The same could be said of the railways; but
when he comes to them he does not say it. What he wants is
enough money for both the 'major industrial routes' to which
the department is committed and a big increase in bypasses
(the benefits of urban roadbuilding 'are less clear').

　　Any kind of national lorry routing, specifying categories of
road which lorries over a certain size either should use or
should not use, is rejected by Armitage. He thus goes further
even the the Road Haulage Association, which told Norman
Fowler a fortnight before Armitage reported that there was
no reason why heavier lorries 'should not be allowed on
Britain's major roads'. Armitage says: 'If diversion costs were
to be kept within bounds there would be few if any environmental benefits.' In other words, any extensive 'getting lorries
away from people' is too much to ask. That leaves piecemeal
local bans. He wants them to be better enforced but he does
not want any more of them. He is cool about further large-
scale schemes such as the Windsor Cordon, and he wants the
diversion costs of bans to be officially emphasised to local
authorities, as they 'do not pay the extra costs they impose'
(which is of course equally true of costs imposed by hauliers).

　　As for transhipment depots or other facilities to reduce the
number of big lorries in towns, Armitage is against any
initiative by national or local government. He follows a series
of contradictory arguments with the statement that heavy
lorries can best be kept out of 'sensitive places' by imposing
weight restrictions and letting hauliers decide how to cope.
This ignores two points: that nearly all weight restrictions are

'except for access', and that the creation of peripheral depots would make it harder for lorry operators to combat proposed restrictions as unworkable or too costly.

Armitage does recommend stricter rules for lorry operators' own depots, to enable licensing authorities to take environmental matters into account; but this is merely one of the many proposals of the Foster report so long ignored by the department. Lorries parked in residential streets are wrong, Armitage says, but what he proposes is hardly severe: the operators' organisations should advise their members that 'their drivers should not take lorries home with them'.

There seems, then, little hope of getting lorries away from people. What of 'improving the lorry'?

Armitage's comment on the fact that lorries have a high involvement rate in fatal accidents is typical of his cosmetic style: 'So lorries can be regarded as more dangerous when they are involved in accidents.' He wants them to be made 'even safer'. He recommends action that ought to have been taken years ago: a reduction of braking distances and the fitting of under-run guards all round. But although anti-locking systems to prevent jack-knifing are used by petrol and chemical companies 'conscious of their reputations', he accepts the department's refusal to make them compulsory. They should be 'kept under serious review'.

'Spray can be frightening', he says, but approves the department's insistence on more research and even questions whether an effective system would be worth fitting, 'because we do not know how many accidents are caused by spray'. He rejects the idea that on motorways during rain lorries should have a special low speed limit. (His only recommendation on speed is for the legalisation of 50 m.p.h. for lorries on fast dual carriageways.)

People upset by lorry noise, Armitage implies, are more sensitive than he is: it 'can sometimes be overwhelming'; it is 'felt to be an important problem'. Though noting the existence of the British prototype quiet lorry, he dashes hopes of an eighty-decibel limit by 1985. 'It has been suggested to us,' he says (by whom?), 'that it may take as long as until 1990 to get agreement, with implementation in 1995.' He would move more speedily. 'Noise is probably the most important specific nuisance created by lorries', so he wants eighty-decibel lorries to begin coming on the road by—when? 'Not later than 1990.'

As for the idea of annual tests to see that lorries at least meet the easy standards now laid down, he calls this 'secondary in importance to reducing the noise of lorries as constructed' (secondary, that is, to something he has just said may not begin to happen until ten years after the time of writing). Besides, there is a difficulty: 'The Department of Transport is not convinced that any of the existing methods for static testing of noise from lorries have any close correlation with noise from lorries in use on the roads.' If this is true, the testing of *new* lorries to meet any standard must equally lack that 'close correlation'.

Official failure to do research into vibration damage brings not a word of complaint from Armitage. There is 'no comprehensive objective evidence'; the effect on buildings 'is a matter of unresolved controversy'; there is 'particular ignorance' about old buildings; but he does not even call for more research. Then out of all this obscurity he is able to pluck some certainties: 'Further improvements in suspension systems and the building of new roads will help to contain the problem . . . There are likely to be some individual places which will continue to suffer from vibration . . . These problems are very localised.' This is false, and the growth of heavy lorries will heighten the falsity. He does recommend two useful (long overdue) measures: a limit on airborne low-frequency vibration and a requirement that all new lorries should have suspensions meeting 'at least the best of today's standards'. But even if the less harmful lorries are eventually made mandatory, the phasing out of all old ones will take up to ten years.

Armitage's remarks on fumes show the hand of his assessor, Professor Patrick Lawther, whose views on exhaust gases have been noted earlier. 'Lorries make only a small contribution to total air pollution,' says Armitage. '. . . Less than 1 per cent of all sulphur dioxide emissions, 2 per cent of carbon monoxide, 3–4 per cent of all hydrocarbons, 6 per cent of smoke and 8 per cent of oxides of nitrogen.' The clever word there is 'total'. People in the street are affected relatively little by the smoke from high chimneys and other non-traffic sources. The percentage contributions of diesel to traffic fumes are rather different (see page 98). Armitage does record that there is 'some concern' about carcinogenic and mutagenic hydrocarbons. The increase in fumes from the forecast rise in lorry traffic would not, he says, 'present a general threat to health'—a slightly worrying phrase. He reports that the department has established 'a viable method' of monitoring a lorry's smoke emissions, for annual tests and for prosecutions; he says it ought to be used.

Overloading, Armitage says, is costing the country millions and stronger action is needed. Axle-weight indicators could be fitted on lorries to help operators to avoid 'inadvertent overloading'. They would not need to be reliable enough to be quoted in prosecutions: in roadside checks 'they could be used as a filter, so that possible offenders could be picked out for weighing'. Good; but then comes an instant back-track: 'We understand that fully reliable axle-weight indicators are still not available.' A pretty phrase follows: the department and manufacturers 'should jointly continue to attempt to develop' them. Meanwhile overloading must remain a non-endorsable offence, for making it endorsable 'would put a large burden on drivers, who on many occasions will not know whether axles are overloaded' (a striking criticism of the intrinsic virtues of heavy haulage). The department's bad record over modern weighbridges suggests that the indicators will take some time. And Armitage says nothing about bringing the enforcement staff up to an effective strength, whether for catching overloaders or all the other offenders who now escape each week in thousands.

The most remarkable thing in Armitage's 'Improving the lorry' chapter is concerned with size. He begins promisingly: 'It is their size which leads to apprehension and fear about lorries. In evidence it was persistently claimed that there is an inappropriateness of scale between lorries and people and their environment'—and he mentions complaints about big lorries on unsuitable roads mounting pavements, cutting corners and so forth. However, the biggest will go on increasing in numbers. A worthy statement follows: 'The official approach hitherto has been concerned more with matching regulations on dimensions to the needs of the haulage industry than with approaching the matter from the point of view of the size of lorries which roads and local environments can take. This tends to act like a one-way valve.'

Only seven paragraphs later, however, he presents the argument of the hauliers and the department for a half-metre

length increase to 50 ft 10 in (see pages 58–9). This 'need' of
the haulage industry arises almost entirely from its enthusiasm
for drivers' bunks, which incidentally help it to compete more
sharply with rail. Armitage does not say: 'The one-way valve
again!' No: 'We have been particularly influenced by the need
to improve the driver's comfort and facilities, including the
provision of an adequately sized sleeper cab, and to help him
in the difficult task of manoeuvring an articulated lorry' (how
an extra half-metre helps him to get round corners is not
explained). So he recommends the 'small increase'.

What is especially challengeable about Armitage's way of
proposing this is that elsewhere he gives the impression that
he is against making lorries longer. For example, in a later
chapter: 'Each heavier lorry could not be larger than existing
lorries.' Indeed, at his press conference to launch his report he
distributed a summary that said 'NO BIGGER LORRIES'.
When questioned, he would not say this was untrue. The
result must have pleased the department: on that night's BBC
news and elsewhere, the public was told, 'Lorries will not be
bigger.'

When Armitage considers taxation he says nothing to disturb
the department. He notes its longstanding (unfulfilled) statement that social and environmental costs should be 'taken into
account' but he produces two long paragraphs of arguments
against any general environmental tax on lorries. It would
help people 'only through a reduction in lorry traffic', he says,
forgetting that the extra revenue could finance much-needed
remedial measures for suffering communities.

The effect of a tax rise on lorry traffic would be only
marginal, he asserts, but the effect on prices would be
'immediate, direct and lasting'. Those words imply something
serious without actually saying so. His economic assessor,
Professor Ray Rees, ought to have done a calculation at this
point. According to *Motor Transport*'s cost tables for the
haulage trade, the correct charge to customers in 1980 for a
32-ton lorry doing an average annual mileage was about £1 a
mile, of which about 10p was to cover taxes. Assume that
taxes were increased by a tenth for the social/environmental
element: the haulier's cost per mile would go up 1 per cent.
Transport accounts for about 5 per cent of the cost of goods.
Therefore the 'immediate, direct and lasting' price rises would

be 0.0005 of £1.

Armitage is on sounder ground when he says that such a tax would give no direct incentive to lorry manufacturers or operators to reduce lorry nuisance. He considers a specific tax on noise, and begins with some excellent points. Mandatory standards 'tend to be set at or not much above the pace of the slowest manufacturer and take a long time to agree and implement', Manufacturers who could do better have no incentive to do so 'because there is no market in environmental goods'; a graduated tax could create one. But once again the back-tracking begins. 'Such a tax would be a major departure from present policy' (the supreme Whitehall argument for inaction). Next sentence: 'Industry itself wishes to rely wholly on regulation' (yes indeed, when regulation has caused it so little trouble for twenty years). Final argument: 'The worthwhileness of a specific environmental tax can be judged only by reference to the toughness of minimum mandatory standards. If those standards are stringent enough there is no need for them to be supplemented by a tax . . . We recommend that rigorous minimum standards should be adopted . . . If these are adopted, they overtake the need for a specific environmental tax.'

Is that clear? The word 'overtake' deserves special admiration. A noise reduction which Armitage thinks might begin to take effect after 1990 becomes a justification for rejecting an immediate measure that has been proposed *because* rigorous standards 'take a long time to agree and implement'. Passages like this—and the report has many of them—make it hard to admire the intellectual power of Armitage and his helpers.

Armitage does better on road track costs. Though he does not question the department's cost-allocation methods, he does say that its failure fully to tax the heaviest lorries must be put right 'at the earliest opportunity'. The department must also 'seek to ensure' (oddly unrigorous phrase) that in succeeding years each class of lorry continues to pay its full costs. Of course these are things that the department has been saying for years it ought to do. With gentle understatement, Armitage criticises the department's longstanding failure to add a sum for public accident costs. Its argument that any calculation would be 'tentative and arbitrary', he says, is 'not sufficiently strong'. 'To treat these costs as zero . . . is more arbitrary than many other possible figures' (*many other?*) and zero is 'the figure most advantageous to the lorry'. Here at any rate one deviousness of Marsham Street is found too much to uphold.

Armitage also opens the way to other additions to the road track calculation by saying that although not enough is yet known about the damage lorries do to underground services for a reasonable estimate to be made of the cost, 'in the meantime a notional element should be included'. Not enough is yet known, either, about damage to buildings; now there is an argument for including a notional element for them as well.

He suggests a further tax innovation that would 'reflect crudely but more accurately' the environmental damage that various classes of lorry do. 'By and large . . . heavier ones do more damage than lighter ones,' he says. So after the track-cost allocation has been put right, if the Chancellor of the Exchequer wants further revenue, 'in the main the excess should be taken from the heaviest lorries'. This would merely be a long-overdue reversal of the present irrational arrangement by which small lorries pay excessively and the most environmentally damaging are the only ones heavily in debt. All in all, Armitage says, his tax proposals would have 'some effect in encouraging the transfer of freight to modes [i.e., rail, canals] which do less environmental damage'.

What might be the effect of all the recommendations so far analysed? Armitage himself sees 'the prospect of improvement in many places'. But not everywhere: 'There will we fear still be places where the problems . . . will remain apparently intractable and exceptionally acute. In some of these places the problems may get worse as the number of the heaviest lorries on the major routes increases. There will be increasing polarisation between those places which enjoy the benefits of effective measures to reduce lorry nuisance and those places where already severe problems will get worse.' I shall not for the moment discuss the clever suggestion that despite a great increase in the heaviest lorries most places will enjoy a pleasanter life. The question here is, What to do for the rest? In a brief chapter Armitage proposes Lorry Action Areas where special grants would enable local authorities to do the following things: install double-glazing; repair houses 'physically damaged by lorries'; maintain roads to high standards to reduce vibration; make minor road improvements to reduce accidents and to reduce noise ('eg by the use of noise-absorbing road surfaces'); build up pavements and erect bollards to deter corner-cutting; and in exceptional cases, close down 'a specific generator of lorry traffic' that causes 'intense local nuisance'.

Armitage concedes that this proposal does not deal with causes but only ameliorates effects; but to do nothing will 'condemn some places to continue to suffer . . . on what seems to us an intolerable scale'. Knowing the Whitehall mind, however, he goes on to put severe limits on the cost. Consider the following sentences: 'The worst problems caused by lorries are very localised. The potential total expenditure in this field is very high and beyond the realms of practicality.' I am not being unfair: those are successive sentences. Armitage quotes the Noise Advisory Council's estimate of the cost of double-glazing all houses already exposed to unacceptable noise (though without converting to a 1980 value, more than £2,100 million), and he says: 'What we are suggesting is infinitely more modest . . . As an illustration, £6 million each year would allow an average of about £¼ million to be spent in twenty-four of the worst affected places.' Modest indeed: for on this basis, even if the annual grant were *all* used for double glazing, it would make life less intolerable inside fewer than 6,400 houses; so even if traffic noise became no worse, it would take 360 years to double-glaze all the houses which, according to the Noise Advisory Council's cautious estimate, are now suffering unacceptably.

'By and large,' Armitage says, 'grants should be once and for all'—which hardly seems meaningful for 'physically damaged' houses, still less for smooth road surfaces. And who will decide among all the pleas for help from people suffering on an intolerable scale?

As possible Lorry Action Areas, Armitage mentions the Archway Road in London with its 7,000 lorries a day (he and his colleagues went to look and listen, which inspired the comment that the effects 'seem to us to be unacceptable'), and also such places as Chapel-en-le-Frith, Derbyshire, and Drighlington, near Leeds, with more than 2,000 a day. They did not greet the notion with much enthusiasm. At Chapel-en-le-Frith, where a bypass has been talked about for thirty years but still won't be built for years, a councillor said: 'You can get used to the noise and the smell, but most people resent being

trapped on the pavement. They cannot cross over to shop o.
the other side of the street. If double-glazing was any real use
people would have done it themselves. Giving towns like ours
special status looks like a payoff for allowing heavier lorries.'
At Drighlington, Mrs Edith Rushforth, who once had her
housefront smashed in by a lorry, said: 'I've been fighting for a
bypass for years. Help with double-glazing is just a sop. At
times I'm reduced to tears. I've even slept in the bath at the
back of the house when I couldn't stand any more.'

When Armitage considers Britain's overwhelming dependence
on road freight, he does little beyond restating what the
department, the Freight Transport Association and the Road
Haulage Association told him. Roadbuilding 'facilitated' the
growth. 'Changes in industrial structure' expanded demand.
At the same time, demand for road transport was 'heavily
influenced by its relatively low price'. Chicken/egg? Here is a
consequence: 'Entire distribution systems and indeed industries have been built around lorries . . . A large part of our
industry is irretrievably committed to the lorry.' Haulage was
something that industry could buy cheap: a haulier 'does not
have to make a larger initial capital outlay for the infrastructure
he uses,' and furthermore, 'hauliers are successful in externalising some of their costs' and there has been a 'tendency' to
undertax the heaviest lorries. But be judicious: this success
and this tendency (both the work of the department) 'are not
likely to have made a big difference'. While hauliers enjoyed
cheap roads, cut-price depots and other benefits, 'it seems
likely,' says a rather separate paragraph, 'that the failure to
invest more in the railways and waterways has been the result
of their inability to produce a sufficient rate of return'.
    Armitage describes what has happened to the railways.
'Factories no longer have to be near the railway' (nobody in
authority has ordained that they should be). 'New industrial
areas have developed with no rail access of any kind . . . There
has thus been a bandwagon effect. As the proportion of
factories linked to the railway has fallen, the incentive for
their suppliers and customers to remain directly connected to
the rail system has progressively declined.' Besides, lines
have been axed and British Rail has been instructed to pursue
only the traffic 'likely to be most profitable' which means
'rejecting other traffic'. There are wider effects: 'The dispersal

of industry affects personal and public transport. Getting to dispersed sites must have encouraged the use of cars . . . Changes in industrial location have affected the viability and prosperity of the older industrial areas and city centres.' This is the nearest Armitage ever comes to suggesting that the growth of apparently cheap freight transport has had bad economic, as well as environmental, effects.

When he discusses the 'popular' proposal that more freight should go by rail, he retails every much-used official argument against the 'apparent advantages'. Lorries not actually in competition with rail cause 'much' of the environmental nuisance. And the big long-distance lorries? 'Much' of their traffic is on motorways (and there, by implication, they bother nobody). He plays down rail's safety and energy advantages, and also the potential ton-mileage switch calculated by British Rail (see page 165). Using an old transport department ploy, he says that if BR took 40 million tonnes of existing road freight, that would 'be only 2½ per cent of the tonnage carried by road'—meaning all tonnage in anything from vans upwards—and it would reduce lorry tonne-miles by 8 per cent. He does not say it would reduce the tonne-miles of big artics, on trips over 125 miles, by a quarter.

Although he recognises that the government's command, 'make rail freight pay', combined with other restraints, is forcing more tonnage on to the roads, he rejects a general rail freight subsidy: it would not 'necessarily' reduce the impact of lorries. Despite the 'bandwagon effect', he spurns proposals that planners should aim to locate industry where rail and water transport are possible, or that county councils 'should have a duty to adopt policies to stabilise or reduce road freight'. He says 'a single council would be in no position' to assess such things, as if they could not confer. 'However, since even a marginal switch is desirable', he recommends that Section 8 grants (see page 169) should be more generous— perhaps by £3 million a year.

At his press conference, Armitage said: 'We've done quite a bit for rail.'

What lorries should he recommend for the good of mankind? He takes two bites at the question, interrupted by a hiccup.

He spends 13,000 words finding virtues, or at worst tolerable minor flaws, in the lorries advocated by the EEC.

With Britain's present road freight tonnage, they would cut operating costs by £150 million a year, he says, and reduce by 8½ per cent the mileage run by lorries over 25 tonnes: estimates dependent on many assumptions, and especially on a maintenance of load factors (see page 00). Of course the forecast growth in long-distance haulage would mean that there was not an *actual* reduction in mileage. It would merely increase a little less than it would otherwise have done. This he counts as an environmental gain. For example, in the context of the promised decibel reduction: 'Allowing heavier lorries would bring forward the time at which this very desirable reduction would start to occur because it should mean fewer lorries than there would have been.' This sentence cannot be too much admired. At the simplest level, it ignores the fact that the engines of heavier lorries must be far bigger—up to 350 horsepower for a 44-tonner, against about 220 for 32 tons—and are thus harder to quieten. More seriously, the reasoning of this sentence is used again and again to justify a claim by Armitage that the heavier lorries would be environmentally 'a positive improvement'. Indeed 'fewer than there would have been' is quickly translated into 'a reduction in the number of the heaviest lorries', a phrase Armitage then uses repeatedly.

One must regretfully forbear to discuss Armitage's questionably soothing claims about the effect of the EEC's lorries on safety and on underground pipes; his dismissal of all suggestions that a higher road-damaging power should be ascribed to the heaviest axles; or his assertion that 'the most likely outcome' of using these lorries would be reduced road maintenance costs, or at worst an increase of £5 million by 1990. One must come to bridges.

His chapter on the EEC package achieves an odd climax. Armitage does what he can to soften the warnings of the bridge specialists (see pages 149–51); saying, for example, that the costs estimated by Husband & Company are maximums not minimums. The operational gains claimed for the EEC lorries 'would more than outweigh' the bridge costs, he says, and in any case there would be 'a strong case for grants from EEC funds' (a new subsidy, that is, for the haulier's infrastructure). But then comes a last-minute 'however': 'However . . . the government might be unwilling to accept the additions to public expenditure on bridges.'

So Armitage abandons a package which he has just found to be worthy and adopts a formula handed him by the transport department in October 1980, just when he thought his task was nearly done. This reduces the EEC's worrying 11.55-tonne drive axle and 24-tonne tri-axle to 10½ tonnes and 22½ tonnes. The favoured lorry configurations and maximums then become: four axles, 34 tonnes; five axles (two-axle tractive unit), 38 tonnes; five axles (three-axle tractive unit), 40 tonnes; six axles, 44 tonnes.

Having abandoned the EEC package, Armitage now finds it possible to say things against it. With his modified lorries, axle overloading would be less frequent; there would be less vibration risk; good braking would be easier to achieve; and as those over 38 tonnes would have to have three-axle tractive units, they would be 'more stable and resistant to jack-knifing'. It is surprising that the flaws indicated here in the EEC lorries were passed over by Armitage a few pages earlier.

More surprising still is the untenable claim that Armitage makes on a crucial point. He says that his proposed lorries 'would not cause additional damage to our bridges', compared with Britain's existing lorries. He makes the claim five times within eight pages. But the department itself, anxious though it had been to minimise the bridge worry, said no such thing. Its specialists were asked what maximum axle-loads would be 'acceptable', and they said a 10½-tonne axle 'is the most that could be accepted . . . without undue risk'. The fatigue damage it caused would be 'substantially less' than that of the EEC drive axle; but it would be greater than now. Each 10½-tonne axle would in fact cause 10 per cent more bridge fatigue than the current 10-ton axle. As for tri-axles, the specialists said that at 24 tonnes they were unacceptable because, among other things, on a six-metre span they would have a 'bending moment' 9.6 per cent greater than that of the worst current British lorry trailer (which itself worries the experts). At 22½ tonnes the excess bending moment would not be eliminated—merely reduced to 2.6 per cent. Furthermore, the 22½ tonnes is 'acceptable' only if the three axles are widely spaced. This spacing adds to the difficulty that a tri-axle bogie has in going round corners. Its front and rear sets of tyres would put enormous sideways strains and pressures on the road: something Armitage says nothing about.

He demands to be challenged, too, when he claims that his

four-axle 34-tonne lorries, which by his own reckoning would do nearly 16 per cent more road damage per ton carried than a 32-tonner, would bring only a small increase in total road damage. And this, he says, would be only in 'the first two or three years', until numerous five-axle and six-axle lorries came into use. But as about 40,000 tractive units designed to operate at between 32 and 40 tons were registered during 1976–80, and as under Armitage's proposals a new investment in tri-axle trailers would allow their owners to operate at no more than 38 tonnes, it is likely that a large proportion of these vehicles would go on being operated instead with their present trailers and at the damaging 34 tonnes.

An assertion by Armitage that by the nineties there could be 'actual reductions in expenditure' on roads is still more questionable. By then there might well be so many five-axle and six-axle lorries in the fleet that long-distance freight would be shifted less damagingly per ton than it is by the present damaging 32-tonners. However, even on Armitage's own reckoning the grand total of damaging axles on the roads would be far greater than now. He estimates that by 1990 the miles run by all lorries over 25 tonnes will be at least 28 per cent more than now and possibly 40 per cent more; and among those lorries he is assuming a large proportion running at over 32 tons. The grand total of road-battering heavy axles could not help but be enormously increased. To achieve 'actual reductions' a quite different policy would be needed: requiring the present juggernauts to have five-axles, and getting more freight on to rail.

Armitage's presentational summing-up is even less troubled than what has gone before by any judicious glances towards disbenefits. He says the lorries he proposes would reduce the cost of moving the present tonnage of freight by up to £130 million, and the expected 1990 tonnage by up to £190 million. (He goes for the top range of the Corcoran/Glover/Shane estimates.) Against this claimed benefit he tots up no costs whatever, neither direct ones, such as damage to bridges, roads, mains or buildings, nor less direct ones, such as the swelling environmental impact from a great growth in juggernaut mileage. When asked why he did not attempt to set out the costs, he said, in words worthy of the department itself: 'They couldn't all be ascertained.'

His lorries would save fuel, his report says; but earlier he has noted, without drawing any useful conclusion, that during the period 1967–77 (when the vast shift to heavier lorries occurred) fuel productivity in terms of diesel used per ton-mile declined by 8 per cent. His only comment is that the price of diesel had fallen in real terms, so haulers had 'less incentive to economise'. Nowhere does he note the evidence presented to him (see page 161) of a fall in load factors with the rise in lorry sizes. When the point about load factors was put to him at his press conference, he said: 'I am not aware of that.' Perhaps Philip Wood failed to make him aware. The knowledge would have made it difficult for him to put a number of unqualified assertions in his report, such as, 'Heavier lorries are intrinsically more efficient and economic.' It would have cast doubt on his estimates of cost savings— estimates which in any case seemed high even to some haulage experts, such as Peter Thompson of NFC.

Armitage's task was to report on the best way of moving freight; but he gives not a hint that he thought of assessing the possible economic benefits of carrying a less overwhelming proportion of long-distance freight by road. Instead he merely says that the amount of freight that his heavier lorries might abstract from the railways 'is not likely to be very significant' and that the generation of new demand for road transport through cost savings would (contrary to past experience) 'be likely to be small'.

His boldest claim is that his heavier lorries would 'considerably reduce the effects of heavy lorries on people and the environment'. It is understandable that he should wish to say so, in view of his declaration at the start that there must be 'an absolute reduction' in the impact. His first justification for his claim is that he proposes stricter controls of various kinds. However, all such long-overdue improvements of course apply equally, and also more easily, to existing lorries; and thus count for nothing in the argument. His second justification is that thanks to his promised bigger payloads, the annual traffic of lorries over 25 tonnes would not increase by 1,980 million miles by 1990, as forecast by the department, but perhaps only by 1,520 million miles. It is not a very cheering figure. It means that the mileage of such lorries might be 40 per cent greater than now; and more daunting, a big proportion of it would be run by lorries of more than 32 tons. Would many people by saying in 1990: 'Thank you, Sir Arthur, for this absolute reduction'?

Armitage recognises that the ill effects of big lorries have grown worse and are affecting more people. Nowhere does he say that this worsening occurred after lorry weights and sizes were last allowed to go up. He asks the sufferers to believe that with still heavier lorries, no such thing would happen. Far from it! Life would be 'absolutely' better. His arguments are delusive. He has made a mockery of his task: to weigh all the facts, look to the future and advise the nation objectively.

The report left 'the departmental view' almost unquestioned in its robust perfection, and gave the minister, Norman Fowler, no reason to stop saying at Road Haulage Association dinners (as he did just before publication): 'It is not the government's job to decide how freight should be sent. That decision should be left to the customer.'

At this late date, what can be done? Whoever joins in a campaign to change the department's thinking has two large facts to lend him fervour: that the department's record shows that it has failed in its public duty, and that the Armitage report is little more than a speech for the defence. Only public pressure can force the department to evolve a new view, one that would bring not only environmental justice but also a shift to an economic realism which has been puzzlingly lacking in a department guided by a permanent secretary who came to it as a high-flyer from the Treasury.

Such a change is not impossible. Some men in the department have hitherto lived lives of dissatisfied acquiescence. Devoted departmental philosophers can detect when it has become wise to change. They can learn to apply the adjectives 'significant' and 'robust' to unfamiliar things.

Armitage himself, early in his report, glimpses the potential power of a public whose servants in Marsham Street have failed it: 'There must be environmental improvement, both for the sake of the quality of people's lives and because, without it, resentment and hostility towards the lorry will increase and put at risk the economic advantages of the lorry.' He sees a danger that organised protesters could become a force too great to dismiss as an anti-social, freakish 'environmental brigade'. What he sees as a danger, the sufferers must see as their hope. Apathy is the polluter's friend.

Appendix

Making Your Voice Heard

Lone voices of dissent achieve little. If your neighbourhood or district suffers from lorries, it probably already has an action group or amenity society concerned with them. If there is no such body, it will not be hard to find people to help you organise one. The Civic Trust (address below) has a 'guide pack' of advice on setting up and running a local society (25p including postage). It also has the addresses of nearly 1,200 amenity societies round Britain.

An immediate issue—whether it is local, such as a controversial road-widening scheme, or national, such as a lorry weight increase—is a great help for launching a group or for putting new life into an existing one. A public meeting and a petition make a good start. What is difficult is to keep things going. Patient work and continual vigilance are essential. A few hints:

Be clear about your targets (you may want both a change in national policy and a local night-time lorry ban). Learn which public authorities are responsible: Department of Transport, county council, district council or a combination of them.

Make sure your MP and your councillors hear from you. Learn the names of the chairmen and members of council committees concerned with lorry matters ('planning and transportation' is a common title). *Before* decisions are made, see that they know your views.

Get to know local government officers concerned with transport and planning. Learn from them; educate them. They can have great influence.

Know what you are taking about, whether it's on Dykes Act powers or the control of lorry depots. ('You will probably end up more expert than the experts,' says a Civic Trust official.)

Make intelligent use of local newspapers and local radio (you will have to have something special to attract national papers or television). Stories of conflict usually have appeal. Timing is important: get your case over when it can change minds. Although reporters and editors sometimes need educating in environmental matters, they will generally find a place for you, especially if you do some of the work for them in clear English and at modest length. Learn their deadlines. If you are engaged in a hot fight, think up picturable events and don't be above using children or pretty girls. A letter to the paper from the association carries weight, but be sure also to encourage members to write their own individually-worded letters (and to MPs and councillors as well). Do not be querulous and abusive; above all, do not be wordy and boring.

Useful Addresses

Association of County Councils (47 councils, England and Wales), 66a Eaton Sq, SW1W 9BH, 01-235 1200

Association of District Councils (333 towns and large districts, England and Wales), 25 Buckingham Gate, SW1E 6LE, 01-828 7931

Association of Metropolitan Authorities (GLC, six metropolitan counties, 36 large towns and cities), 36 Old Queen St, SW1H 9JE, 01-222 8100

British Rail, 222 Marylebone Rd, NW1 6JJ, 01-262 3232

British Road Federation (umbrella group for road-users and road-builders, from AA to Sand and Gravel Association), 388 Oxford St, W1N 9HE, 01-499 0281

Civic Trust, 17 Carlton House Terrace, SW1Y 5AW, 01-930 0914

Conservation Society, 12A Guildford St, Chertsey, Surrey, KT16 9BQ, 09328 60975

Convention of Scottish Local Authorities (combining the function of the three English associations), 3 Forren St, Edinburgh, 031 225 1626

Council for Environmental Conservation (umbrella for 30 societies), Zoological Gardens, Regent's Park, NW1 4RY, 01-722 7111

Council for the Protection of Rural England, 4 Hobart Place, SW1W 0HY, 01-235 9481

Council for Protection of Rural Wales, 14 Broad St, Welshpool, SY21 7SD

Environment, Department of, 2 Marsham St, SW1P 3EB, 01-212 3434

European Parliament Information Office, 2 Queen Anne's Gate, SW1, 01-222 0411

Freight Transport Association (15,500 users of freight transport; chiefly manufacturers, etc, operating their own lorries), St John's Rd, Tunbridge Wells, Kent, TN4 9UZ, 0892 26171

Friends of the Earth, 9 Poland St, W1V 3DG, 01-434 1684

Georgian Group, 2 Chester St, SW1X 7BB, 01-235 3081

Inland Waterways Association, 114 Regent's Park Road, NW1 8UQ, 01-586 2556

London Amenity and Transport Association, 13 Alwyne Place, N1, 01-226 3404

National Association of Local Councils (8,600 English parish councils and Welsh community councils), 100 Great Russell St, WC1B 3LD, 01-636 4066

National Council on Inland Transport, 5 Pembridge Crescent, W11 3DT, 01-727 4689

National Federation of Women's Institutes, 39 Eccleston St, SW1W 9NT, 01-730 7212

Noise Advisory Council, 1 Lambeth Palace Rd, SE1, 01-211 8960

Railway Development Society, BM/RDS, London, WC1N 3XX

Rambler's Association, 1/5 Wandsworth Rd, SW8 2LJ, 01-582 6878

Road Haulage Association (18,000 operators of lorries for hire), 22 Upper Woburn Place, WC1H 0ES, 01-387 9711

Scottish Development Department (environment and transport matters), New St Andrew's House, Edinburgh, EH1 3TD, 031 556 8400

Scottish Women's Rural Institutes, 42 Herriot Row, Edinburgh, EH3 6EV

Socialist Environment and Resources Association, 9 Poland St, W1V 3DG, 01-439 3749

Society for the Protection of Ancient Buildings, 55 Great Ormond St, WC1N 3JA, 01-405 2646

Town and Country Planning Association, 17 Carlton House Terrace, SW1Y 5AS, 01-930 8903

Transport, Department of, 2 Marsham St, SW1P 3EB, 01-212 3434

Transport Department Licensing Authorities (licensing and control of lorries and depots): Scottish, 24 Torpichen St, Edinburgh EH3 8HD, 031 229 9166; Northern, Westgate Rd, Newcastle-upon-Tyne, NE1 1TW, 0632 610031; Yorkshire, 386 Harehills Lane, Leeds, LS9 6NF, 0532 499661; North-western, Parsonage Gdns, Deansgate, Manchester, M60 9AN, 061 832 8644; West Midland, 200 Broad St, Birmingham, B15 1TD, 021 643 5011; East Midland, 14-16 Trinity Sq, Nottingham, NG1 4BA, 0602 45511; Eastern, 13-15 Hills Rd, Cambridge, CB2 1NP, 0223 358922; South Wales, 1-6 St Andrews Place, Cardiff CF1 3PW, 0222 24801; Western, Denmark St. Bristol, BS1 5DR, 0272 297221; Metropolitan, PO Box 643, Bromyard Ave, Acton, W3 7AY, 01-743 5566; South-eastern, 3 Ivy Terrace, Eastbourne, BN21 4QT, 0323 21471

Transport 2000, 40 James St, W1M 5HS, 01-486 8523

Ulster Society for the Preservation of the Countryside, Carney Hill, Holywood, Co Down, BT18 0JR

Victorian Society, 1 Priory Gdns, W4 1TT, 01-994 1019

Welsh Office, Cathays Park, Cardiff CF1 3NQ, 0222 28066

Bibliography

Place of Publication is London unless otherwise stated.
TRRL = Transport and Road Research Laboratory, Crowthorne, Berkshire.

Abelson, Peter (1979), *Cost-benefit analysis and environmental problems*, Farnborough

Advisory Council on Energy Conservation (1977), *Freight transport: short and medium term considerations*

Advisory Council on Energy Conservation (1978), *Energy for transport: long-term possibilities*

Alexandre, Ariel, ed. (1975), *Road Traffic Noise*

Alexandre, Ariel, and Barde, Jean-Philippe (1976), 'The economics of traffic noise abatement', *Traffic Quarterly*, Westport, Connecticut, April 1976

Armitage, Sir Arthur (1980), *Report of the inquiry into lorries, people and the environment*, HMSO

Association of Metropolitan Authorities (1980), *Road and rail freight: a study group report*

Aston, University of (Joint Unit for Research on the Urban Environment) (1976), *Environmental policy and the heavy goods vehicle*, Birmingham

Bartlett, R.S., Edmondson, D.R., and McCarthy, S.P. (1978), *Hull freight study: assessment of possible area lorry controls* (LR 829); *Hull freight study: assessment of possible lorry network and proposed road improvements* (LR 846), TRRL

Battilana, J.A., and Hawthorne, I.H. (1976), *Design and cost of a transhipment depot to serve Swindon town centre* (LR 741), TRRL

Beesley, Professor M.E. (1979), *Influence of measures designed to restrict the use of certain transport modes*, European Conference of Ministers of Transport, Paris

Benn, Tony, MP (1980), 'Manifestos and mandarins', in *Policy* and practice: the experience of government (Royal Institute of Public Administration)

Bouladon, Gabriel (1979), 'Costs and benefits of motor vehicles', in *Urban transport and the environment* (report of seminar of Organisation for Economic Cooperation and Development), Paris

British Rail (1976), *Environmental and social impact study*

British Rail (1980), *European railways' performance comparisons*

British Road Federation (1979), *No time to stop: the case for the road programme*

Buchanan, Colin, et al (Ministry of Transport Study Group) (1963), *Traffic in towns,* HMSO

Burt, M.E. (1972), *Roads and the environment* (LR 441), TRRL

Castle, Barbara (1973), 'Mandarin Power', transcript of talk to senior civil servants, *The Sunday Times,* 10 June 1973

Chapman, Leslie (1978), *Your disobedient servant*

Christie, A.W., Bartlett, R.S., Cundill, M.A., and Prudhoe, J. (1973), *Urban freight distribution: studies of operations in shopping streets at Newbury and Camberley* (LR 603), TRRL

Christie, A.W., and Hull, Mrs M. (1977), *An analysis of the study by Hertfordshire County Council for the Heavy Commercial Vehicles Act* (LR 759), TRRL

Christie, A.W., Hornzee, R.S., and Zammit, T. (1978), *Effects of lorry controls in the Windsor area* (SR 458), TRRL

Civic Trust (1970), *Heavy lorries*

Civic Trust (1979), *Heavy lorries nine years on* (submission to Armitage inquiry)

Corcoran, P.J., and Christie, A.W. (1978), *Review of the results of planning studies* (SR 381), TRRL

Corcoran, P.J., Glover, M.H., and Shane, B.A. (1980) *High gross weight goods vehicles—operating costs and road damage factors* (SR 590), TRRL

Corcoran, P.J., Hitchcock, A.J., and McMahon, C.M. (1980), *Developments in freight transport* (SR 580), TRRL

Crockett, J.H.A. (1973), 'The effects of traffic on older buildings', paper presented at Planning and Transportation Research and Computation conference, Warwick

Cundill, M.A., Deaves, C, Edmondson, D.R., and McCarthy, S.P. (1977), *Swindon freight study: assessment of possible 'no entry except for access' controls* (LR 792), TRRL

Cundill, M.A., and Shane, B.A. (1980), *Trends in road goods* transport 1962–1977 (SR 572), TRRL

Currer, E.W.H. (1974), *Commercial traffic studies* (LR 628), TRRL

Currer, E.W.H., and O'Connor, M.G.D. (1979), *Commercial traffic: its estimated damaging effect, 1945–2005* (LR 910), TRRL

Davies, C.H., and Dawson, R.F.P. (1980), *The costs of conforming to standards for noise from road traffic* (SR 475), TRRL

Environment, Department of (1976), *A study of some methods of traffic restraint; and Transport policy, a consultation document*

European Conference of Ministers of Transport (1972), *Studies on the social costs of urban road transport*, Paris

European Conference of Ministers of Transport (1978), *Economic prospects for railways*, Paris

Foster, Professor Christopher, et al (1978), *Road haulage operators' licensing: report of the independent committee of inquiry*, HMSO

Geddes, Lord et al (1965), *Carriers licensing*, report to minister of transport, HMSO

Gissane, William, and Bull, John (1973), 'Fatal car occupant injuries after car–lorry collisions', *British Medical Journal*, 13 January 1973

Grime, Professor Geoffrey, and Hutchinson, T.P. (1979), 'Vehicle mass and driver injury', *Ergonomics*, vol. 22, no. 1

Gwilliam, Professor Kenneth, and Mackie, Peter (1975), *Economics and transport policy*

Gyenes, L. (1978), *Fuel utilisations of articulated vehicles: effect of gross vehicle weight* (SR 424), TRRL

Hamer, Mick (1978), *A load on your mind*, Transport 2000

Harland, D.G. (1974), *Rolling noise and vehicle noise* (LR 652), TRRL

Harland, D.G. (1976), 'Forecasts of exposure to traffic noice in residential areas', unpublished paper

Hasell, B.B., and Christie, A.W. (1978), *The Greenwich–Lewisham freight study* (SR 407), TRRL

Heggie, Ian (1979), 'Economics and the road programme',

Journal of Transport Economics and Policy, January 1979

Heimerl, Gerhard, and Holzmann, Ekkehard (1980), 'Valuation of traffic noise—different nuisance of street and rail traffic', paper presented at world conference on transport research, Imperial College, London

Hensher, David, ed. (1977), *Urban transport economics*, Cambridge

House of Commons (1972), debate on motion against heavier lorries, *Hansard*, 29th November 1972; *Urban transport planning*, report of Expenditure Committee (environment sub-committee)

House of Commons (1974), *Public Expenditure on transport*, report of Expenditure Committee (environment sub-committee)

House of Commons (1980), *The roads programme*, report of the Transport Committee

House of Lords (1978), *EEC transport policy*, report of Select Committee on the European Communities

Kemp, R.N., Chinn, B.P., and Brock, G. (1978), *Articulated vehicle roll stability: methods of assessment and effects of vehicle characteristics* (LR 788), TRRL

Langdon, John (1977), *The effects of road traffic noise in residential areas*, Building Research Establishment, Garston, Watford

Langdon, John (1978), 'Monetary evaluation of nuisance from road-traffic noise', *Environment and PlanningA*, vol. 10

Lecomber, Richard (1975), *Economic growth versus the environment*

Leitch, Sir George, et al (1977), *Report of the advisory committee on trunk road assessment*, HMSO

Leitch, Sir George, et al (1979), *Trunk road proposals—a comprehensive framework for appraisal*, HMSO

Leonard, D.R., Grainger, J.W., and Eyre, R. (1974), *Loads and vibrations caused by eight commercial vehicles with gross weights exceeding 32 tons* (LR582), TRRL

Levin, Dr Peter (1979), 'Highway inquiries: a study in governmental responsiveness', *Journal of Public Administration*, spring 1979

Lister, Norman (1977), 'Heavy wheel loads and road pavements—damage relationships', in *Heavy freight*

vehicles and their effects, OECD symposium report, Paris
Lister, Norman (1980) 'Strengthening and reconstruction: design criteria', paper presented at Institution of Highway Engineers conference, Leamington Spa
Llewelyn-Davies/Forestier-Walker/Bor (1972), 'Freight transport and the environment', four-volume consultants' report to Department of the Environment, unpublished
Lorries and the Environment Committee (1976), *Report on transhipment*
Lorries and the Environment Committee (1979), *Improved goods delivery*

Margason, G., and Corcoran, P.J. (1977), 'Operational evaluation of the effects of heavy freight vehicles', in *Heavy freight vehicles and their effects*, OECD symposium report, Paris
Martin, D.J. (1978), *Low frequency traffic noise and building vibration* (SR 429), TRRL
Martin, D.J., Nelson, P.M., and Hill, R.C. (1978), *Measurement and analysis of traffic-induced vibrations in buildings* (SR 402), TRRL
Mason K., and Nash, C.A. (1979), *A note on the rail share of the freight market in certain western European countries*, Institute for Transport Studies, University of Leeds
Metra Consulting (1979), 'Costs and cost effectiveness of means of abating road traffic noise, aircraft noise and industrial noise', study for Netherlands ministry of public health and environment
Morton-Williams, Jean, Hedges, Barry, and Fernando, Evelyn (1978), *Road traffic and the environment*

Nash, C.A. (1976), *Public versus private transport*
Nash, C.A. (1979), *The influence of transport policy on the competitive position of the Deutsche Bundesbahn*, Institute for Transport Studies, University of Leeds
Neilson, Ian, Kemp, R.M., and Wilkins, H.A. (1979), *Accidents involving heavy goods vehicles in Great Britain* (SR 470), TRRL
Nelson, Jon P. (1978), *Economic analysis and transportation noise abatement*, Cambridge, Mass.
Noise Advisory Council (1974), *Noise in the next ten years*, HMSO

Olson, Mancur (1977), 'The treatment of externalities in net income states', in *Public economics and the quality of life*, Johns Hopkins University, Baltimore

Organisation for Economic Cooperation and Development (OECD) (1972), *Environmental damage costs*, Paris

OECD (1975), *The polluter pays principle*; and *Strategies for urban noise abatement*, Paris

OECD (1977), *Heavy freight vehicles and their effects* (symposium report, three vols), Paris

OECD (1979), *Urban transport and the environment* (seminar papers, three vols), Paris

OECD (1980) *Noise abatement policies* (conference report), Paris

Pearce, Professor David (1976), *Environmental economics*

Pearce, Professor David, ed. (1978), *The valuation of social cost*

Plowden, Stephen (1980), *Taming traffic*

Plowden, Stephen, and Sinnott, P.R.J. (1977), *Evaluation of nuisance* (SR 261), TRRL

Plowden, Willian (1970), 'MPs and the roads lobby', in *The member of Parliament and his information*, ed. Anthony Baker

Pryke, Richard, and Dodgson, John (1975), *The rail problem*

Riley, B.S., and Bates, H. J. (1980), *Fatal accidents in Great Britain in 1976 involving heavy goods vehicles* (SR 586), TRRL

Road Research Laboratory (later TRRL) (1970), *A review of road traffic noise* (LR 357)

Roads Campaign Council (1961), *Urban survival and traffic* (proceedings of symposium at King's College, Newcastle upon Tyne)

Rodgers, William, MP (1980), 'Westminster and Whitehall: adapting to change', in *Policy and practice: the experience of government* (Royal Institute of Public Administration)

Sharp, Clifford (1973), *Living with the lorry*

Southampton, University of (Department of Civil Engineering) (1973), *Transportation and environment* (symposium proceedings)

Straw, Jack, MP (1978), 'Power in government—a Chinese

puzzle', *University of Leeds Review,* vol. 21
Sumner, R., and Baguley, C. (1978), *Close following behaviour at two sites on rural two lane motorways* (LR 859), TRRL
Suurland, Jan (1979), *Noise charges in the Netherlands,* Organisation for Economic Cooperation and Development, Paris

Thompson, Peter (1977), 'Road haulage—a healthy industry?', paper presented to Chartered Institute of Transport
Thompson, Peter (1979), 'Increasing productivity and efficiency', address to *Commercial Motor* fleet management conference
Thompson, Peter (1980), 'Productivity in road haulage', lecture to Chartered Institute of Transport (Irish section)
Transport, Department of (1977), *Transport Policy* (White paper)
Transport, Department of (January 1979), *Comparative trials of articulated goods vehicles between 32,5 and 44 tonnes gross weight*
Transport, Department of (April 1979), *Water spray from heavy goods vehicles*
Transport, Department of (1980), *Policy for roads: England;* and *Report on study into the effects of heavy vehicles on bridges* (Husband & Company)
Transport, Ministry of (1966), *Transport Policy*
Transport, Ministry of (1967), *The transport of freight;* and *Public transport and traffic*
Transport, Ministry of (1968), *Road track costs*
Transport, Ministry of (1970), *Roads for the future*
Transport and Road Research Laboratory (1975), *Swindon freight study; collection of data and construction of computer model* (SR 158UC)
TRRL (1977), *The management of urban freight movements* (proceedings of seminar, May 1976)
TRRL (1979), *Symposium on energy and road transport* (Proceedings, April 1978).
(For other TRRL reports, see: Bartlett, Battilana, Burt, Christie, Corcoran, Cundill, Currer, Davies, Gyenes, Harland, Hasell, Kemp, Leonard, Martin, Neilson, Plowden (S.), Riley, Sumner, Tyler, Whiffin, Williams.)
Tyler, J.W. (1979), *TRRL quiet vehicle programme* (SR 521), TRRL
Tyme, John (1978), *Motorways versus democracy*

Urban Motorways Committee (1972), *New roads in towns* (report to Department of the Environment)

Whiffin, A.C., and Leonard, D.R. (1971), *A survey of traffic-induced vibrations* (LR 418), TRRL

Williams, Marian (1980), *Tabulations of 1977 road casualties indicating risks of injury to road users in relation to vehicles involved* (SR 576), TRRL

Wilson, Sir Alan, et al (Committee on the Problem of Noise) (1963), *Report*, HMSO

(Both the Department of Transport and the Department of the Environment submitted unbound Background Papers to the Armitage inquiry. In addition the Department of Transport submitted 51 short supplementary papers. All are available from the departments.)

Index